Bangladeshis in Manchester
Oral History 2nd Part

Mustak Ahmed Mustafa

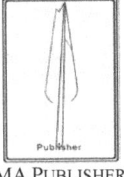

MA PUBLISHER

Mustak Ahmed Mustafa

The right of Mustak Ahmed Mustafa to be identified as the author of this work has been asserted in accordance with sections 77 and 78 of the Copyright Design and Patent Act 1988.

Copyright © Mustak Ahmed Mustafa 2024
Email: news4mustak@gmail.com

Published by MA Publishing (Penzance)
Website: www.mapublisher.org.uk   Email: mapublisher@yahoo.com
Released on December 2023

Printed in their region of sale: Australia | Canada | Europe | UK | USA

ISBN-13: 978-1-915958-20-4

All rights reserved. No part of this publication may be reproduced, stored in a retrieval system, or transmitted, in any form or by any means, electronic, mechanical, photocopying, recording, public performances or otherwise, without prior written permission of the copyright holder, except for brief quotations embodied in critical articles or reviews.

Disclaimer:

All expressions and opinions of the work belong to the artists and PA does not share or endorse any other than to provide the open platform to publish their work. For further information on PA policies please email: pennyauthors@yahoo.co.uk for further information and submission guidelines.

Document layout and pagination by Mayar Akash
Cover image Typeset in Times Roman

Paper printed on is FSC Certified, lead free, acid free, buffered paper made from wood-based pulp. Our paper meets the ISO 9706 standard for permanent paper. As such, paper will last several hundred years when stored.

Contents

Preface:	13
Summary Of History Project	15
Chapter 1 – Introduction	16
1.1 Introduction to the Organisation:	16
1.2 Introduction of the Oral History Project:	18
1.3 Objectives:	20
1.4 Introduction of the Author:	20
Chapter 2 – Interviews	23
2.1 Alhaj Moboshor Ullah:	23
2.2.1 Life in Bangladesh:	23
2.2.2 Journey to the UK & Immigration:	24
8.2.3 Life in the UK:	26
8.2.4 Employment:	28
8.2.5 Housing:	30
8.2.6 Social & Family:	30
8.2.7 Conclusion:	32
8.3 Alhaj Md. Abdur Rashid	33
8.3.1 Life in Bangladesh:	33
8.3.2 Journey to the UK & Immigration:	33
8.3.3 Life in the UK:	34
8.3.4 Employment:	34
8.3.5 Housing:	36
8.3.6 Social & Family:	36
8.3.7 Conclusion:	37
8.4 Alhaj Sunawar Ali	38
8.4.1 Life in Bangladesh:	38
8.4.2 Journey to the UK & Immigration:	38
8.4.3 Life in the UK:	38
8.4.4 Employment:	39
8.4.5 Housing:	39
8.4.6 Social & Family:	40
8.4.7 Independence of Bangladesh:	40
8.4.8 Conclusion:	40
8.5 Alhaj Aklas Ali	41
8.5.2 Journey to the UK & Immigration:	41
8.5.3 Life in the UK:	43
8.5.4 Employment:	44
8.5.5 Housing:	45
8.5.6 Social & Family:	45
8.5.7 Conclusion:	45
8.6 Alhaj Johur Uddin	46
8.6.1 Life in Bangladesh:	46

8.6.2	Journey to the UK & Immigration:	46
8.6.3	Life in the UK:	46
8.6.4	Employment:	47
8.6.5	Housing:	48
8.6.6	Social & Family:	49
8.6.7	Independence of Bangladesh:	49
8.6.8	Conclusion:	50
8.7 Alhaj Munsif Ali		50
8.7.1	Life in Bangladesh:	50
8.7.2	Journey to the UK & Immigration:	51
8.7.3	Education in the UK:	51
8.7.4	Employment:	51
8.7.5	Housing:	52
8.7.6	Social & Family:	52
8.7.7	Conclusion:	53
8.8 Alhaj Rois Ullah		54
8.8.1	Life in Bangladesh:	54
8.8.2	Journey to the UK & Immigration:	55
8.8.3	Employment:	55
8.8.4	Housing:	56
8.8.5	Social & Family:	56
8.8.6	Independence of Bangladesh:	56
8.8.7	Conclusion:	57
8.9 Bimal Kanti Bhattacharjee:		58
8.9.1	Life in Bangladesh:	58
8.9.2	Journey to the UK & Immigration:	59
8.9.3	Life in the UK:	59
8.9.4	Employment:	59
8.9.5	Housing:	60
8.9.6	Social & Family:	61
8.9.7	Independence of Bangladesh:	61
8.9.8	Conclusion:	61
8.10 Alhaj Noorfor Ali		62
8.10.1	Life in Bangladesh:	62
8.10.2	Journey to the UK & Immigration:	62
8.10.3	Life in the UK:	63
8.10.4	Employment:	63
8.10.5	Housing:	64
8.10.6	Social & Family:	64
8.10.7	Independence of Bangladesh:	65
8.10.8	Conclusion:	66
8.11 Haji Tozomul Ali		67
8.11.1	Life in Bangladesh:	67
8.11.2	Journey to the UK & Immigration:	68

8.11.3	Life in the UK:	69
8.11.4	Employment:	70
8.11.5	Social & Family:	71
8.11.6	Housing:	72
8.11.7	Conclusion:	72
8.12	Alhaj Shomsher Khan	73
8.12.1	Life in Bangladesh:	73
8.12.2	Journey to the UK & Immigration:	73
8.12.3	Life in the UK:	74
8.12.4	Employment:	75
8.12.5	Housing:	76
8.12.6	Social & Family:	76
8.12.7	Conclusion:	77
8.13	Alhaj Kari Abdul Baki	77
8.13.1	Life in Bangladesh:	77
8.13.2	Journey to the UK & Immigration:	78
8.13.3	Employment:	78
8.13.4	Housing:	79
8.13.5	Social & Family:	80
8.13.6	Independence of Bangladesh:	80
8.13.7	Conclusion:	81
8.14	Alhaj Md. Dilwar Khan	81
8.14.1	Life in Bangladesh:	81
8.14.2	Journey to the UK & Immigration:	82
8.14.3	Life in the UK	83
8.14.4	Employment:	83
8.14.5	Housing:	85
8.14.6	Social & Family:	85
8.14.7	Conclusion	86
8.15	Alhaj Abdul Aziz	87
8.15.1	Life in Bangladesh:	87
8.15.2	Journey to the UK & Immigration:	88
8.15.3	Life in the UK:	88
8.15.4	Employment:	88
8.15.5	Housing:	89
8.15.6	Social & Family:	90
8.15.7	Independence of Bangladesh:	90
8.15.8	Conclusion:	91
8.16	Alhaj Abdul Mannan	91
8.16.1	Life in Bangladesh	91
8.16.2	Journey to the UK & Immigration:	92
8.16.3	Life in the UK:	92
8.16.4	Employment:	92
8.16.5	Housing:	93

8.16.6	Social & Family:	93
8.16.7	Independence of Bangladesh:	96
8.16.8	Conclusion:	96
8.17	Alhaj Muktar Ali	98
8.17.1	Life in Bangladesh	98
8.17.2	Journey to the UK & Immigration:	98
8.17.3	Life in the UK:	99
8.17.4	Employment:	99
8.17.5	Housing:	100
8.17.6	Social & Family:	100
8.17.7	Independence of Bangladesh:	101
8.17.8	Conclusion:	102
8.18	Alhaj Muslim Ali	102
8.18.1	Life in Bangladesh:	103
8.18.2	Journey to the UK & Immigration:	103
8.18.3	Life in the UK:	103
8.18.4	Employment:	104
8.18.5	Housing:	104
8.18.6	Social & Family:	105
8.18.7	Conclusion:	105
8.19	Alhaj Md Nasir Ali	106
8.19.1	Life in Bangladesh and Other Places:	106
8.19.2	Journey to the UK & Immigration:	107
8.19.3	Employment:	109
8.19.4	Housing:	110
8.19.5	Social & Family:	110
8.19.6	Conclusion:	111
8.20	Alhaj Mohammed Ali Annjab	111
8.20.1	Life in Bangladesh:	111
8.20.2	Journey to the UK & Immigration:	112
8.20.3	Life in the UK:	112
8.20.4	Employment:	112
8.20.5	Housing:	113
8.20.6	Social & Family:	114
8.20.7	Independence of Bangladesh:	114
8.20.8	Conclusion:	115
8.21	Alhaj Mohammed Anis Ali	116
8.21.1	Life in Bangladesh:	116
8.21.2	Journey to the UK & Immigration:	116
8.21.3	Life in the UK:	117
8.21.4	Employment:	118
8.21.5	Housing:	118
8.21.6	Social & Family:	119
8.21.7	Independence of Bangladesh:	120

8.21.8	Conclusion:	120
8.22	Alhaj Mohammed Bashir Ali	121
8.22.1	Life in Bangladesh:	121
8.22.2	Journey to the UK & Immigration:	121
8.22.3	Life in the UK:	122
8.22.4	Employment:	122
8.22.5	Housing:	123
8.22.6	Social & Family:	123
8.22.7	Independence of Bangladesh:	123
8.22.8	Conclusion:	124
8.23	Alhaz Ismail Hussain Shiraji (Jomir Ali)	124
8.23.1	Life in Bangladesh:	124
8.23.2	Journey to the UK & Immigration:	125
8.23.3	Employment:	125
8.23.4	Social & Family:	126
8.23.5	Conclusion:	128
8.24	Alhaj Shah Husiar Ullah	129
8.24.1	Life in Bangladesh:	129
8.24.2	Journey to the UK & Immigration:	130
8.24.3	Employment:	130
8.24.4	Housing:	131
8.24.5	Social & Family:	131
8.24.6	Independence of Bangladesh:	132
8.24.7	Conclusion:	133
8.25	Mohammed Fozlu Miah	134
8.25.1	Life in Bangladesh:	134
8.25.2	Journey to the UK & Immigration:	135
8.25.3	Employment:	135
8.25.4	Social & Family:	136
8.25.5	Conclusion:	138
8.26	Alhaj Mohammad Azmal Khan	139
8.26.1	Life in Bangladesh:	139
8.26.2	Journey to the UK & Immigration:	140
8.26.3	Employment & Business:	140
8.26.4	Housing:	141
8.26.5	Social & Family:	141
8.26.6	Independence of Bangladesh:	143
8.26.7	Conclusion:	144
8.27	Alhaj Hafiz Ekhlasur Rahman Chowdhury	145
8.27.1	Life in Bangladesh	145
8.27.2	Journey to the UK & Immigration:	145
8.27.3	Life in the UK:	146
8.27.4	Employment & Business:	146
8.27.5	Housing:	148

8.27.6	Social & Family:	148
8.27.3	Conclusion:	149
8.28 Alhaj Keramoth Ali Ahmed		149
8.28.1	Life in Bangladesh:	149
8.28.2	Journey to the UK & Immigration:	150
8.28.3	Life in the UK:	150
8.28.4	Employment & Business:	151
8.28.5	Social & Family:	152
8.28.6	Independence of Bangladesh:	152
8.28.7	Conclusion:	152
8.29	Alhaj Khondokar Abdul Musabbir MBE	153
8.29.1	Life in Bangladesh:	153
8.29.2	Journey to the UK & Immigration:	153
8.29.3	Life in the UK:	155
8.29.4	Employment & Business:	155
8.29.5	Housing:	157
8.29.6	Social & Family:	157
8.29.7	Conclusion:	159
8.30	Alhaj Ayubur Raja Chowdhury	160
8.30.1	Life in Bangladesh	160
8.30.2	Journey to the UK & Immigration:	161
8.30.3	Life in the UK	161
8.30.4	Employment:	161
8.30.5	Housing:	162
2.30.6	Social & Family:	162
8.30.7	Independence of Bangladesh:	162
8.30.8	Conclusion:	163
8.31	Alhaj Atar Miah Chowdhury	163
8.31.1	Life in Bangladesh	163
8.31.2	Journey to the UK & Immigration:	164
8.31.3	Life in the UK:	164
8.31.4	Employment:	164
8.31.5	Housing:	165
8.31.6	Social & Family:	165
8.31.7	Conclusion:	166
8.32	Alhaj Surab Ali	167
8.32.1	Life in Bangladesh:	167
8.32.2	Journey to the UK & Immigration:	167
8.32.3	Life in the UK:	167
8.32.4	Employment & Business:	168
8.32.5	Housing:	169
8.32.6	Social & Family:	169
8.32.7	First in the Town:	170
8.32.8	Independence of Bangladesh:	170

8.32.9	Conclusion:	170
8.33	Alhaj Mohammed Rafique Uddin	171
8.33.1	Life in Bangladesh:	171
8.33.2	Journey to the UK & Immigration:	172
8.33.3	Employment & Business:	172
8.33.4	Social & Family:	173
8.33.5	First in the Town:	174
8.33.6	Conclusion:	174
8.34	Alhaj Mohammed Wajib Ali	174
8.34.1	Life in Bangladesh:	175
8.34.2	Journey to the UK & Immigration:	175
8.34.3	Employment:	175
8.34.4	Housing:	176
8.34.5	Social & Family:	176
8.34.6	Independence of Bangladesh:	177
8.34.7	Conclusion:	177
8.35	Faruk Ali	177
8.35.1	Life in Bangladesh	177
8.35.2	Journey to the UK & Immigration:	178
8.35.3	Life in the UK:	178
8.35.4	Employment:	180
8.35.5	Housing:	181
8.35.6	Social & Family:	182
8.35.7	Independence of Bangladesh:	183
8.35.8	Conclusion	184
8.36	Phul Bhanu Ali	185
8.36.1	Life in Bangladesh	185
8.36.2	Journey to the UK & Immigration:	185
8.36.3	Employment:	185
8.36.4	Housing:	186
8.36.5	Social & Family:	186
8.36.6	Conclusion	187
8.37	Nazrul Islam	188
8.37.1	Life in Bangladesh	188
8.37.2	Journey to the UK & Immigration:	189
8.37.3	Life in the UK:	189
8.37.4	Employment & Business:	190
8.37.5	Housing:	191
8.37.6	Social & Family:	191
8.37.7	Liberation of Bangladesh:	193
8.37.4	Conclusion:	194
8.38	Amir Miah	194
8.38.1	Life in Bangladesh	195
8.38.2	Immigration:	195

8.38.3	Employment:	195
8.38.4	Housing:	197
8.38.5	Social & Family:	197
8.38.6	Independence of Bangladesh:	198
8.38.7	Conclusion:	198
8.39	Alhaj Abdul Rouf Chowdhury	198
8.39.1	Life in Bangladesh:	199
8.39.2	Immigration:	199
8.39.3	Employment:	199
8.39.4	Housing:	200
8.39.5	Social & Family:	200
8.39.6	Conclusion:	201
8.40	Alhaj Amir Ali	202
8.40.1	Life in Bangladesh:	202
8.40.2	Immigration:	202
8.40.3	Life in the UK:	203
8.40.4	Employment:	204
8.40.5	Housing:	205
8.40.6	Social & Family:	206
8.40.7	Independence of Bangladesh:	206
8.40.8	Conclusion:	207
8.41 Alhaj Mokbul Ali		207
8.41.1	Life in Bangladesh:	207
8.41.2	Immigration:	208
8.41.3	Employment:	209
8.41.4	Housing:	210
8.41.5	Family and Social Life:	210
8.41.6	Independence of Bangladesh:	211
8.41.7	Conclusion:	211
8.42	Mohammed Kacha Miah	212
8.42.1	Life in Bangladesh:	212
8.42.2	Journey to the UK & Immigration:	213
8.42.3	Employment:	215
8.42.4	Housing:	216
8.42.5	Social & Family:	216
8.42.6	Independence of Bangladesh:	216
8.42.7	Conclusion:	216
8.43	Abu Taher Md Mohiuddin Chowdhury MBE, JP, B.Com	216
8.43.1	Life in Bangladesh:	217
8.43.2	Journey to the UK:	217
8.43.3	Early Life in the UK	217
8.43.4	Employment & Achievements:	218
8.43.5	Family:	218
8.43.6	Independence of Bangladesh:	219

8.43.7	Conclusion:	219
8.44	Alhaj Masrurul Hasan Choudhury	220
8.44.1	Life in Bangladesh	220
8.44.2	Journey to the UK & Immigration:	221
8.44.3	Early Life in the UK:	221
8.44.4	Employment:	221
8.44.5	Housing:	222
8.44.6	Social & Family:	222
8.44.7	Independence of Bangladesh:	223
8.44.8	Conclusion:	223
8.45	Lion Gulam Mustafa Chowdhury MBE	224
8.45.1	Life in Bangladesh:	224
8.45.2	Immigration:	225
8.45.3	Life in the UK:	225
8.45.4	Employment:	226
8.45.5	Social & Family:	228
8.45.6	Independence of Bangladesh:	231
8.45.7	Conclusion:	233
8.46	Alhaj Sazzad Khan	234
8.46.1	Life in Bangladesh:	234
8.46.2	Immigration:	234
8.46.3	Employment:	236
8.46.4	Social & Family:	239
8.46.5	Independence of Bangladesh:	240
8.46.6	Conclusion:	245
8.47	Shamsuddin Ahmed MBE	246
8.47.1	Life in Bangladesh:	246
8.47.2	Immigration:	246
8.47.3	Life in the UK	247
8.47.4	Employment:	249
8.47.5	Housing:	250
8.47.6	Social & Family:	251
8.47.7	Independence of Bangladesh:	252
8.47.8	Conclusion:	253
8.48	Alhaj MA Aziz Nunu Miah	254
8.48.1	Life in Bangladesh:	254
8.48.2	Immigration:	254
8.48.3	Life in the UK:	254
8.48.4	Employment:	255
8.48.5	Housing:	257
8.48.6	Social & Family	257
8.48.7	Independence of Bangladesh	258
8.48.4	Conclusion	259
8.49	Alhaj Makhon Miah	260

8.49.1	Life in Bangladesh:	260
8.49.2	Immigration:	260
8.49.3	Life in the UK:	260
8.49.4	Employment:	261
8.49.5	Housing:	262
8.49.6	Social & Family:	262
8.49.7	Independence of Bangladesh:	263
8.49.8	Conclusion:	264
8.50	Abdul Kadir Jilani (Bodor Uddin)	265
8.50.1	Life in Bangladesh	265
8.50.2	Journey to the UK & Immigration:	266
8.50.3	Life in the UK	266
8.50.4	Education in the UK:	267
8.50.5	Employment:	267
8.50.6	Housing:	268
8.50.7	Family & Social:	268
8.50.8	Independence of Bangladesh:	269
8.50.9	Conclusion:	270
8.51	Syed Ansaf Miah	271
8.51.1	Life in Bangladesh	271
8.51.2	Journey to the UK & Immigration:	271
8.51.3	Life in the UK	272
8.51.4	Education in the UK:	272
8.51.5	Employment & Business:	272
8.51.6	Housing	273
8.51.7	Social & Family:	273
8.51.8	Independence of Bangladesh:	274
8.51.9	Conclusion	274
8.52	Conclusion	274
8.53	Muhammad Abdul Matin Chowdhury	275
8.53.1	Life in Bangladesh:	275
8.53.2	Journey to the UK & Immigration:	276
8.53.3	Family and homes:	277
8.53.4	Employment & Business:	277
8.53.5	Life in the UK:	277
8.53.6	Social & Family:	277
8.53.7	Independence of Bangladesh	285
8.53.8	Conclusion	286
Acknowledgements:		287
Bibliography		288
References		289
Source of Information from Internet:		293
Photo Album		294

PREFACE:

It gives me great pleasure to introduce you to one of the most important projects Tigers International Association (TIA) has undertaken in its 25-year history. This project will be an addition to the existing local history and the community will be benefitted not only locally, but globally.

The Oral History of Bangladeshis in Greater Manchester is a hugely significant project that charted the arrival and settlement of Bangladeshis in this area of the UK. What this project has enabled us to do is capture the invaluable experiences of people who paved the way for generations with their experiences in a foreign land. It has enabled us to recognise the pioneering early migrants to the UK. By writing this history book we are acknowledging their achievements and thanking them for creating the future the public enjoys today.

Of course, this history project would not be possible without all those people who participated and gave us an insight into their lives. It would not have been possible if we were not successful with the help from the Heritage Lottery Fund and subsequently the support of many partners, volunteers, sponsors, and supporters. We extend a very heartfelt thank you to all the people who were involved in and supported us with this project.

This project brought together a unique set of first-generation Bangladeshis' who settled in the Greater Manchester area. We could have done hundreds of interviews and gathered the experiences of many more but naturally, there were limitations in resources. Those who did participate were a cross-section of the very diverse group of first-generation Bangladeshis' who give us a snapshot of the types of life and experiences.

We offer our heartfelt thanks to them and their families for supporting this project and helping to preserve their journey for generations to come. The success of this project is down to the many people, businesses, and organisations that have supported us from day one. Without the commitment, resources, and generosity of the sponsors, we would not be able to accomplish the project.

This "Oral History of Bangladeshis' in Greater Manchester" project has been in our thoughts for several years but without the resources and support, we would not have been able to realise the potential that we have unlocked.

We have acknowledged the support of the Heritage Lottery Fund (HLF) to undertake the unique history project. What the HLF has enabled us to do is capture a piece of history that will now remain with us for years and play a role in educating and informing others of the history and origins of the people that make up the diversity and richness of Greater Manchester. Now we can present to you the findings of our project.

Our objective is to record the previous history of the first generation of Bangladeshi people for the benefit of the wider community to share the experience. Also, this will be a good resource for the researcher or even the Bangladeshi generations to come to understand their roots and how they are living in Britain.

Summary of History Project

Early settlers in Greater Manchester from the Indian subcontinent can trace their roots back nearly 100 years. The first wave of migrants in sizeable numbers from Bangladesh came in the 50's. It is over 70 years since and many of those early migrants are no longer with us. As they have passed, so have their experiences, hardships, and successes.

15 years ago, a group of people at Tigers International Association considered a project which could capture and keep some of the experiences so that future generations could see how the experiences of the past, first generations helped to shape their lives.

As ever, funding and resources held the project back. However, 17 years ago, we received support from the Heritage Lottery Fund to help us undertake the Oral History of Bangladeshis in Greater Manchester. This would capture accounts of the lives and experiences of some of that first generation, early settlers into the area. The aim was to obtain this invaluable information and keep it alive and with it, the memories of so many who have helped to make this area what it is: a rich, vibrant, and dynamic place.

We put together a team of dedicated people, and researchers to find people with an interesting tale to tell. We found many. Sadly, we could only work with a limited number. Over 4 years, we spoke to no less than 50 people about their lives, early days, experiences, hardships, and much more. They gave us an insight that was eye-opening, fascinating, full of happiness, and sadness, hardship and hope, and aspiration.

To undertake this very demanding piece of work, we worked with a range of agencies that supported us in a variety of ways including The Manchester Metropolitan University & Huddersfield University, local colleges, businesses, and voluntary organisations.

We captured the conversations in audio and video, and they have been archived and captured in DVD format so that they are preserved for years to come. They have already proven to be an excellent tool for our youngsters to learn about their past and an educational tool for everyone in Manchester who is interested in tracing the rich diversity of the people of this area.

All this has been made possible by the volunteers who have worked tirelessly on this project. Their commitment was a fitting testimony to those they were researching, interviewing, and working with. We will work with schools, libraries, and other organisations to get this resource to large audiences so that these experiences can be shared and appreciated. It is hoped that similar projects will spring up elsewhere so that the rich history of Bangladeshis in Britain can be truly captured, shared, and celebrated.

CHAPTER I – INTRODUCTION

1.1 Introduction to the Organisation:

Tigers International Association (TIA) was formed by a group of British Bangladeshi professionals, inspired to work with and help Bangladeshi people residing in the UK and abroad. We are working with local government offices and other various voluntary organisations to provide support in the fields of education, employment, health, leisure, and recreation.

TIA is based at 259 Featherstall Road North, Oldham, a terraced property, which has been adapted to provide office space together with a moderately sized meeting room. Its Management Committee is drawn from members of the local community, and the services that it provides benefit the local community.

It is a registered charity that has been in existence for over 25 years. Since it was founded, TIA and its team of volunteers have worked tirelessly to support the Bangladeshi community in the Greater Manchester area with advice, guidance, and basic training to empower people to play their part in society.

Over the 25 years of its existence, the TIA has created and still enjoys many useful and strong partnerships which help it deliver real benefits and services to the residents of the Greater Manchester community.

Our charity is simple, supportive, and effective. Our objective is to increase confidence in education and better chances in life. TIA is based in Oldham to primarily work with the local people and make a positive impact in the community

TIA's vision for the organisation was sixth-fold. Firstly, to promote the benefit of the public especially the Bengali community in the UK and abroad without distinction of sex, race, religion, political or other opinions by associating together with the public and voluntary organisations in a common effort to advance education, training, leisure, and recreation.

Secondly, to work with the Bangladeshi community in the UK and abroad to create a social network to share the cultures of the various host communities to propagate understanding and tolerance by educating people in the cultural diversity of various communities and promoting understanding of the different cultures of the world (community cohesion).

Thirdly, the relief of persons who are in need by the provision of advice and information in such matters as immigration, money debts, welfare benefits, housing, health, education, training, and employment.

Fourthly, TIA aims to provide relief, whenever necessary to the victims of natural disasters in any community in the world.

Fifthly, advance the education of the public in the arts and cultural activities in particular through exhibitions, workshops, and performances to promote the development of a public appreciation of music, drama, and literature.

Sixthly, TIA aims to advance education and provide relief of unemployment for the benefit of the public by the establishment of an institution to deliver vocational training courses, provide work experience, and develop relationships with job centres, employers, and other agencies to provide assistance to find employment.

More specifically, TIA works with the local community to set up various educational training and provide efficient help and support within Education, Training, and advice projects based on local needs or community benefits.

TIA is focusing on developing activities in each of the areas, advice centres, training, and community projects. We want to take advantage of our unique emphasis on educational and cultural learning and development opportunities.

This is truly a community-based charity organisation with membership open to individuals who will share our aims and objectives. General members are recruited to the TIA development committee, which has been formed. Through these local committees, a professional network has already been created. This will help immensely in delivering TIA's objectives.

TIA's strengths are ongoing support from volunteers, effective financial management, effective communications between staff and community members, the heart of the community, an only organisation aiming primarily for Bangladeshi people although open to all, strong link with Local authority and other committee members, well known and respected organisation activities, and proven track record over 10 years of community and voluntary activities.

Over the years, the TIA has gained the respect of local people who rely heavily on the services including advice and information. TIA successfully delivered numerous projects for the benefit of local people, working with the statutory and voluntary sectors and the business community. This partnership approach has enabled it to go further and faster in helping people meet a variety of needs.

TIA aims to promote volunteering and provide opportunities for individuals to become involved in volunteering activities. TIA aims to provide a great standard of customer service to its communities and provide them with a simple effective service for all their personal and development needs. TIA has structured this very carefully so the support provided by TIA will be proficient.

Today's Bangladeshi community in Greater Manchester is very different from those who arrived as the first wave of migrants. Our Project "The Oral History of Bangladeshis in Greater Manchester" highlights this progress four generations on. Today, the community is well integrated into mainstream society but inequality and disadvantage in accessing services still exist, which is why TIA exists.

However, over the years, we have had to adapt to the changing needs and expectations of the community. Whereas in the early days, it was about language, access to basic services, and communication issues, today, the challenges are mirroring those experienced by mainstream communities.

Unemployment, drugs, crime, etc are affecting the community. We are working with mainstream agencies in a partnership role to better inform them of the needs and expectations of our still hard-to-reach community. As ever, we work with very limited resources, supporting ever-increasing numbers and higher demands for our services.

TIA's is connected with the worldwide community by Facebook and other social networks. The community benefited from exchanging news and views through these online services. In the past, the TIA has developed two projects in Bangladesh, one in Sylhet and another one in Barishall. We also plan to do two projects; one is re-housing projects for poor people and another one is to develop a medical college and a hospital in Sylhet.

We are creating a growing number of role models representing diverse fields and are all proud to be British and Bangladeshi. Their success is down to the hard work and dedication of many of our volunteers. More importantly, their success, our success is down to many of the parents and grandparents, respected elders who took part in the Oral History Project, and who are now reaping the benefits of the hard work.

Our young people and community are progressing, moving forward, achieving success, and creating role models for future generations. TIA is proud to play its part in helping to bring about the small changes that will have a huge impact in the future.

TIA has and continues to work with volunteers to provide most of our services. Encouraging local people in the community to give something back has been our greatest success and this is the most powerful way to show the community that change, and improvements are possible.

1.2   Introduction of the Oral History Project:

The long-term migration from Bangladesh is a well-known phenomenon. A good number of people who are of Bangladeshi origin now reside in different countries of the world as long-term migrants. Industrialised countries of Europe, North America, and Australia are the most important destinations of these long-term emigrants.

The People of Bangladesh have made their marks in many fields ranging from economic activities to the academic arena. They have developed successful enterprises. The restaurant industry is one such enterprise that brought long-term emigrant Bangladeshis to the forefront. Due to the hard work done by the Bangladeshis, curry has become the second staple food of the UK.

Along with host countries, Bangladesh has also made significant gains from the long-term immigration of a section of its population. Long-term emigrants played a glorious role during the war of independence of Bangladesh. The continuous flow of remittance is another of their well-recognised contributions. New export markets have opened for Bangladesh. Bengali ethnic goods and cultural and spiritual materials are being exported to different countries of the world to cater to the demand created by long-term emigrants.

The emigrant population is also showing interest in investing. Regular visits to Bangladesh by the emigrant population play a positive role in developing the economy in general. The UK immigrants Bangladeshis are also getting involved in local and national politics.

This opens new opportunities for influencing public policies in favour of the Bangladeshi community. The emigrant population has certain emotional, social, and cultural requirements for which they want to maintain a certain degree of relationship with Bangladesh. This in many cases results in economic, social, and cultural interactions.

Different studies on migration have shown that the migrant community can work as a bridge between the host (UK) and their home country, and migrants' economic and social interaction can be beneficial for all three parties: the migrant, the host country, and the home country.

The Governments of Bangladesh have gradually realised the importance of its emigrant communities. The seventh parliamentary Government took the most decisive step in this respect and created a separate ministry, the Ministry of Expatriates' Welfare and Overseas Employment, to efficiently manage the migration sector. The Ministry has been entrusted with managing both long-term and short-term migration.

Since the mid-1970s, the Government of Bangladesh has been involved in regulating and controlling short-term labour migration, and long-term migration. However, is a completely new area of Government intervention. The Ministry in this area aims to ensure the well-being of long-term immigrants, as well as to create space for them to participate in the development process of Bangladesh.

To do so, the Government needs to develop a concrete plan of action. Moreover, there hardly exists any systematic information base to plan the sector. There is no information about the nature of emigrant Bangladeshi communities abroad, their professional expertise, and the types of problems they face either in the country of immigration or the country of their origin. Besides, the Government also requires identifying the needs for capacity building of its functionaries for the efficient management of this sector.

Hence, it is important to undertake an in-depth study on the issue to ensure efficient use of the limited resources of the Government. This study is a modest attempt to provide policymakers, civil society organisations, the private sector, and the emigrant community with the necessary information to develop policies and strategies in this regard. The Long-term emigrant community of Bangladesh is much dispersed.

However, most Bangladeshi immigrants reside in the UK. Due to time and resource constraints, this study was based on the experiences of emigrant Bangladeshis in the UK.

1.3 Objectives:

The objectives of the study can be divided into two parts: policy objectives and, research objectives.

The research objectives of the studies are:

Review existing literature and studies on long-term emigrant Bangladeshis living particularly in Greater Manchester (UK).

Trace the processes of their migration and settlement patterns.

Sketch social, economic, and cultural profiles of emigrant Bangladeshi communities.

Gather data and analyse those to identify their needs, concerns, and priorities.

Gauge the level and nature of links of such emigrants with Bangladesh, particularly of the first-generation Bangladeshi immigrants.

Assess the scope and the role of immigrant Bangladeshis on the political and economic machinery in formulating policies towards British Bangladeshis.

The policy objectives of the studies are:

Suggest policy measures to the relevant authorities for addressing immediate and long-term issues and concerns of the emigrant communities of Bangladeshis living in Greater Manchester.

Suggesting policies and recommendations for the relevant authorities to develop policies and projects for the benefit of the local community.

Recording the history of first-generation Bangladeshi immigrants who migrated to the UK, to share the experience with the wider community and to get benefit from our research.

1.4   Introduction of the Author:

Mustafa Ahmed Mustak

Mr. Mustak is a highly intelligent, educated, and perceptive person. His natural carelessness, knowledge, and experiences have been of great influence and assistance to the Bangladeshi community which has been recognised and appreciated widely throughout the UK and Bangladesh.

Whilst he was in Bangladesh, he successfully ran 2 businesses with the full assistance of his father and was a news reporter and contributor for the "Weekly Sylhet Songbad", "Daily Sylheter Dak", "Potrika" and the monthly magazine "Tiloth-Thoma". In 1986 he successfully produced a film named "Shuk Duker Pritibi"; he also took an acting role in the film.

Mr Mustak came to the UK in 1989 and has made an impact within the various communities through volunteering and in the management of voluntary organisations. He first became involved with the "Tower Hamlets Homeless Families Campaign" in East London. He has contributed to the delivery of key objectives such as timely re-housing, school admission, and welfare benefits for homeless families. He eventually became one of the management committee members making a direct contribution to the planning and development of the project.

He has also worked with the "Tameside Metropolitan Borough Council" as a housing development officer. Whilst he was working there, he was also working as a tutor at "Mossley Hollins High School" for GCSE students. He worked with the "BACP" in Rochdale as a senior advice worker and worked for the "Glodwick SRB project" in Oldham.

Mustak was actively involved in developing a Credit Union in Hyde and he became the director of the "Hyde Credit Union". He also played a key role as the trustee of "Croft Millennium Trust", which negotiated with Tameside Council for a piece of land in Hyde to develop as a children's play area. This space is being utilised by children and the elderly for socialisation and recreation. He had taken the initiative to set up a community learning centre in Hyde by securing funding from the National Lottery.

He had done an action research project for Tameside MBC to investigate the employment, business, education, housing, and health of the Hyde and Bangladeshi communities. He was also involved in doing the Bangla audio dubbing for a documentary video project called "Catering for whom?" and translated a part of a poetry book called "Untold Words" which was published in 1996.

Mustak was involved in interviewing 50 participants of the oral history project, and he gave support to the volunteers by doing the recordings, editing, transcriptions, translations, and finally the publication of it all. He also used his previous experience in undertaking the research work for this history project giving this book extra strength and adding more valuable information for the researcher and the future generation to study this material.

In 2000, Mustak wrote & published a history book called "Bangladeshis in Great Britain", particularly for the Hyde Bangladeshi community. He also contributed as an editor of a Bangla literature magazine called "Setu Bandhan" published in March 2002 by the Tigers International Association -TIA. He published a book called "Life in the UK Test Guide" in 2007; He also published his poetry books "Spondon" & "Chetona" in 2013. In 2021, he also published his translated version of his poetry book "Consciousness" and "Bangladeshis in Manchester.

He has taken the leading role to set up several different groups in Hyde, Ashton-u-Lyne, Oldham, Rochdale, and Manchester. These groups are as follows: Shapla Forum (Community consultation group) Surma Bangladeshi Group (Senior citizen group), Job Club (Bangladeshi unemployed group), Bangladesh Mela Steering Group (Arts & culture), Bangladesh Social Club, and Tigers International Association -TIA. Throughout the years he has organised several community events such as seminars, workshops, festivals, and children's play schemes, which benefited the Asian communities. In doing so he has given the opportunities to volunteers to develop their various skills including being organised, having leadership, and using teamwork.

In 2004 Mustak successfully set up an Immigration Law Practice focusing on the UK immigration law in Manchester, Birmingham & London. The practice was well well-established and busy organisation with offices across the Northwest and London.

He is the chief editor of "Probash Barta 24.com" and presenter of PB24TV hosting various programmes including "community matters", poetry, music, legal advice and so on. The Probash Barta 24.com online newspaper aims to accommodate various topics including health, education, employment, training, business, literature, history, politics, and sports for the benefit of the wider community. This publication is targeting the creation of a new audience. Mr Mustak hosted a programme known as "Community Probin" at ATN Bangla and contributed as a regional reporter for Channel S.

Since 1991, Mustak has been involved with various organisations such as Manchester TEC, Oldham Business Enterprise, RMBC, Tameside Racial Equality Council (TREC), Oldham Development Agency for Community Action (ODACA) now known as Voluntary Action Oldham - VAO, Manchester Business Link, First Step Project, Stuart Ridgeway, Princes Youth Business Trust, Salford NHS Trust.

Furthermore, he has successfully obtained funding from the National Lottery Charities Board, BBC Children in Need, Northwest Arts Board, Princess Youth Business Trust, Tameside MBC, Oldham MBC, Glodwick SRB, Greater Manchester Community Trust, Commonwealth Youth Exchange Council, and BICA for various organisations he worked for.

Mustak has dedicated his life to serving various community sectors, fostering collaboration and unity among diverse groups. His efforts have been widely recognized not just in the UK, but also internationally. Throughout his career, he has actively engaged with residents, advocating for their concerns to relevant authorities, and ensuring the delivery of quality public services.

He received various Awards such as the Channel S Community Award, Oldham Chronicle Pride in Oldham Award in 2003, Writers Award in 2013, SEFC Award in 2014 and Mayor's Appreciation Award in 2015.

He seeks truth in every area of his life, whether in learning, discussing values, or relating to his fellow community members and others. He is seen as one of the most distinguished community and social workers in Greater Manchester. In 2024, he also received a prestigious honorary doctorate from the American University of Business and Social Sciences for his profound and transformative impact on community development, public service, and social cohesion over his impressive 30-year career.

CHAPTER 2 – Interviews

2.1 Alhaj Moboshor Ullah:
(Interviewed on 17 November 2007)

2.2.1 Life in Bangladesh:

Alhaj Moboshor Ullah was born in 1953 in the area of Shingerkas, Mazgaow village of Bishwanath, Sylhet. His father's name is the late Haji Mohammed Saif Ullah and his mother's name is Hajini Aymuna Bibi. He completed his primary education at 'Shingerkas Primary School' and was admitted to a local high school called 'Aklimur Raja High School'.

His high school was two miles away from home. Ramsundor High School was about five miles away. The road combination wasn't very good to travel on, for that reason he used to go to school on foot. He studied till year eight in high school and after that, he migrated to the UK.

In 1966, the prices of goods were reasonable, but people did not have enough money to afford them. So, it wasn't easy either. For example, he said that people who didn't have enough money wouldn't be able to afford to buy fish and had to find good places to go fishing to see if they could retrieve some food for themselves, but there were sufficient fish available in the ponds, canals, lakes, and rivers. And the ordinary people used to catch the fish to survive. There were so many fishing tools people used to use them I.e. fishing nets.

He said that people in the 1960's were quite gentle, easy-going, and open-minded. The curriculum in the school was very much related to real life. The method of teaching was very good and advanced. Teachers were very friendly and caring with delivering the curriculum. The students were affectionate towards the school - teachers.

There was no need to employ a house teacher after receiving good tuition from the school. The students were able to do the homework on their own after receiving the tuition from the school - teachers.

Most of the fishing area is controlled by private owners now, so it is difficult for ordinary people to catch fish from the lakes. More specifically, the poorer population was in a more difficult situation. During the Pakistan period, if there was any crisis, the government used to provide relief to the ordinary public. At that time Ayub Khan was the president of Pakistan. He did not see anyone deprived when it came to getting relief from the government.

23

Nowadays you will see the complete opposite, the poor do not get their goods. He has many poor relatives living in Bangladesh, but he has never seen anyone receiving help from the government. The poor people were entitled to receive relief goods from the government, but some people abused the system and began looting the goods. There is a lack of a distribution system that exists in Bangladesh due to political corruption.

The village economy was dominated by agriculture. He had seen that there were people involved with the production of rice, if someone did not have the land, but was able to get some land from the landowner and become partners in the rice cultivation the people could easily keep their families fed for at least six months.

The rich people were lazy when it came to doing the cultivation work; they'd rather purchase the rice from the local stores. Moulana Shikondor Ali and Moboshir Khan had made a tremendous contribution to their village school and many people had the opportunity to become educated. He appreciates their contributions, which have benefited the local people.

He said it was very hard to obtain an education as there was no transport facility going to and coming from school. The road was disabled for the time being, if there was rain sometimes it would flood due to the cracks in the road. He used to bring one extra set of clothes to school to change it before he entered. There were no culverts over the channels, so he did not have much choice.

Sometimes, people came forward to put a bridge made of bamboo, but people used to break the temporary bridges. He was very keen to do the study; especially with his parents encouraging him. If he had never come to Britain, then he would have been able to continue his study. His father was so simple man, before his father came to Britain he was engaged in agriculture. His father used to cultivate his lands and sometimes he used to hire the lands from someone else.

2.2.2   Journey to the UK & Immigration:

His father Saif Ullah came to Britain in 1957. His father came to realize that he would be able to bring his son to the UK. His eldest brother is deaf, so his father decided to bring him instead. At that time his father used to live in Oldham. On 6th November 1966, he arrived in the UK. He was only 14 years old. When he first came to Britain he lived at 57 Belmont Street, Oldham, with his father. In 1966, there were only a few families that had lived in the UK. Most of the people were single at that time.

In 1963, the Queen visited Pakistan, at that time Ayub Khan (President) requested the Queen to allow some people from Pakistan to come to Britain to work. Since then, the labour voucher was started and many people had the opportunity to come to Britain during that time. Entering Britain was so easy to migrate to.

In 1963, the British government had given the "Labour Vouchers". Since then, many people "especially the men" utilised the opportunity and came to Britain. No women came to Britain with the Labour Voucher, he did not see anyone come or hear from anyone about this. His teacher Moulana Shikondor Ali helped him to file the forms. He signed the form and sent it to the British High Commission. He received an interview call letter from BHC and met with the school - teacher.

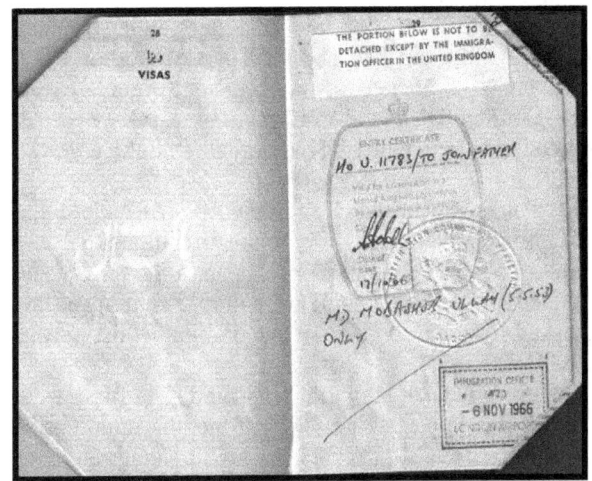

His teacher then told him that you are only 14 years old, and you needed to decide whether he would like to go or not. If you decide not to go then this opportunity should be given to someone else instead. His teacher also told him that when he was old enough he would be able to come to Britain. He accepted his advice and the letter was given to his father. His father then gave this letter to his friend.

The Second time, his father arranged paperwork from one of the rubber factories. He submitted these papers to the British High Commission, Dhaka. At that time the interview procedures became a bit harder compared to the previous years. The entry clearance officer used to ask unnecessary questions like: what do you eat? Where did you stay last night? Who came with you? How many houses do you have? Who came to your house yesterday? Etc.

He also thinks that the interpreter made up these unnecessary questions. For example, he said that he had taken his brother to the interview and his brother found that the interpreter wasn't an interpreter at all, his brother objected, and the interpreter had to leave the interviewing room.

In 1966, it was the first interview of his life; it was in a foreign embassy, which he can't forget. During the interview, he was very nervous because he had to answer so many questions. He was worried that if he didn't answer the questions correctly the outcomes could be negative. His father told him to tell the truth during the interview.

At the age of 14, whilst he was going through the interview process "whether or not this process was right" he could not understand and he thought it wasn't logical at all. After all, Moboshor Ullah was successful, like many other young people. The formal interview lasted for about an hour, there was a long queue on that day. On that day he received the visa. On the way back to Sylhet from Dhaka, his mother started crying. When he arrived finally at his new home, his brothers and sisters started crying. After seeing this scenario, he was a bit nervous and afraid too. He told his mother that she should contact her husband to let him know that he is coming to the UK.

After all that, his family members (mother & other siblings) made compromises and accepted the reality and had accepted that Moboshor Ullah should go to the UK. Finally, the airline ticket was booked from Surma Travels in Sylhet town. The owner of Surma Travels also asked him a question which was "you are so young, and you are going to the UK, the weather in the UK is so cold, how can you live there?"

He paid 16,000 Rupees "Pakistani Currency" and flew from Dhaka by PIA. He was so young that an air hostage had to carry him to the aircraft and put him in a seat. There were no known people on that flight. At that time only a few people used to go abroad. Other Bangladeshi people were on the same flight, his family talked to them and asked for them to keep an eye on him, whilst he was on the flight.

When the flight took off from Dhaka, he was a bit scared. The flight went to Karachi and arrived at Heathrow Airport. When he first met the Immigration Officer, he was unable to understand the English Language, the interpreter was called and asked him a question asking whether his father came to the airport to pick him up. He answered yes to this question.

As he was coming out from the flight, he had seen his father in the crowd and his father was waving his hand to show that he was at the Airport. His father embraces him at the airport. His father hired a taxi from Oldham; the taxi driver was called Abbas Ali. This taxi driver Abbas Ali had helped his father to prepare his declaration paper.

Abbas Ali was an educated person; therefore, he helped many Bangladeshi people sort out their Immigration. His father offered him some food, but he was so tired, within about three minutes he had fallen asleep in the taxi.

At the airport he saw some people working with long beards and turbans, he asked his father are these people Imam (priests). His father replied and told him that they were sheikhs, Indian people.

In 1982 he brought his family when the British government passed a law for the commonwealth citizen to bring their family to the UK (NB: Immigration & Nationality Act 1981). Before that, there was no provision within the immigration Law to bring many families to the UK.

8.2.3   Life in the UK:

His father worked in the stadium as a line marker. His father used to get £7.00 per week. There was a time when many jobs were available in the factories and people were able to find employment very quickly.

The bus was the main transport to go anywhere, but it was not adequate. The people used to wait 3-4 hours at the bus station. Waiting in the cold weather, their feet used to get cold. The people used to wear 2/3 sets of stockings and long boots to protect their bodies from the cold weather. It was a very hard life in Britain during those times, he added.

The weather conditions were very bad. Heavy snow fell during winter, most of the time they used to remove the snow/ice from their doorstep to open the door. The thickness of the snow/ice falling was high over feet. One person used to hold the other person's hand, when they used to go out.

At that time, there were no Bangladeshi or Indian grocery shops, which has now changed drastically. The first grocery shop was on Rochdale Road, Oldham, owned by Mona Ullah, who was from the Doulothpur village of Biswanath. Almost all the Bangladeshis used to go there to do the shopping. They used to do the shopping once a week; it was easy to split the cost between them. The English women used to deliver straight to their doorstep.

One person was responsible for paying the grocery bills. They did not like to eat sheep meat; instead, they used to get live chickens from the farms. They prepared halal meat, which was the main reason not to buy the meat because that was not halal at that time.

Nowadays you get everything you need; fish, vegetable pan, etc, battle nuts were not available at the beginning. He said sometimes when they felt that they wanted to eat fish then they would buy herring or sardines from the Market.

On Saturdays and Sundays, they used to buy chickens and cook their food in a big cooking pot. The price of a hen was 2 shillings 5 pence (1/2 crown). The prices of goods were very cheap. Usually, on a Saturday, he used to go to the public bath. There were always long queues and people used to wait in the queue for about 3 to 4 hours to get the serial. Half an hour maximum time was allowed to have a bath, and the charge was only 2 shillings. The soap and towel were included in this price.

There were language difficulties when he first arrived in the UK, he was able to understand but was not able to speak. The English people used to show their affection to the Bangladeshis. If there was any problem in finding an address they used to show the address, and sometimes they used to drop you off at the destination address.

They used to give money for the travel expenses if anyone was struggling with funds. Some people used to advise the newcomers to keep their medical cards, to show the address where they were living. For those people who were unable to speak the English language, it was useful to keep the medical card in their pocket. The police were very helpful too. He never faced any discrimination just because of his race or nationality. The English men and women were very affectionate and caring too.

In the house his father used to live in, the rent was £2.50 per head. Three/four people used to share the cost of the meals. There were insufficient fresh vegetables available. There were big unions from Spain. People used to think twice about whether to buy the vegetable or not, due to the prices being a bit high.

The people used to consider their income before they spent their money. When he used to do the shopping, he'd remember his family back home. If he spent all his income in the UK, then how could he send money abroad to support his family? It will be very difficult for the Bangladeshi family members to maintain themselves.

At that time people used to save most of their money and send it to their loved ones. Many people sent money abroad to buy land and to build houses. Due to this, the people were so careful when spending money. He was saddened about not completing his secondary school certificate exam, this was because he had left Bangladesh and had come to Britain. He also added that the most enjoyable time of his life was when he was living in a village, he thought that he'd never see home again and would worry about it quite a lot.

In the past, the people who established a business were educated and intelligent, nowadays the setup of a business is much easier than in the past. Many businesses have been set up in different towns and cities, in the past, the business was more profitable because there was less competition. Elderly people would usually get jobs in the factories but for the younger generation, only restaurant jobs were available.

Before coming to Britain, he did not know anything about this country, he was too young to learn about foreign countries. He was at a very young age when he came to the UK. He recalled some of the memories of when he used to go out with his father, and then white people used to give him sweets and show affection to him. He won't forget that he has also never seen any discrimination.

At the factory where his father used to work, the white workers used to tell his father to bring his child with him. He used to go with his father and used to get around 4-5 packs of sweets, which was more than enough. There was some racial tension though, he can't remember the exact year, but he said in the past the black and Asian people were welcomed by the British white people. The people used to come forward and offer help.

In 1995, the total Bangladeshi population in Hyde was around 3,500; in 2007 the total population has doubled. Housing issues are not the only issue within the Bangladeshi Community, this is an issue for the wider community. For example, he said there is a two years waiting list for the New Charter Housing. Many Bangladeshis are now living in their own houses, so it is for the minority group who are not able to purchase due to their circumstances.

8.2.4 Employment:

His cousin owned a restaurant business in Salisbury; he started his first job in the restaurant and worked there for about two and half years. He did not receive any pay, but he learned the English language and had gotten a lot of work experience from there. The accommodation and food were free and sometimes he used to get £5.00 - £6.00 for his pocket expenses.

When he was 16 years old, he told his cousin that he was not going to work for him unless he was paid. He asked his cousin to help him find a new job for him. He was also told that his father's income was not sufficient for maintaining his family in Bangladesh, so he needed to earn some money and would like to support his father.

He imagined that working in a factory would be hard, even if he had the chance to work there, he would not be able to do so. He has seen his father and other people working in factories.

His father then contacted a man who had a restaurant in Liverpool; he was originally from the same village. His name was Dipok Chowdhury, and the name of the restaurant was Asha. Dipak Chowdhury finally agreed to offer a job to him. He started his employment as a coffee waiter in mid-1968. The wages were £6.00 per week and accommodation and food were included; he had worked there for about 12-14 years.

Dipak Chowdhury's father was an advocate in the Judge Court, Sylhet, Bangladesh. Dipak Chowdhury helped him to learn English all the time to improve his communication skills. Dipak Chowdhury also insisted that he should go to college to learn English. He also took Faruk Miah with him to college to learn English.

Moboshor Ullah described one of his experiences and said, "One of the teachers came to our restaurant and he recognised us, he first saw us at college and told us that we're able to speak good English, why do you come here?", The teacher also told them that they can speak English and therefore have no need to come to college and waste their time.

Moboshor Ullah was gradually promoted from his position which was a coffee waiter to a full waiter. He remembered some of his colleagues whilst he worked at the Asha Restaurant in Liverpool, those were Abu Talib-chef, Subrotho Kanti – Assistant Chef, Rafiq Miah, Barindro Chondro Biswash, Musleh Uddin Ahmed, and Hussain Ahmed.

He went to the Milk factory in Dukinfield, Cheshire and he met the manager. He had a job for three weeks on a trial basis. The manager also told him that all the training would be given, and if he could show that he would be able to do the job then a permanent position would be offered. He completed his trial period with success and had a permanent job with the Milk Company. His job was to operate a computer. He worked there for about three years and used to get £135.00 - £150.00 per week. In 1981, he established a takeaway business in Penny Meadow in Ashton-under-Lyne.

In 1986 he sold his Takeaway in Ashton and opened another Takeaway in Liverpool. He ran the takeaway for about 7-8 years and then sold the business. He then opened another takeaway in Stockport. In 1995, he sold his third business and dedicated his time to the Bangladeshi Community in Hyde.

8.2.5   Housing:

In 1977 he left the job and moved to Dukinfield, Cheshire where he bought a two-bedroom house for the price of £1,600.00. The toilet was outside; there was also no central heating, the main reason for moving to Cheshire was due to his father working in that area and his father requested that he should come to Cheshire.

8.2.6   Social & Family:

In 1969 he returned to Bangladesh for the first time and got married to Afia Khatun from Chuto Polir Ghaw, a village of Chattak. He stayed there for about 14-15 months and then returned to the UK, when he returned, he also rejoined his old employment at the Asha Restaurant.

In 1975, he brought his wife and son to the UK. He had started living in a house next to his workplace and paid the rent of £12.00 per week. Within his friends' circle, he was the first person to get married and pass his driving test. These were the great achievements in his life, he added. In 1986 he performed his Hajj (Pilgrimage to Makkah). In the same year, he had an invitation from the

Hyde Bangladeshi Welfare Association (HBWA) and joined with them.

In 1995, there were activities by the HBWA because the centre was closed. Since he became involved, he started to do some lobbying with some agencies and was able to bring some of the services to the centre. He also visited other associations in Greater Manchester, to see how the other associations were run and what sort of activities they were doing. More specifically he appreciates the support he received from the Oldham & Rochdale Bangladesh Association.

He was a member of the Tameside Racial Equality Council, Age Concern, Shahjalal Housing Association, Probin Mela Luncheon Club, and the school governor for Hyde Technology School. He worked towards developing the Bangladeshi Community in general but he used to participate and provide support to social activities. His contribution to the Hyde society will be remembered by the Bangladeshi Community, he added.

He said, "we need to educate our children, then they will lead the community, they will have better jobs and will bring prosperity in the future. We will then feel proud to our community". If you put the national interest first and work together as a team, then we will succeed, he also added.

In 1996, he became the general secretary of the Hyde Bangladeshi Welfare Association. In 1997 he became the chairman of the same Association. He continuously served this community until 2004.

He is the father of 9 children, 4 sons, and 5 daughters. The eldest son

Kashem Uddin has graduated from Birmingham University and is now working as a teacher in Dubai, his second son is working for British Gas as an engineer, his two daughters are married (Nasima & Halima & Rajima), Naima is working in the legal sector in an office and his other children are in the school and College.

8.2.7 Conclusion:

He shared his experience in working with the community and his life in the UK. He said "You never get 100% support; some people will always oppose your actions by criticising or not co-operating with you. You must ignore those kinds of people, and you must work towards a good cause and projects, then you will see success". He also said, "Do not look backwards and try to move on, helping other people is helping mankind and this is purely community work; you will get rewarded from the creator".

He also said, "If any community works as a team (united not divided) when dealing with any issue, you will see success". There was an incident with the

local police in 2000. The Police played a negative role and arrested a few young people for throwing some rubbish (chips and wrapping paper).

The community was united, a public meeting was called, and the Chief Inspector of Police had to apologise in public for their wrong action. That police officer was suspended later. There is some provision for the elderly people at the HBWA, which has been running for about 20 years.

He said, "after qualifying Bangladesh, there is no guarantee that you would be able to get a job but, in the UK, there are many opportunities for an educated person to find employment". Many relatives are living in Bangladesh, and he travels to Bangladesh on a regular basis to see his close relatives. He wishes for his retirement life to be spent in the UK with his family.

8.3 Alhaj Md. Abdur Rashid
(Interviewed on 1 July 2010)

8.3.1 Life in Bangladesh:

Md. Rashid was born in 1940 in the village of Syed Mandaruka, Balagonj, Sylhet, Bangladesh. He mentions that he remembers his primary school in Mandaruka and the times he had been there. During that time most people used to complete their studies right after their primary education. He was studying at high school in class 6 before he came to Britain.

His father used to work onboard a ship; he cannot recall when his father started work due to his young age. During the 1940s and late 1960's some people travelled to Calcutta to gain employment by working onboard ships. His father had no intention of travelling to Britain and living there. During this period many people from India and Pakistan travelled to Britain to live and his father decided to settle in Britain.

8.3.2 Journey to the UK & Immigration:

When Md. Rashid came to Britain at that time his father was already living in Britain, in 1958 Md. Rashid came to Britain with a work permit, he found out from his friends that there were some opportunities for working in Britain as a work permit holder. At that time a visa was not required to come to Britain, but permission was required from the relevant authority.

During that time Bangladesh was under Pakistan's government rule. He flew from Dhaka to Karachi and arrived at Heathrow Airport in London. He travelled with two of his friends to Britain; before their arrival, they contacted relatives to meet them at the airport but unfortunately due to poor communication they did not receive the message and were unable to meet them at the airport. The people from Bangladesh came to Britain to work and earn money, and he followed in their footsteps.

The main communication was written letters, but a telegraph was used in emergencies. From Heathrow Airport, Mr Rashid travelled by taxi to Birmingham to his father's house and he stayed there for 6 -7 weeks.

8.3.3 Life in the UK:

They used to go to the public bath every week to have a bath, there weren't any Mosque facilities either. There was a grocery shop in Manchester; Maulana was the owner of the shop. Everyone had known this butcher, Mr. Matin Miah from Bangladeshi used to own an Orient Restaurant in Manchester. There was a grocery shop next to the restaurant which they used to buy spices, rice, and other things.

In 1958 when he first came to Hyde his uncle Haji Wahab Ullah had mentioned that he was the first Bangladeshi man in Hyde. He used to live on 86 Victoria Street and used to work in a cotton factory. **He also said that the Late Mr Jomsher Ali, his brother Mr Yaor Bakth Chowdhury, Mr Abu Tahir, Mr Shuna Miah, Mr Gulam Kibria, and his cousins' brother were amongst the first Bangladeshi settlers in Hyde.** They all used to live in one house and work in the cotton mill. At that time single people used to live in one house. If it was a big house then 10-15 people would live in that house and they used to cook their food by themselves.

Mr. Ahsan Ullah from Jogonnatpur Sylhet, Bangladesh used to own the "Dhaka Restaurant" and he was the first Bangladeshi restaurant owner in Hyde. There was another restaurant in the same place called "Kashmir Restaurant" and Mr. Hason Ullah was the owner of the restaurant. **The first grocery shop was owned by Late Mr Hason Khan from Sikondpur, Sylhet,** Bangladesh. That was a small shop and didn't have a sign or a name; they used to pray on top of the shop. It was on Union Street. People used to know it as the Bangladeshi shop. Before the Mosque was established people used to pray at the shop.

During the work in the factory, he used to get an hour lunch break. There were not any facilities to pray at work, so after work, he used to pray at home. The main reason that would stop them from praying at work was the lack of facilities to do Wudhu. At that time everyone used to pray at home because there were not any Mosques nearby.

They used to get a weekend off from work, on the weekends they used to do cooking, go out, and some even used to go to the English cinema hall. Some people used to go to Manchester to watch Indian Hindi movies, and 2-3 people used to go together. Also, they used to go to friends' and relatives' houses.

During the holiday period, they used to go to different towns to visit friends and relatives. From 1981 all the prices started increasing. Before that, everything was very cheap, including the rent for the houses. He also said during 1960-1980 everything was very positive, a happier time even.

8.3.4 Employment:

During his stay with his father, he looked for employment but at that time there was a job crisis in Britain. He had written to his relatives living in London and met up with them to discuss finding a job. From what his relatives had told him he realized that it is hard to get a job. He tried for about 5-6 weeks to get a job but unfortunately, there were no jobs available for him.

During these times there were no telephones available in most houses. His father sent him a letter asking if he'd found a job yet, he replied: "At the moment, there is a really bad job crisis in London". In 1957-1958 there was a terrible job crisis. At that time his father wrote a letter to his brother regarding a job for his son.

His uncle replied to his Father confirming that he had found a job in Hyde and that his son needed to go there to get the job. Mr Rashid's father went to London and then came to Birmingham with his son. After that day he came to his brother's house in Hyde with his son. Mr. Rashid's uncle found him his first job in Britain.

His first job was in the Ashton Manchester Cotton Mill; his starting wages were 6 pounds per week. He worked there for 6 months as a trainee labourer, although he did not have any experience, he slowly learned the necessary skills to work in the factory. It was difficult for him because, without any previous experience in the UK or Bangladesh working in a mill, he soon started as a spinner. In that factory, they used to make the thread and export them to other countries.

In 1959, Britain started to take more and more people for jobs, every factory had a job vacancy. He started a new job in a rubber factory with good wages; he used to make gloves from plastic. His wages were 15 pounds per week, and after 15 months he went to Bangladesh for a holiday.

He stayed in Bangladesh for 9 months and then came back to Britain, as he returned, he started a new job in the Godley area in Hyde, they would make pies, sausages, and other things. His wages were 60 pounds per week. He worked there for 2 years then he returned to Bangladesh. At that time, the people did not stay in Britain for a long time. After 1 or 2 years they used to go back to Bangladesh.

After that, he again returned from Bangladesh and found another job in the Ashton Brothers cotton factory. After that, he worked in a factory in Hyde where they used to make clothes. He worked there for a long time and that was his last job in Britain. In 1979 he started a restaurant business in Liverpool. He stayed with the restaurant for 2 years; it was also a partnership business with 4 other people.

The business's name was Sher-E-Punjab Indian food shop. It was a good business, He then decided to leave the business due to his partners being gamblers and putting the business at risk, also he wanted to return to Bangladesh. In 1980 he stayed in Bangladesh for 6 months, he then came back to Britain with his family, he found out from the staff that the restaurant business was not doing good and that his partners had spent the money on gambling.

He asked his partners to provide the business accounts, but they did not give back a good answer. His partners had left all the gas, electricity, and tax bills unpaid which had added up to around 40-50 thousand pounds worth of debt, they initially bought the business and paid 40 thousand pounds. He had to make a hard decision, with 40 – 50 thousand worth of debts; he had taken over control of this business.

Then in 1981, he decided to sell the business. After paying all the outstanding bills and taxes, he received only 3 thousand pounds by the end of it. His business was in a really bad situation, and he had lost one freehold house. During 1981 he wasn't involved with any jobs or businesses due to his pension age.

8.3.5 Housing:

During that time, he used to live with his uncle at his house in Hyde, he did not have to pay any rent, but he used to pay 50 pence every week for the food. During that time everything was cheap, i.e. 45 kg rice was 50 pence, now the same rice was £50.00.

Throughout that time there weren't many telephones compared to this day and age where every family either has a telephone or a mobile phone. They used to contact each other by writing letters to one another. They didn't have a television or a carpet in the houses which is very shocking to this generation. They used to use Coal to warm the house, in those times in Britain the weather conditions were very bad, there was no difference between day and night, and it was always cold.

The weather conditions were bad, it was too foggy, and snowy and during the daytime, it would be cloudy. In these times he used to socialize and spend time with other people in the living room, when they went out, they had to wear big coats and gloves because of the cold. They didn't have a bathroom inside the house either; they used to use the toilet outside of their house.

In 1960, he bought a 2-bedroom house for 600 hundred pounds. At that time, they didn't have radiators or bathrooms inside the house, after 1970 they started to put radiators and bathrooms inside the houses. He sold the house and bought another 2-bedroom house for 1200 hundred pounds. Then the Council demolished the house. Then he bought another 3-bedroom house, and he gave this house to his daughter and her husband as a gift. In 1990 he bought another house for 27 thousand pounds and now he is living in this house.

8.3.6 Social & Family:

Before his family came to Britain there were 10-15 families who used to live there, currently, about 700 hundred families and more than 5 thousand people are living in Hyde. There is a Bangladeshi Welfare Association to provide help to the community. Since 1981 he has been involved with the association and at this present time, he is an executive member and member of the Hyde Probin Mela Luncheon Club.

This is how he involved himself with the community work. There was a housing association called "Shahjalal Housing Association" and he was a member of the association. At the moment Ashiana is in Rochdale had taken over the Shahjalal Housing Association.

Mr. Rashid claimed to be one of the first Bangladeshi settlers in Hyde amongst other people and there are a lot of things that we can learn from him. At first, when he came to Britain, he had problems speaking English but slowly improved. He did not go to school or college to learn English; he learned it from other English-speaking people.

In 1964 he got married in the Anorpur village in Bangladesh. He has 1 daughter and 2 sons. His sons are married, and His mother and brothers are living in Bangladesh. After every 1 or 2 years, he goes to Bangladesh to see his family and relatives. He loves his country Bangladesh.

He was involved with the Mosque; in 1981 he used to go to the Mosque to Pray in Hyde, Manchester. He became the Chairman of the Mosque, and he was involved with the Mosque for 10 years, he gives thanks to Allah. They used to donate money for the Mosque on Fridays. Slowly the number of people had increased. They bought 2 houses for the Mosque and rebuilt it. After 1992 he became a Mosque Trusty.

In 1982 he went to Makkah to do his first pilgrimage (Hajj) then in 1992 he did his second Hajj. Mr Rashid is an established person in Britain; in 1960 he got British Citizenship. He is now retired and spends his time watching television, going to the library, Luncheon club, shopping, and going to the Mosque and praying. Sometimes he goes to relatives' houses or spends time with his family and grandchildren. During the rest of his life, he wants to spend it in Bangladesh and Britain.

8.3.7   Conclusion:

He has been living in Hyde for a long time; he also said that in the time he had spent in Britain everybody used to show respect, they were caring, supportive and helpful to each other. Slowly everything is changing unfortunately he mentions. He also said this is because everyone is either living in a different town or area or not going to each other's houses and communicating with the family.

In the past, everyone used to live together and communicate with each other, they were caring, loving, and helpful. The new generation needs to show respect, have a loving nature, and be helpful towards the community; also, they must follow their cultural route. He said Britain is a free country, but the new generation must follow a good way and must respect their parents. They will do well in their personal, family, and educated lives. This is an important message to pass on to the new generation.

8.4 Alhaj Sunawar Ali
(Interviewed on 15 Jan 2008)

8.4.1 Life in Bangladesh:

Alhaj Sunawar Ali was born in the village of Silaura, Jaganath Pur, Sunamgonj. His father's name was the late Mohammed Rashid Ali. When he was 5 to 6 years old his father passed away and in 1970 his mother died. Out of 4 brothers and two sisters, he is the only successor left of the family.

Before coming to Britain, he was responsible for looking after the land property. From the income of the property, he was able to support his family. His family was well-maintained, and everyone lived peacefully. The poor and rich people in the village weren't divided, everyone used to live together.

8.4.2 Journey to the UK & Immigration:

In 1942, his elder brother came to Britain. In May 1962, his elder brother obtained a 'declaration' for him, which allowed him to enter the UK. The flight expenses cost around 1800 to 2000 Rupees. His departure to the UK began from Dhaka Tejgaon Airport to Karachi. He had to stay in Karachi for three days due to some technical problems. He then flew to London Heathrow and then to Manchester Airport.

After arriving at the Manchester Airport, his elder brother came to receive him and then took him to his house. At the time Britain's weather was very cold and he endured the cold British weather. He and his brother travelled together to Britain, and they stayed in their elder brother's house. When he arrived in the UK, he was only 25 – 26 years old.

8.4.3 Life in the UK:

His life in the UK was heard at the beginning as he said no Bangladeshi families were living in the UK. People used to cook their meals, wash their clothes, and work hard either in restaurants or factories.

8.4.4 Employment:

At first, he began work in a restaurant where he received £7.00 wages every week. He eventually worked in the Manchester Airport as a kitchen potter; the wages were £10.00 per week. Then he got a job in a paper mill in Manchester. When at work Mr. Ali did not face many difficulties communicating with the workers.

He had to work for 9 hours from 8 am till 5 pm. The average weekly wages for this job were £10 to £12 as the pay was not fixed. Sometimes there was an opportunity to do overtime.

During that time the weather condition was extremely cold so he would wear two pairs of socks and warm insulated clothes when going to work as the workplace did not have heating facilities. He worked there for one and a half years before moving onto a cotton mill in Rochdale which was called Dunlop; he worked there for one year.

He then got a job in another cotton mill in Hyde called Ashton Brothers. He used to work 12-hour shifts, and his weekly wages were £15.00 to £16.00. He went to Bangladesh in 1970 and returned to the UK in 1972 and he was re-employed at Ashton Brothers. His weekly wages were £20.00 per week. The night shift was 10 pm to 5 am. He used to go to work by bus; he worked there for 10 years. The factory work was hard and boring, throughout his career he worked in several other factories due to competitive pay.

In 1978, he went to Makkah for a pilgrimage and then went to Bangladesh. Upon his return to the UK, he found that the Ashton Brothers was closed, where he used to work. He also said, "At the end of the 1970s factories in Britain were closing and people became unemployed". After that, he was not able to work much and the house he owned was demolished by the local council.

The behaviour of the English people was very friendly. In the factories, the English people used to care for foreigners. He said that if he had to go to Bangladesh, upon his return to the UK, it was possible to re-engage with the employment.

8.4.5 Housing:

At that time, while he was living with his brother, the houses did not have central heating and the houses had to be heated via coal fireplaces, there were only a few Halal shops where they bought their groceries. There were not sufficient mosques to pray in, during the occasion of Eid, Bengali people would have to pray in an Arabian mosque in Manchester.

He lived in Manchester for twelve years. Then in 1975, he moved to Hyde where he rented a house.

8.4.6 Social & Family:

He got married before he came to Britain. He had to leave his wife and his eight-month-old son in Bangladesh. In 1976 he was able to bring his wife and children into the UK where they lived in a flat in Manchester. The children were enrolled in school but because of frequent visits to Bangladesh, the children were unable to study properly. However, one of his sons was educated in a Madrasah (Islamic School) in the UK. The rest of his children are working.

8.4.7 Independence of Bangladesh:

At the time of liberation, he was in Bangladesh. During the war, he was a witness to the events that unfolded. During his stay in Bangladesh, his passport was destroyed (bug). After that incident, he received a new passport from the British High Commission in Dhaka and flew back to the UK.

Remembering the memory of liberation, he said that the anti-war group behaved very rudely and caused chaos. The members of this group are known as Rajakar, and they worked against the liberation of Bangladesh and cooperated with the enemy. His hometown was not affected during the liberation movement, but Pakistani troops captured the local chairman Haris Miah and then later released him.

8.4.8 Conclusion:

In 1978 for religious purposes, he spent a few weeks inviting people for religious talks, and then he went to Hajj. The savings were spent on maintaining the family and visiting Bangladesh; therefore, he did not have enough money to invest in businesses back in Bangladesh. He is pleased that he has been able to raise his children well who have been able to pursue their ambitions. Now he is enjoying his retirement life with his family in Britain.

8.5 Alhaj Aklas Ali
(Interviewed on 1 July 2010)

8.5.1 Life in Bangladesh:
Alhaj Aklas Ali was born in the village of Boruni, Bishwanath, Sylhet. He completed primary education at "Baushi Primary School", and then he went to "Palbari High School" and studied in that school for 1 and a half years. They had a paddy field and agricultural work.

His father died when he was little, He used to work on a ship. His father had a chance to settle in Britain, but he did not stay, but the people with who he used to work decided to settle in Britain.

8.5.2 Journey to the UK & Immigration:

In 1963 Mr. Ali came to Britain using an employment voucher, he went to Sylhet to visit, and he found out that people were going to Britain by voucher. He used to play football in Bangladesh, and he used to come to Sylhet to play football matches, from that he got to know new friends and people from Sylhet. From Sylhet, one of his friends used to work in the Dhaka British High Commission.

He went to Dhaka British High Commission to get the voucher form, he had to stand in a huge queue, and then after 2 days, he went to the hotel because he didn't get the form. This is because there was a long queue for collecting voucher forms, sometimes they would even fight in the queue. After the Fazer prayer, he went to the British high commission and saw 200-250 people standing in the queue, police used to control them because the people used to argue with each other. British High Commission guard wall was sooner or later broken due to the people.

Whilst these things were happening Mr. Ali had an idea that he could go inside the office because his friend worked there. Then people asked him where he was going due to them standing there for the last 3 days waiting to get inside. Then he said, "My friend works there, and I am going to see him", it took him 4-5 hours to get into the office gate. Then he mentioned his friend's name and managed to go into the office. Then he was confused because he didn't know where to go, he soon saw some stairs though. He went up the stairs and met a fair lady who was wearing a skirt and half of her hair was cut, he thought that she might be from another country.

She asked him "What do you want?" He did not understand, so he resorted to saying his friend's name. She told him to go to the 3rd floor of this building and that he'll find him there, she also said 2 ladies were the same age as her on the 3rd floor. He then went to the 3rd floor and repeated his friend's name, and then the gentlemen asked him again what his friend's address was.

He gave the correct answer then the gentlemen took him to his friend. When he finally found his friend asked, "What are you doing here?" He told him about collecting a form voucher. While he was drinking tea his friend went to another room then came back and asked him "How many forms do you want?"

His friend gave him 3 form vouchers and his friend told him about the people who were standing outside and that they might take the form from you so be careful. He said goodbye to his friend, and he met with the lady again, he found out that she was 40-45 years old, first, he got scared but she could speak in Bangla too.

Mr. Ali was talking to the lady for a while; she told him to be careful about the people outside and not tell them that you have got the voucher form. These things happened before, when he came outside the office people asked him about the form, and he said he did not get one. Then he went to the hotel, and he discovered that he had another problem, he did not have any money to pay for the hotel or to get home.

When he came to Dhaka, he thought about the possibility of getting a form, so he stayed in Dhaka for a couple of days, and then he went back to his home. Then afterwards he thought there would be someone from Sylhet at the train station waiting for him. He went to the train station and started looking for someone from Sylhet, and then he noticed that someone touched his shoulder, and it turned out to be his niece's husband.

He asked about the family and how they were keeping it, he then asked his niece's husband which hotel he was in. Then his niece came to the hotel and asked when he is going home. Then he told me about everything including the hotel, the money and why he went to the train station. Then his niece and her husband took him to the train station, and they said their goodbyes. Also, they pay for the bills of the hotel. After he came to the village he told his brother about the form, hotel, and everything.

He gave one (1) voucher form to his next-door neighbour who was a poor man, but they knew someone who came to Britain by cheating, so he did not come to Britain. He gave another form to one of his friends he used to contact. He went to the agency with his form, and they sorted out everything, and they called to get the main voucher but Mr. Sad Miah who used to work in the agency was ill, and he went to his village. Mr. Aklas Ali was worried that there was a possibility of him not going to Britain.

Then he went to Dhaka to see Chuto Miah for help who is from Sylhet, Mr. Chuto Miah sorted things out for him then he went to Chittagong. After a few days, Mr. Ali went to Chuto Miah's house and told his wife everything and she said he didn't mention anything about you at home.

Then he went back to where he used to stay and found out where he could get the voucher to go to Britain. There was a long queue, so he went back. He went back to his friend; he told everything to the person who was at the office gate. He asked are you here with any agency he said no, and he told him to sit and wait. Then he came back with some papers and asks his name, father's name and what village he came from, this was all written down on the paper then he went off again.

He came back and said he had given all the details to someone and that certain someone would call you. He was waiting but no one came, Bangladeshi people were walking past but he did not say anything. After a while a fair lady came and asked him how long he had been waiting, he said: "I don't know exactly but roughly 2 and half hours". She said, "My God!" Then she went to the next room and called him to follow.

She told him to sit and asked his name, date of birth, and address and after that, she gave him a Visa. He was happy and went home with his Visa; he booked his ticket from a travel agency in Sylhet for British Airways. It cost him 15 hundred Takas. He spent all the money from his savings and his brother sold his Paddy field for his brother to buy suits and other special things. Everyone came to Mr. Ali's house to say goodbye to his wife's family, friends, and relatives.

He came to Heathrow by British Airways; at that time, he was 25 years old. No one came to Heathrow to receive him because he didn't let anyone know that he was coming to Britain but one of his cousins' lives in Britain and Mr. Ali has his address from Bangladesh. He stayed in London and lived in someone's house that he knew.

8.5.3　　Life in the UK:

At that time there weren't many good facilities for the telephone. He stayed in London for 12 weeks and looked for a job; he did not find any jobs there, so he went to Yorkshire in Leeds to his friend's house. The reason he came to Leeds was to find his nephew, he knows that his nephew lives in this area, and he is an Association chairperson for this area, also he is the community chairman for the Mosque. His nephew came to Britain when he was 10 years old. He came to Britain a lot earlier than Mr. Ali came.

8.5.4   Employment:

Mr Ali's first job in Britain was in a factory in Mossley. In that factory, they used to do wool and cotton work. As a learner he used to do 12-hour shifts 5 days a week and on Saturday 4 hours, including overtime, his wages were 7 pounds for the first week. He worked there for 3 months. Then he found another job in a factory which was much closer to his home where he used to live. He went there because it is near and has good wages. The factory's name was John King Foundry, in that factory he used to do cutting work, and his wages were 14 pounds per week.

He worked there for 5 years and during that time he got himself British citizenship. When he came back from Bangladesh he started working again in the John Kings Foundry factory. The reason he found the job again was that the manager used to like his work very much. He used to do overtime because the manager used to offer it to him every time. He worked in that factory for 3 and a half years.

Then he found another job in an iron factory, 12 hours shifts 5 nights including a bonus, he used to get 25 pounds per week. After 5 years of working, he went to Bangladesh and stayed there for 4 and a half months and then came back to Britain. Then he started work in Leeds in a Yorkshire foundry. That was a metal factory, and they used to make lorries, car engines and train parts.

He worked there for 5-6 years and then went back to Bangladesh for the 3rd time. When he came back from Bangladesh, he found another job in a glass factory in Leeds and it was near the Yorkshire factory. He used to do 8 hours shifts and they had overtime facilities. He used to get 60-70 pounds per week because if anything was urgent then he used to take a day off otherwise he used to work 7 days a week.

During Bank holidays or other holidays, he used to tell his manager that he wanted to keep on working. Every time he used to do overtime job. After that he went to another metal factory which was in the same area, the factory's name was Catton Factory, and he worked there for a year and a half. He spends his work life in a factory in Britain.

In 1990 he went to Bangladesh, and when he came back to Britain, he noticed that for VAT purposes the factory job was not making good business and there were not many vacancies. They used to fill up forms for the factories, but they didn't get the job. Then he came to Hyde.

He also said he used to work as a supervisor in the John King factory. His duties were to tell the workers what time they came in for work, what are they doing, how they had to do the work, and people who were working overtime. During the work at the factory, he had friends and out of them, he used to talk about one of his friends from Africa. He used to get a 1-hour lunch break. Some people's jobs were less dangerous, so they used to go to the canteen to have lunch.

8.5.5 Housing:

Within 5 years in Britain, he bought a 6-bedroom house for 500 pounds, in total he bought the house for 5 and half thousand pounds. The mortgage was 10 pounds per week. In that house, he had 2 kitchens, 1 sitting, and a dining room.

He also said that during that time they didn't have toilets inside the house, they used to use the toilet outside of their house. They used to go to the public bath to have a bath because they didn't have a bath inside their house. They did not have any radiator facilities also, he used to go to town for shopping and there was one grocery shop in the town. He didn't face any problems with speaking English during work at the factory.

8.5.6 Social & Family:

In 1968-1969 he went to Bangladesh to see his family and relatives. He stayed there for 5 and half months and then came back to Britain because of his house. When he first came to Britain his eldest son was 2 and half years old and his wife was pregnant. After 12 days of coming back to Britain, his 2nd son was born.

He got married before he came to Britain and his wife and children were in Bangladesh. The reason he came to Britain was to work and to establish himself. In 1986 Mr. Ali's wife and 5 sons came to Britain but his eldest 2 sons got married in Bangladesh and they continued to live in Bangladesh with their family. Sometimes they come to Britain to see their father and Mr. Ali goes to Bangladesh to see his son's family and relatives.

In Britain, his 2 sons work in factories and 1 son works as a waiter. In 2006 he went to Makkah to do his Hajj. He had a heart problem now he's recovered from that but now he has an illness called arthritis.

8.5.7 Conclusion:

He thanked Allah and said he is happy in his personal and family life because he came to Britain. He thinks he has this illness because of his work at the factory. The Doctors did examinations, and they said they found bruises on his feet. During their work in the factory, they used to wear metal boots. He also said if anything that weighed 10 kg had fallen on his feet nothing would happen to his feet.

When they used to go outside of the factory for a walk the boots would make a sound like horseshoes, He has bruises on his feet because of wearing safety boots. Now he is retired and has health issues but still working for the community. He is a member of the Bangladesh Welfare Association and Hyde Jameh Mosque. Then he said he enjoys living in Hyde now and is happy with his family.

8.6 Alhaj Johur Uddin
(Interviewed on 4 July 2010)

8.6.1 Life in Bangladesh:

Alhaj Johur Uddin was born in 1938 in the village of Shahbajpur, Bishwanath, Sylhet. His father's name is Late Md. Rahat Ullah. He has 8 brothers and sisters, and he is the eldest, his father used to maintain the family from agricultural work. Also, his uncle was in Britain, and he used to work on a boarding ship and he settled in Britain.

They all used to stay together; most of the families in the village were very poor except for 7-8 families, he passed primary education from his local school in Shahbajpur and then he went to Khujkipur High School in Balagonj. When he was in class 7 education he finished his education.

8.6.2 Journey to the UK & Immigration:

Md. Johur Uddin came to Britain in February 1962; his uncle prepared everything for him to come to Britain. His Uncle sent a letter with an address to go to Dhaka and with contact information and more information about going to Britain. They told him to come again with a photo and passport. At that time, they didn't need a Visa to come to Britain; they only needed a Passport to come to Britain.

He booked his ticket to come to Britain from Sylhet. When he came to Britain he started work the next day.

8.6.3 Life in the UK:

At first, he did not like living in Britain because he didn't know how to speak the language. His grandfather used to live in Halifax and work there, his grandfather managed to get a job in this factory which his grandfather used to work at. It was an engineering factory in north Halifax. He worked there for 2 years. First, he used to get 7-8 pounds per week as a learner.

In 1976 he came to Hyde and about 15-20 Bangladeshi families were living in Hyde. Since he came, people have started to come and live in Hyde. Now, 7-8 hundred Bangladeshi families are living in Hyde, and about 6-7 thousand people are living in Hyde. There was a restaurant called 'Dhaka Intercontinental' and a Grocery shop in Market Street in Hyde and the owner was Bangladeshi.

In 1962 1/2 Bangladeshi people were able to speak English; if certain Bangladeshi people couldn't understand English words they used to understand English by their sign language. At that time British people were helpful. They used to like Bangladeshi people. For example, if anyone was lost or didn't know how to get to their house then the person would show the address to the English person, then they used to take the person to their house address. It is very rare for this time generation.

In 1962 - 1963 during that time it was very cold in Britain. It used to snow very much. He used to live in Halifax at that time. It started snowing when he was going to his uncle's house to give him his wages. That night he stayed in his uncle's house, and it was snowing all night. After that day when he went to the bus station and saw the bus, but it wasn't moving because of snow. He stood there for 2 hours when finally, the driver started to drive to Halifax. Then the bus had become stuck in the Halifax area because of snow. All the passengers were on the bus. Then the truck came and put sand on the road and the bus managed to go to Halifax at 7.30 at night. He said that time people used to use the bus to go to work or anywhere.

During the weekend he used to go to the public bath to have a bath and he used to play cards, chest, etc. Also, they used to go to the cinema to watch Indian and Urdu films, on Sundays. At that time, they used to have a cinema in that area, and they all used to like to watch films at the cinema; they used to go to the cinema in the evening. When they used to finish watching the cinema then they used to get prepared for cooking. The next day some people must work at night or in the morning. He used to take his lunch or dinner with him to work, during the summer holiday he went to Black Pool and Southport from his company.

8.6.4 Employment:

He used to work 5 days including 4 hours on Saturday. His wages were 10 pounds and 50 pence. He used to do various work in that factory-like using drill machines, sanding machines, or melding. He used to like working there; he never thought it was too hard. His uncle used to live there. During his work in Halifax, he used to live with his grandfather and Uncle, he worked there for two years, and then he went to Bradford Textile Mill where his other Uncle used to live.

When he first came to Britain, he stayed 1 or 2 days with his uncles. His grandfather found a job for him in Halifax; he went to Halifax and lived with his grandfather and Uncle. After trying hard he found a job in the Bradford textile mill. Weekly he used to get 18 pounds, at that time he used to live with his other Uncle. He worked there for 2 years; He used to look for good jobs and good salaries.

Then he found another job in a factory in Show Bridge town. They used to work in 3 shifts. The job routine was if you work 5 days in a day shift then you get 3 days off and if you work in a night shift then you get 3 days off after. He used to work a 1-week day shift and 1 weeknight shift. It was good, per week he used to get 19-20 pounds. He used to do welding, spinning, and doubling in that factory, about 7 years he worked in that factory.

During his work in that factory, he used to look for different jobs and good wages. Then he found another job in the James Turner factory. After 3 months he went to Benson Turner, during work in the factory in 1969 he went to Bangladesh. In 1970 he came back to Britain and found out that the factory was closed. Then he found another job at Hill Brothers Textile Mill in Bradford, he worked there for 4 years.

In 1977 he went to Bangladesh for a Holiday. When he came back to Britain in 1978, he found out that most of the factories were closing, during that time in Hyde his grandfather, brother, and one of his uncles used to live there. He called his grandfather and brother and told them he was searching for a new job.

He came to Hyde to see them, but the intention was to find a job. They told him to stay for that day so that he could go to their workplace and meet some new people, they also said you could speak English, and you are an experienced worker which would make finding a job easier.

They told him "If you speak to the Manager then you might get a job" On the next day he went to the factory, he spoke to the Director of the factory and the Director said we need a person like you but not at the minute, we will let you know by phone. He then went to Bradford, and after 3 days they called, the caller's name was Mr John, and he said to Mr Uddin that he could start work.

Then he came back to Hyde and started working. It was in 1978; the factory's name was Kingston Mill, and it was in Hyde. He came to live in Hyde and now he is living in Hyde. He was Forman of the factory, and he worked there till 1997, and he retired from there. That was his last job in Britain.

8.6.5 Housing:

He used to catch the bus to go to work when he was in Bradford. In Bradford, he used to live in his own house with his uncle. Before his uncle went to Bangladesh, he put Mr Uddin's name on the house. It was a 6-bedroom house. His uncle bought this house for 600 pounds, and he had to pay a 150 pounds deposit. He used to pay 10-shilling mortgages per month. That time if you rent out 1 bedroom then you can get 5 shillings per month. This is impossible nowadays. That time they used to have 10-shilling notes. He sold the house in Bradford when he came to Hyde.

At that time there weren't radiators inside of the houses, they used to use Coal to warm the house. They used to warm water using a Coal fire and a gas cooker, they also used to go to the public bath on Saturday to have a bath. If there are too many people in the public bath then it used to take time to have a bath, otherwise, it didn't take time to have a bath. He used to go to the public bath once a day during the week and he used to warm water to have a shower at home.

People used to go to have a bath in a public place after work; they used to pay 6 pence or 1 shilling to have a bath in the public bath. At that time everything was cheap. For example, one packet of cigarettes was 1.6 pence which is 6 pounds to this time. At that time if a single person used to get 14-15 pounds in wages, then they used to save 10 pounds. But then it was impossible when their family was here.

8.6.6 Social & Family:

In 1959 he got married before he came to Britain. At that time, he had 3 daughters. After he came to Britain he went to Bangladesh a few times. Then he realized that other Bangladeshi people were bringing their families to Britain. In 1980 his wife, one son, and one daughter came to Britain.

He has 2 sons and 6 daughters. His eldest sons and daughters got married. His eldest son owns a restaurant business. Another one of his daughters is studying religious education and his youngest son is studying in college. In 1998 this successful gentleman went to Makkah with his mother to do Hajj.

In 1972 there was a Bangladeshi Welfare Association in Hyde, but it was closed. They used to do meetings in Town Hall when it was started new. Then it became a large association, 27 people used to work for the project. It was at 19 Chapel Street which is still there. He was involved with the association as Vice-chairman for a long time. Now he is a member of the Luncheon Club and a general member of the Mosque.

8.6.7 Independence of Bangladesh:

In 1971 during the war in Bangladesh, Mr. Uddin used to do meetings and demonstrations and helped people in Bangladesh with money. Like other people, he used to give all of his wages away to support the war in Bangladesh. Every week he used to go to London for meetings and demonstrations. When he used to work in a factory the Pakistani people used to work there, and they would argue with Bangladeshi people.

Bangladesh had Victory on the 16th of December 1971. It is shown on this information BBC channel. That time he finished work and was heading home. One Pakistani person was listening to the radio that Bangladesh had a Victory, and 93 thousand Pakistani people were arrested after he heard the news, he smashed the radio on the road.

At that time, he used to live in Bradford. Lots of Pakistani people used to live there but the Bangladesh people were not scared. At that time 700-800 Bangladesh people used to live in Bradford. During the meetings and demonstrations, they did not face any problems with the Pakistani people.

In 1971 they formed the 'Shogram Porishod committee' in Bradford. They didn't think about themselves, they used to help raise awareness about the war and people in Bangladesh. All the Bangladeshi people used to give all their wages to war in Bangladesh. The only thing all the Bangladeshi people wanted is the Victory of Bangladesh.

8.6.8 Conclusion:

Mr. Uddin retired in 1997. Now he is living with his family in Hyde. His father was in Britain, but he went back to Bangladesh because he did not like Britain, he never came back to Britain. His father came to Britain in 1983, and he went back to Bangladesh in 1984. Mr. Uddin goes to Bangladesh to spend time with some of his family.

It was the last time he went to Bangladesh, and he stayed there for 6-7 months. In 1972 he had gotten his British Citizenship. In Bangladesh, he has 5 sisters, 1 brother, and their family. At the moment he spends his free time with his grandchildren and sometimes he goes shopping with them. Mr. Uddin is an established gentleman in Britain and our Community. He is an established person to our new generation. In his personal life, he is happy with his family.

8.7 Alhaj Munsif Ali
(Interviewed on 30 November 2007)

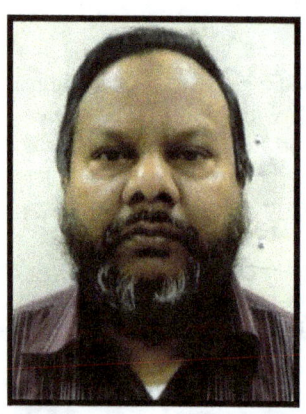

8.7.1 Life in Bangladesh:

Alhaj Munsif Ali was born in 1951 in the village of Doyamir, (Balagonj) Osmani Nagor, and Sylhet, Bangladesh. His father's name is the late Alhaj Kasim Ali (Shareng) and his mother's name is the late Gulu Bibi.

His father was living in the United Kingdom; he has 4 brothers & 3 sisters. He studied at Abdus Subhan Primary School & Sodrunnessa High School, then he studied up to the class of seven due to taking up residence in the UK.

8.7.2 Journey to the UK & Immigration:

Mr Ali's father used to work on a boarding ship and took up residence in the UK. When his father went to Bangladesh to bring him to the United Kingdom his father was 60 years old. Alhaj Munsif Ali's main intention was to study in the UK and look after his father who has reached the age of 60.

In 1966 he came to the UK with his father and arrived at Heathrow Airport. From there they took a taxi and went to London where his father's friend was living. He and his father stayed there for two days. Then they took a train from King Cross Train station and came to Manchester where his cousin was living.

8.7.3 Education in the UK:

He joined Greenfield Primary School in the year of four. His father had taken a job in a Textile Mill, which was in Oldham. He had to move with his father, and he then joined Chadderton County Secondary School, he completed his GCSE at the age of 15. He was encouraged to study the Textile Diploma on a part-time basis, the course was for 5 years, and he completed it in 3 years. He received a certificate from the college which is intermediate level.

8.7.4 Employment:

After completing his secondary education, he started to work in a textile factory. His starting wage was £8.00, and he used to work 40 hours a week. He used to get a day off with pay to go to college.

In 1969, his father went back to Bangladesh and Mr. Ali moved to Hyde in Cheshire. He worked in a paper factory for about a year. Weekly wages were £10 but if anyone worked on Saturday, he used to get £2 on top of the weekly wages. In 1970 he worked in the Eastern Restaurant as a trainee waiter. The wages were £12 per week with free food and accommodation.

The reason for changing employment was that people enjoyed working in the restaurant, and the people who came from Bangladesh; enjoyed working in restaurants. There were many facilities like free food and accommodation which were provided by the employer. Working in the restaurant was much better than working in the factory. That was the main reason for the change of employment.

He worked there for about 5 years, and after that, he opened a restaurant on Union Street in Oldham town. That was a partnership business with Mr Alhaj Ismail Ali. The name of the restaurant was Eastern Tandoori. He was running this business for about 3 years. The weekly business taking was 15/1600 pounds. After receiving the wages, he used to get £25-£30 profit per week.

While he was running the first business he opened another restaurant. In 1984/85 he sold his share to his partner. Thereafter, he opened a takeaway business. In 1993 he sold his takeaway. In 1994 he went to Makkah to do the pilgrimage. He opened another takeaway but due to low turnover, he sold the business. During the present time, he is working as a private taxi driver. Whilst he was involved with the business, he was a bus contractor and then he worked as a bus driver with the Greater Manchester Transport.

There was an opportunity for a contractor who worked for at least 2 years and would like to become a bus driver. He had been given the chance to sit for a test and undertake some training. He successfully passed the test and got the job offer.

His wages were £4 - £5 per hour and he worked there for about 7 years. He left the bus driver job and went back to run his own business. His partner was not happy to run the business on his own. Therefore, Mr. Ali decided to leave the bus driver job and take over the business management. Mr Ali still feels that the driving job was very good for him. There were some benefits which were very useful such as sick benefits.

The relationship with staff was also very good. There was no racism. There were no differences between white and black workers either, everyone was treated equally and had gotten the same benefit. Mr Ali said there were no regulations in the factories such as safety regulations and wearing a uniform to do the work. There was half an hour for a lunch break and for using the canteen facility, if people go to the canteen to take their lunch, they could not finish in half an hour. So, people used to get their meals from home and just used the microwave to warm up the food.

Mr. Ali used to get the food from home, and they used to sit somewhere convenient to eat. Some other people used to do the same. He enjoyed working in the factory. The house consisted of 9 bedrooms. Some people used to live in a single room and some people used to share rooms. At that time there was a good relationship with people. People used to accept other people as their brothers.

8.7.5 Housing:

His father used to share accommodation with one of his friends; he was living there with them for the time being. There was no bathroom, no hot water, or central heating system in the house, the toilet was outside the house, and the coal was the only source of heat in the room. He used to use the bath once a week at the public bath.

One shilling per person was the charge to have a bath and the soap was 6 pence. Depositing 1 penny to get a towel and when you return the towel you get your 1 penny back. The room he was living in was with his father, another person was living there as well. For the accommodation, he used to pay £1 per week. The landlord used to change the bed sheet every week.

8.7.6 Social & Family:

He used to send money to his family members who were residing in Bangladesh. Mr. Ali and his 2 brothers are living in the UK. One brother is residing in Bangladesh. His Bangladeshi brothers are responsible for looking after the property in Bangladesh and in some time they can come to the UK to see them.

In 1972, he went to Bangladesh and got married, he has nine children. His eldest son was born in Bangladesh and the rest of them were born in the UK. Two of his daughters and two of his sons got married. One son is working in the Gas office, other children are studying. He has many relatives living in Bangladesh; he goes regularly to Bangladesh to see them.

He sometimes takes his children and family to Bangladesh. His childhood was very good; the Bangladeshi community is doing better compared with the previous period. His children are now going to universities and obtaining degrees. He thinks that the parents and community both need to be more anxious and provide necessary guidance and support to their children. All parents should have the responsibility to maintain family ties with Bangladeshi relatives, taking children to Bangladesh is also important.

8.7.7 Conclusion:

In his conclusion, he says that **our community needs to focus more on education.** He is working as a volunteer with the local Bangladeshi community in Hyde. He was involved with the Hyde Welfare Association and served as an official. He is now involved with Hyde Jameh Mosque. He also said that he and his children have been educated because they are in the UK. If he never had the opportunity to come to the UK then it would have been more difficult for his family to study, studying in Bangladesh is more difficult, unfortunately.

8.8 Alhaj Rois Ullah
(Interviewed on 30 July 2009)

8.8.1 Life in Bangladesh:

Alhaj Rois Ullah was born in 1930 in the village of Moinpur, Chattok, Sunamgonj. His father's name is the late Ayub Ullah Master. As the son of a schoolteacher, he was not able to get more qualifications. He concentrated on education as his mind was set on doing something else, and after that, he migrated to the UK.

His father had huge sums of land; he'd employ workers to do the cultivation. Income from the teaching and the cultivation was sufficient to maintain his family without any difficulties. The financial status of the family was also good due to the earnings of his father. The village's economic condition was good, as was the socio-culture. During that time everyone lived friendly and peacefully, and the old people were also highly respected and loved by all.

There was peace in the society because there was no jealousy. The correctors of villagers were very good too, so there were never any corrals or fighting. Although most of the people were dependent on agriculture there were not any highly ambitious diseases in their minds and hearts. Therefore, the people were happy and peaceful. He found those days were beautiful and everything quite stunning.

"Today's present is a bit different from the earlier time. Today's present is quite devoured by drugs and drunken issues. The past we know no longer exists. People's feelings and attitudes toward each other are vanishing."

Many Bangladeshi people were dependent on cultivation, and only a few had the opportunity to do different things. Earnings from selling crops were sufficient to meet the general expenses of the families. The prices of goods were very cheap, nowadays people want to earn more money and most of them are running after wealth, but no peace and happiness.

He made his quick remarks by saying **"The main reason for unhappiness is that people are forgetting Allah (the creator)"**. He was very active in sports; in particular, he became a good football player. He earned his name and fame as a football player and became very popular in his village.

At that time there were three football teams, but they did not have any individual team names. All the football teams were known as Moinpur Football Teams. He was confident as a right forward and as a striker position.

He played against different towns and cities, i.e. Balagonj, Sylhet, and Sunamgonj. He recalled some of his football teammates; are Abdul Kuddus, Afruj Miah, Abdul Wahab, Abdul Rashid, and Modoris Ali. He was very keen to be a football player, which was the main reason, not to complete or make any progress in education.

8.8.2   Journey to the UK & Immigration:

In 1961, at the age of 25, he came to Britain with a labour voucher. At that time people came to the UK with student and medical vouchers. He came to know many of his friends including one of his cousins had come to the UK, and then he decided to come to the UK.

He flew from Dhaka to Calcutta by Air India, and then soon arrived at London Heathrow Airport. When he arrived at London Heathrow Airport, he showed the address to an English man. The Englishman then told him to follow him as he was taking him to the train station.

He had taken the train from London to Coventry. The English gentleman told him, as soon as he arrived in Coventry, then he needed to show the address to the Taxi driver. The taxi driver then would be able to take you down to the destination address. He did the same thing and arrived at the house where his relative was living. He did not notify his relatives that he was coming to the UK. So, when his relative saw that he had arrived in the UK, he was surprised. He stayed there for about six years.

He has been living in Hyde, Cheshire for nearly 40 years. There was a small Mosque in Hyde. He has taken the initiative along with Mr. Abdul Jalil and Abdus Subhan. They were able to purchase a warehouse, which has been converted into a proper Mosque. Similarly, the Hyde Bangladesh Welfare Association was established and provided services to the Community. Since the foundation of the two establishments, he has been involved with its activities.

8.8.3   Employment:

In Coventry (1961), there was a bread factory known as "Sutton Bakery". He started his first job at this company. He used to work 6 days a week, 12-hour shifts and his wages were £13.00 per week. He used to give all the money to his relatives. His relative used to give him £2.00 - £2.50 for his pocket expenses and leftover money was kept as savings. After that, he continuously built up his savings. In 3-4 years, he had about £12,000.00 - £14,000.00 in his hands.

He went to Bangladesh and upon his return re-joined the same factory in Coventry where he had previously worked. At that time the weekly wages were £24.00. He became a sleeping partner at a well-known restaurant in Hyde, known as Dhaka Restaurant. He did not work in the restaurant until 1969. He decided to spend some time with the business; therefore, he finally came to Hyde, where he is residing now. He worked there as a chef and earned good money. After receiving the drawing, they used to earn £200.00 - £300.00 profit per week.

In 1981, he went to Bangladesh with his family and stayed there for six months. Upon his return, he found that his other partner did not pay the VAT, and his name was misused therefore, he decided to close the business. Later, he opened another restaurant known as Raj Mahal but could not succeed, therefore had to sell this business. Since 1985 he has not set up any more businesses and chose to spend some time with his family.

8.8.4 Housing:

About a year later, he bought a house for Ullah. The price of a bedroom house was only £150.00. He reflected on his Coventry life and said the toilets were outside the house. He used to go to the public bath once a week. There was no central heating or bath inside the house. The people used to use coal for the fire and make some heat.

The weather conditions were so bad; sometimes the water pipe had been frozen due to cold weather. Sometimes it was difficult to open the door due to heavy snowfall. The people used to cut the ice to open the doors, he can't forget those days in the 1960s having to cope with the bad weather and the icy cold.

8.8.5 Social & Family:

During the post-liberation war, he decided to bring his wife with him and duly applied for entry clearance. When he arrived in the UK with his wife, they did not have any children. In 1981, he went to Bangladesh with his wife, 4 sons, and 1 daughter. He stayed there for about six months.

He is a father of five sons and one daughter. All his children are married except for the youngest son. Two of his sons are involved in the curry business and there other two are working in different sectors.

He decided to go to Bangladesh to see his close family members and to get married. He stayed over a year got married and returned to the UK.

8.8.6 Independence of Bangladesh:

At the time of the independence war with West Pakistan, he used to get letters regularly and he was informed that the condition of the country was getting worse. He was worried but could not decide what to do, as he was afraid for his life.

One day he received a telegram from his father-in-law, he had written that Mr. Ullah's house had been raided by the Pakistani Military and his wife was living with the in-laws.

Eventually, he had to fly from London by PIA. When he arrived at Karachi Airport, his passport and handwatch had been seized by the Immigration Authority. One of the officers informed him that it was not possible to fly any aircraft to Bangladesh due to the risks of being killed as the war was raging on. He had to stay at the airport for one night. On the next day, one officer came with the information that a flight to Bangladesh had been arranged.

Finally, he arrived in Dhaka safely. When he arrived in Biswanath, Sylhet, he came to know that the Pakistani Military was killing ordinary people. He could not find many people in the town due to the people hiding in different locations. He then went to Sylhet town and arrived at a hotel known as Ramana Hotel, Zindabazar. He felt just a little bit safe but still worried about how he would go to his in-law's house or his house in Moinpur, Chattak.

When he was travelling from Biswanath to Sylhet, during the war period, he was really scared for his life. After he had a meal at the Hotel, he spoke to the restaurant owner, he told him that he wanted to go to Raynagar, where his nephew was residing. The hotel owner arranged a rickshaw for him to travel there.

He arrived at his nephew's house; his nephew's family was surprised and shocked to see him in Bangladeshis during the war. He stayed there for one night and on the next day; he went to his in-law's house. He saw the condition of that area was quiet and safe as no military was there. He stayed there for quite a few days, after that, he rented a house in Sylhet town.

One day he suddenly heard that huge bombardments were going on in Dupder Lake. He went to his next-door relative's house to review the situation. He moved to his relative's house, where they made a bunker to hide and protect them. He sent his wife to his in-law's house by hiring a baby taxi. During the liberation period, he was in Bangladesh and had seen the war.

When the war was over, he went to see his house. He has seen that there are so many bullets that have hit the walls. He has seen many bullets had entered his house. He thought Allah had saved them. He said he took the correct decision, firstly to send his wife back to her parent's house, where there was no war and secondly, he went to his village home. Otherwise, they would have been killed by the Military.

8.8.7 Conclusion:

He believes "post is not important at all; you need a good intention to work for the community" he added. He also said working for the community is good charity work. He also said, "You need to work towards developing the community, not to see your gain".

Many relatives are living in Bangladesh, and he travels to Bangladesh regularly to see his close relatives. He wishes to retire from his life in Bangladesh, but it is a very difficult decision to make considering all his children were born and brought up in the UK.

He believes that coming to Britain has helped him achieve his primary goals. The children have been educated and established here. Living in Bangladesh, the objective may not be achieved. He has six brothers and three sisters. Three brothers lived in the UK, one sister residing in Bangladesh, and two sisters passed away. There was a time when only families were living in Hyde. Now over a thousand families are living in this area. The total Bangladeshi population is about 8-9 thousand.

Finally, he said, if you are honest and want to help the community, then the new generation will benefit from this.

8.9 Bimal Kanti Bhattacharjee:
(Interviewed on 21 January 2008)

8.9.1 Life in Bangladesh:

In 1938, Bimal Kanti Bhattacharjee was born in the village of Daspara, Balagonj (Osmani Nagar), Sylhet. His father's name is the late Krishna Kumar Bhattacharjee. His father was a landlord, businessman, and religious teacher.

His primary education was completed at Lal Koilas Primary School; he then studied SSC at Mangalchandi High School up to Class 10. During his childhood, he enjoyed playing football and Ha-do-do (Kopti) and took part in school sports activities. After the death of his father, he got involved with the family business. He was able to maintain his family's expenses from the earnings of the business.

He inherited 90 Acres of Cultivation land and some property from his father. His grandfather also had huge amounts of land in Gualabazar, Balagonj, and Sylhet. His family life was very good. The village culture was very simple and traditional, people used to celebrate with each other. Most of the villager's occupations revolved around agriculture. The simple living of villagers meant that they weren't interested in attaining wealth. Villagers would live in harmony and peace amongst each other.

8.9.2 Journey to the UK & Immigration:

In 1962, he came to Britain with a "Labour Voucher". When he was a student, he received information about life in Britain from the post office staff. The post office staff mentioned that labour vouchers were a route to gain access to Britain. He then collected a "Labour Voucher" form from the post office filled out the form and posted it to the British High Commission. After a few months, he received a letter from the High Commission. He obtained a Pakistani passport and went to Dhaka British High Commission where he got entry. He bought an airline ticket which cost around 1800 Rupees.

In 1962 he arrived at Heathrow Airport but before arrival, he imagined Britain would be a better country even though he never had any knowledge of the country. However, while he was on the airplane he felt very emotional as it would be a great distance between him and his family. He will be missing his loved ones in Bangladesh. He asked himself why he was leaving his home country and coming to Britain. On the same flight, he had some friends who came to Britain.

8.9.3 Life in the UK:

During that time there weren't many shops. There was only one Bangladeshi grocery shop owned by Kolomdor Ali. They used to buy necessary grocery items from that shop. During that time, Bangladeshi families started to arrive and there were only 10 – 15 families who arrived in Hyde at that time. Sometimes, he used to get live chickens delivered to his home by English people. Sometimes, he used to go to Ashton-u-Lyne to do the grocery shopping.

There was not much entertainment as there were only a few cinemas and theatres. Between 1982 and 1983 the welfare association was established to help the community. There were regular monthly meetings organised by the Hyde Bangladesh Welfare Association to discuss any issues facing the Bangladeshi community and how the people can enjoy a prosperous life in the UK. In the past, it was difficult to find social time due to work. He used to work a 12-hour daily shift; if he had to work the night shift then he used to sleep in the daytime and vice versa.

8.9.4 Employment:

Upon arrival to the UK, he and his friends went to visit a friend in East London. During his stay in London, he visited a Bangladeshi restaurant in Scunthorpe where he started work as a trainee waiter, his weekly wages were £5.00, and free accommodation and food were provided by the employer. He worked there for two years; he used to make some savings and used to send money abroad to support his family. At that time the value of the pound was 20.00 Rupees.

He went to Stockport, Hyde, and moved onto a Rubber Factory, and worked as a trainee worker. He worked as a trainee for three weeks, during this time he stayed at his friend's house, but he had to support himself with food and a place to sleep. He was able to grasp the English language quickly as he studied it back at home. At that time there were about 100 Bangladeshi people employed at the same factory.

He then moved to another factory and worked there for about a year and a half. Then he moved back again to his previous employer, there was an opportunity for many people, it was that they could leave their jobs and go abroad and upon their return, they could re-employ with the same company, but that opportunity was not available in the latter stages.

He also worked at the Hyde CPA Company, which was a cotton mill, where they used to print fabrics. He also worked at a cooker manufacturing company for some time. He worked at the factory for seven years; He then moved to another factory and worked there for 22 years. In the beginning, his weekly wages were £50.00 and then his latest weekly wages were increased to £173.00 – £175.00.

He used to make himself sandwiches for his lunch, no rice and curry were allowed at the beginning. When English people realised that rice and curry were the main food for the Bangladeshi, then it was allowed to be taken to the factory with Tiffin. There was some trouble; he had been attacked by the young stars when he was coming from the factory with the wages. They tried to hijack the money and run away.

8.9.5 Housing:

In 1966, he bought his own house for £500 which consisted of two bedrooms. Inside the house, it didn't have any bathrooms and toilet facilities. The toilet was located outside of the house and people used to have a shower in the public bath; he used to pay 2 shillings for using the facility. He only bathed once a week as it would be very time-consuming due to the long queues.

The public bath was situated in the location of Hyde Library on Union Street. At that time there was no central heating system in the house. To heat, the house coal would be used. The weekly expense for buying the coal was around three pounds. There was also no hot water. Sometimes the house was troubled, and the police dealt with the matter efficiently.

In 1966, there were about six Bangladeshi houses, where all the single people used to live. There were families as such living in the area in the past.

After living at his first home for 12 years, he moved to Boardman Street in Hyde. This house had three bedrooms, and he paid £7,000.00 to purchase the house. He installed the central heating system and a gas cooker in his new house. The bathroom and toilet were inside the house. In 1981, he bought a house on Church Street and paid £46,000.00. This house consists of three bedrooms and two reception rooms.

8.9.6 Social & Family:

He went to Bangladesh in 1970 and stayed there till 1973. During this period Bangladesh achieved independence. In 1973 he brought his wife with his two sons and one daughter to Britain. His oldest son was 16 years old and therefore got a job instead of being schooled. The second son went to school while the daughter was too young to join the school.

During days off he used to go to other towns and watch films at the cinema. When he first arrived in the UK, there were very limited cinema halls. He said, "Very lately there was a theatre hall that was established on Corporation Street, Hyde". He used to take his family to watch English & Hindi films at the cinema. There was no entertainment facility, at the Hyde Bangladesh Welfare Association. There was a lack of video players at that time.

8.9.7 Independence of Bangladesh:

During the liberation period, he was living in Bangladesh (East Pakistan). During the war, he was a witness to the events that unfolded. One day, he and his wife were coming from his in-law's house, when they arrived at Sherpur; they were arrested by the Pakistani Military. Then an army member took them to their camp office, fortunately, a family friend was working at the camp office and was able to recognize them. Then his family friends offered some tea and breakfast and arranged a safe journey to Gualabazar, escorted by the Pakistani Army.

He heard the story from many Bangladeshis that an illiterate person would apply sign language to understand the language which would be seen as funny. For example, seeing the number 100 bus coming it would be known as a bus of one stick and two eggs.

8.9.8 Conclusion:

In his family life, he is a father of two sons and two daughters. His eldest daughter is a social worker whilst the younger daughter is a solicitor. Both of his sons are involved in businesses. Overall, he is a happily retired person who has made the most of his life.

8.10 Alhaj Noorfor Ali
(Interviewed on 30 November 2007)

8.10.1 Life in Bangladesh:

Alhaj Noorfur Ali was born in the village of Sikondor Pur, Balaganj (Osmanagar), Sylhet. His father's name was Alhaj Abdul Karil and his mother's name was Mendira Begum. He has two brothers and two sisters.

Upon completing his primary education, he moved into high school. The high school was known as "Khuski Pur Manullah High School". He studied up to the class of year nine and then left education. Every class year would consist of between 50 to 60 students. The majority of class students were from a Hindu background. In his high school, there were 12 teachers.

He spent his childhood happily, during this time people's living conditions were very good. Fish and milk were widely available. Farmers used to harvest a lot of rice during that period. Remembering memory in 1955 a kilogram of rice would cost around 1.30 – 1.60 Rupees. Villagers owned a fair amount of farm animals.

His father worked on a boarding ship for 30/35 years. His job would transport him to different countries to work in and this took him to America where he worked there for seven and half years. Afterwards, his father went back to Bangladesh.

8.10.2 Journey to the UK & Immigration:

When he was young, he heard that if you obtained a passport from Karachi (West Pakistan) then it would be possible to get entry into the United Kingdom. He also learned that there were plenty of jobs available in the UK. After learning this he and his 14/15 friends went to Karachi, West Pakistan. They stayed there for about one year. 5 of them arrived in Britain. It cost them 1400 Rupees to travel to Britain using Pakistani Airlines (PIA).

He arrived at Heathrow Airport in January 1960. After getting out of the plane, he felt extremely cold as he had not adjusted to the British weather. After exiting the airport, a taxi was reserved for them, he showed the taxi driver the written address of his cousins' house, and the taxi driver took them to the exact destination.

The house was located on Brick Lane, 125 Oldham Street, London, where his cousin's sister and her husband used to live there. The taxi journey took one hour, the taxi journey cost them £50. He knocked on the door and an individual wanted to find out their relation to the homeowner. He replied that he was related to the homeowner.

After that they were invited into the house, the cousin of Mr Ali greeted them, gave them warm clothing and took them to a well-heated place whilst they all dined together. His cousin went to a shop and bought more warm clothes for them, he stayed there for two weeks. This house had around 6 to 7 rooms and it was occupied by 30 to 35 people.

8.10.3 Life in the UK:

In England, there were not enough mosques for people to pray in but if they wanted to send their children to school for education then this option was widely available. He would pray at home but during Eid, he would go to a mosque in Manchester.

When living in Hyde, there were about 15 houses and around 100 to 150 Bangladeshi people living in that area. Most of these people did not have their families living with them. About 2 to 3 people had their families with them. The reason for not bringing their family was that they weren't thinking of settling in the UK.

After 1965 people started bringing their families into the UK. He used to spend his time playing cards and watching Hindi films or meeting friends during his days off.

8.10.4 Employment:

He visited another cousin in North London and was staying there. During his stay, he was introduced into training as a waiter which lasted for one year. In 1961, his cousin went to Bangladesh which made him move to Hyde where there was another relative living in this area. After staying in Hyde for two weeks he received a job where he worked in a factory called Red Firm. It was a rubber factory.

His weekly wages were £20.00 and sometimes a bonus was awarded. Overtime was available for workers, when he learned to operate machinery, his weekly wages were £36.00. Here he worked during day shifts for six months and then moved onto night shifts. The factory conditions inside were well-suited for workers which included heating.

The accommodation and food had to be arranged by the workers themselves, workers used to take their meals to work but he used to live near the factory so he used to go home to eat during the day shifts but at the night shifts, he would take his meal with him. Some of the wages would be sent to his father in Bangladesh after Mr Ali's expenses were covered. He worked there for 9 and a half years and then went back to Bangladesh in 1970. The Pakistani Airlines fare costs £250 but the Airways return costs 1400 Rupees for every passenger.

In 1982, after spending ten years in Bangladesh, he returned to England. He noticed a lot of changes in Britain which he was unaware of. Factory workers were able to get their jobs back after returning from their holidays, however, his factory had closed, and factories were becoming derelict. He found a job in an aluminium factory in Aston where he would make kitchen cookery equipment. He worked there till 1987. The weekly wages were £75.00. He worked with English workers therefore he eventually learned to speak English.

In 1968, he entered a partnership with a restaurant whilst he was working in the factory but later, he sold his share in the restaurant. During those days Mr. Ali used to work 60 hours weekly, the weekly wages were £36. Mr. Ali says that "in those days £36 were good wages". In some weeks he used to work the whole week without taking a day off. In Hyde, there weren't many hard workers like himself available.

Factories were closing in Britain, and this resulted in Mr Ali becoming unemployed like other factory workers. He tried to work in a restaurant but because of his age, he was unable to work and now relied on benefits.

8.10.5 Housing:

He lived in a rented house in Hyde which was shared with other people. The rent would cost per person 12 shillings. He had to share one room with three people, and they would all contribute to cooking. The house did not have central heating and coal had to be used for heating purposes. It was called the 'Terrapin method'.

The toilet was located outside and during winter it was very difficult to access. He lived in this house for one year. This house belonged to his relative and this relative was going back to Bangladesh, at this point he bought the house for £250 in 1963. This house consists of five bedrooms, two reception rooms, and a kitchen. At that time buying houses was not an issue; it was possible to buy a house by paying a £50 deposit.

8.10.6 Social & Family:

In 1970, during his stay in Bangladesh, he got married. One month before the liberation war he returned to the UK with his wife. After spending 14 months in the UK with his wife his first son was born in March 1971. Upon hearing about the birth of the child, his father invited them to visit Bangladesh to see his grandchild and he went back with his family.

During this visit, the liberation war was over, and it was the early period of Bangladesh's independence. Freedom fighters and anti-war groups clashed with each other and a court case followed, he was involved in this incident. He stayed in Bangladesh for ten years and his wife gave birth to one more son and daughter. Thereafter, his wife has given birth to two sons and one daughter.

His oldest son is educated and now works in a law firm in Britain and the second son has passed his A-levels and is working. The third son has passed his GCSEs and is working, and the fourth son is studying at a university while the fifth son is studying in high school. The oldest daughter passed her GCSEs and got married. The second daughter worked in a clinic but could not work anymore due to her illness. The third daughter is a school - teacher and the last daughter is studying in high school.

In 1965, an elderly person from his village did his prayer by using a room which was granted by Mr. Hasan Khan. If a Muslim person died, then the body would be showered and then prayer will be held in Manchester in memory of the person who passed away. The Land was purchased from the council to make a burial ground for Muslim people. This was possible due to Mr. Hasan Khan and others who contributed money towards the purchase of the land in 1966. Muslims in Hyde who wished to pray, bought a house so then they could pray.

For the improvement of the British Bangladeshi community, he has been

involved with activities strengthening links even to this day. He was elected as a Vice-Chairman for the Hyde Bangladeshi Welfare Association. He was regarded as being a very dedicated and religious person who devoted his life to providing voluntary work for the benefit of the mosque. Since 1996 he has been the managing committee Chairman of the Hyde Mosque. Children have been receiving religious education from this mosque. Due to his free time, he decided to go to Makkah to do the pilgrimage (Hajj) in 1991.

8.10.7 Independence of Bangladesh:

He is extremely happy with the independence of Bangladesh, but he is not satisfied with the present situation of the country, especially with the fact that everyone is taking bribes. Government officials are not helping stabilise the country by providing jobs for people and accessing public wealth.

During the war in Bangladesh, Bangladeshi people provided support by holding meetings and talking to British officials to help support the independence of Bangladesh. From different parts of Britain, Mr Islam from Hyde and Mr Motin from Manchester held talks regarding the war.

8.10.8 Conclusion:

In Britain, Bangladeshi children were falling behind in education because their guardians were not focused on their progress in school. Nowadays guardians are becoming more aware to educate their children. He has five sons

and four daughters who have been educated in the UK.

At present, he is a British citizen, but he has deep feelings for the motherland of Bangladesh. With these feelings, he frequently visits Bangladesh. Even his children have affection for Bangladesh. He has been successful in his career in Britain, and he is very happy that he has been able to educate all of his children. This may have not been possible if Mr. Ali had stayed in Bangladesh.

8.11 Haji Tozomul Ali
(Interviewed on 20 June 2009)

8.11.1 Life in Bangladesh:

Haji Tozomul Ali was born in 1939 in the village of Batipara, Bishwanath, Sylhet. His father's name is Md Asod Ullah; he has two brothers and one sister. He completed his primary education at 'Khagata Primary School' and was admitted to a local high school called 'Ram Shundor High School'. He studied till class eight in high school and after that, he migrated to the UK. His father first used to work onboard ships as a crew.

After working for three or four years his father went back to Bangladesh with a one-way ticket. The financial status of the family was also good due to the earnings of his father. At that time everyone lived friendly and peacefully, and the elders were also highly respected and loved by all. He found those days beautiful. Going to college, and teaching the students, he found everything quite stunning. Today's present is a bit different from the earlier time. The past we knew no longer exists. People's feelings and attitudes toward each other are vanishing.

This way everyone was busy helping each other. He has added an example of living with 9 different families in one boundary, if there was one single issue and someone required other people's help, all the family members from the neighbours used to come forward to provide the necessary help and assistance you required. That was a very useful and easy way for people had overcome the problem.

Living together as a family and maintaining relationships with others was great, more specifically helping each other. There was no jealousy amongst any families within the society. Now society is paralysed with frustration, one brother is not helping the other.

He said that people in the 1960's were quite gentle, easy-going, and open-minded. The curriculum in the school was very much related to real life. The method of teaching was very good and advanced. Teachers were very friendly and caring with delivering the curriculum. The students were affectionate towards the school - teachers. There was no need to employ a house teacher after receiving good tuition from the school. The students were able to do the homework on their own after receiving the tuition from the school - teachers.

The village economy was dominated by agriculture, and earnings from selling crops were sufficient to meet the general expenses of the families. There was good cultivation of three kinds of paddy; these are mainly Ayush, Amon, and Buro. There was a good time to catch plenty of fish from the small lakes.

He said that one winter his father went to Bangladesh and his father saw that there was a huge number of Koi, Shing, and Magur fishes that had been retained in big pots. His father then advised other members of the family that at least for a week there was no need to go fishing, this was due to the smell of the fish which had become worse and there was plenty of live fish which had been reserved and would be enough for his family for quite some time.

He also said that during the fishing season, people used to eat enough fish, and people used to get fed up with eating fish every day. During that season which lasted about three months, there was no need to go to the fish Bazar to buy fish. There was a big lake in his village. In the month of Boishak, there was a rainy season, when the paddy field used to be flooded with rainwater.

People used to catch different kinds of small and big fish from the paddy fields. The small fish were very tasty to eat. It was like a tail he felt. He also added there was a time when people used to say rice and fish were the main identity of Bangladesh, now you wouldn't be able to find the fish like you used to get in the old days.

He felt sorry for not completing the secondary school certificate exam because he had to leave Bangladesh and come to Britain. He also added that the most enjoyable time was living in the village with the villagers; unfortunately, this wasn't going to come back in his life.

8.11.2 Journey to the UK & Immigration:

In the year 1963, he arrived in the UK. During that year people started to fill out the forms to get a work permit. He approached two gentlemen, one of them was known as Sudhir Takur who was his next-door neighbour, and another one was known as Moboshir Khan who is now residing in Oldham. Both helped him fill in the application form and post it to the London address. Both told him that he would receive a reply from the UK and that he needed to contact them.

After about 6-7 months he received a reply from the UK and it was advised that he could contact the British High Commission, he then had to complete the paperwork. It was also known as the "Voucher From". When he received the voucher from the British High Commission, he was finally confirmed that he was able to come to the UK. His father paid all the travel expenses. He flew from Dhaka by PIA and arrived at Gatwick Airport; his father came to Dhaka to give him a see-off.

From the Gatwick airport, he went to his nephew Kuddus Miah's house. He was welcomed and offered good hospitality. On the next day, they arranged a ticket for him to come to Luton. At that time one of his cousins used to live in Luton and another cousin used to live in Accrington. He stayed one night with his cousin in Luton and came to Accrington by Bus. His cousin received him from the bus station.

8.11.3 Life in the UK:

There was heavy snow falling during that time, most of the time they used to remove the snow/ice from their doorstep to open the door. The thickness of the snow/ice fallen was high (10 inches to 18 inches). The people who are arriving now, if they saw this weather condition, then they would have said that there is no need to do the work in the UK and they would eventually go back to Bangladesh.

The bus was the main transport to go anywhere, but it was not adequate. The people used to wait 3-4 hours at the bus station. Waiting in the cold weather, the feet used to get cold. The people used to wear 2/3 sets of stockings and long boots to protect themselves from the cold weather. It was a hard life in Britain, only the people who had been through the same experience as he would agree, he added. Two people used to sleep in a double bed, one person in a single bed. If there was an extra guest, then three people would sleep in the double bed.

On weekends they used to buy chickens and cook them in big cooking pots. The price of a hen was 2 shillings 5 pence (1/2 crown). The prices of goods were very cheap. Usually, on Saturday, he used to go to the public bath. There were long queues and people used to wait in queue for 3 to 4 hours to get the serial. Half an hour maximum time was allowed to have time in the bath. The soap and towel were also included in this price.

There were language difficulties, when he first arrived in the UK, he was able to understand but was not able to speak. The English people used to show their affection to the Bangladeshi people, if there was any problem in finding an address, they used to help them find the address, and sometimes they used to drop them off at the destination address. They used to give money for the travel expenses – if anyone had no money.

Some people used to advise newcomers to keep their medical cards, to show the address where they are living. For those people who were unable to speak English, it was useful to keep the medical card in their pocket. The police were very helpful too. He never faced any discrimination just because of his race or nationality. The English men and women were very affectionate and caring too.

They used to do the shopping once a week, it was easy to split to cost between themselves. The English women used to bring the delivery to their doorstep; one person was responsible to pay the grocery bills. They did not like to eat meat; instead, they used to get live chickens from the farm. They prepared to eat halal meat, which was the main reason why they did not buy the meat because that was not halal at that time.

Nowadays you get everything you need, for example, fish, vegetables, and a pan (beetle nut was not available at the beginning). He said sometimes when they felt that they wanted to eat fish, they used to buy herring or sardine fish from the Market.

8.11.4   Employment:

He started to look for a job, but it was very difficult to find a suitable job, during that time when he was approaching the factories, the gatekeepers used to show signals using their hands that there was no vacancy. He was concerned about how he would support himself, to pay for the food and living cost. Considering that there is no vacancy he still made the effort to continue his job search in the factories.

One of my uncles was intermediate passed, he taught him how to speak English, more specifically how to find a job. After so many days later finally he was able to find a job in the factory. This factory was known as "Brine Fabrics and Printers Limited" and it was a cotton factory, where he started his first job in the UK.

Designing and printing fabrics were the main jobs in this factory, he described that after printing, they used to put the fabrics into washing machines and it was dried in another room, his role was to dry the fabrics. There were about six rooms for drying the clothes. There were Bangladeshi workers and there were British workers.

At that time there were about 100 – 150 Bangladeshi who used to work in this factory. There were facilities to do five times prayer within the factory. At the time when the prayer time is due, the management used to say to all the workers that all the machines should be turned off and go to the prayer.

The workers were very obedient to the management. Usually, the shift was for eight hours a day, but sometimes when it was needed to do overtime, everyone was bound to follow the instructions. The shift work was 8 hours to 12 hours but in the absence of another worker, the shift working time was doubled, i.e. 16 hours and there was no hesitation from the workers to do the overtime or double time.

He used to get £7.00 per week for working an 8-hour shift and if he had to work extra 4 hours overtime, he used to get paid £12.00 - £13.00 per week. At that time people used to say his weekly earnings were good. The living cost was minimal compared to the current cost. To pay for a single bed to rent was only ten shillings.

After working 3-4 years working in the "Brine Fabrics and Printers Limited" he then moved to David Cotton Mill in Rawtenstall. There were three shift workers; amongst them, a few of them rented a house. They used to share the cost of living and food. He shared an experience of living with three shift workers; they used to cook the meals at three different times.

They all lived in one house, but they hardly saw each other during working days. The weekend was their usual days off but sometimes, people used to work Saturdays as well as overtime. They used to write notes to communicate with their roommates.

He worked in the David Cotton Mill in Rawtenstall for about five years. After that, he moved to Brian Fabrics Limited in Oldham. This factory used to produce rubber frames for the glass. His weekly wages were £16.00 per week. After working five years in this factory, he moved to another rubber factory in Hyde. He worked there for another five years then the factory closed. While he was working in Oldham, he used to live with his uncle. When he moved to Hyde, he was able to find a house with assistance from the company.

8.11.5   Social & Family:

In 1967 he went back to Bangladesh to see his close family members and got married. He stayed there for about six months. In 1982 he brought his family to Britain when the British government passed a law for the commonwealth citizen to bring their family to the UK. (NB: Immigration & Nationality Act 1981). Before that, there was no provision within the immigration Law to bring many families to the UK.

When the process was started many of them did not like to bring their families to the UK due to their personal choices. He did not have any intention of bringing his family but he realised that one day his children would say that he had the opportunity to bring his family to the UK, but he did not do anything. Just for that reason, he decided to bring his family. Many other people had done the same thing as he did at the beginning.

In 1970, when his father passed away, he travelled to Bangladesh for a second time. In 1981 he went to Bangladesh to do the paperwork for his family (application for entry clearance). In 1982 he brought his family (wife & children) with him and lived in the Hyde area. He took a two-bedroom house and used to pay rent which was £15.00 - £20.00 per week. He was unemployed by then and was receiving benefits.

He was a father of seven children, four sons, and three daughters. The eldest son is a qualified electrician, the second son is working with NHS in the Diabetics section, his third son is a Hafiz (Memorised the Holy Quran) and his fourth son is studying at the University, his two daughters are married and the other daughter is studying at the University doing Masters Degree.

He is living his retirement life by doing shopping and visiting friends and relatives. He goes to the Ashton-U-Lyne James Mosque regularly to perform his prayers. While he was living in Hyde, he was involved with the Bangladesh Association and Hyde Jameh Mosque Committee but in Ashton-Under-Lyne he is not involved with any Community Organisation. After 2-3 years interval he goes to Bangladesh to see his close relatives. His eldest brother is living in Bangladesh. Sometimes, he takes his family with him. He has taken his second son to Bangladesh and arranged marriage from there, it has proven that he has got the patriotism for the country where he was born and maintaining the connections.

8.11.6　Housing:

He used to live with a group of five people during his time in the mills; everyone was responsible for bearing the cost of food equally. The toilet was in the backyard, nowadays that is impossible to believe. It was very cold weather; he used to feel very cold whilst using the toilet outside. There was no carpet inside the house either, but people used to use the lining instead. There was no central heating but there was a fireplace inside the house, the coal was used to warm up the room, but it was not sufficient to warm up all the rooms. Five to ten people used to sit in front of the fireplace at once, the front side of the body used to get warm enough, but the backside was always cold.

In 1987 he came to Ashton-Under-Lyne to live. The house is owned by the West Pennine Housing Association. He had to apply to the housing association before getting this offer. As soon as he received the offer, he accepted and moved there. Now he is paying £92.00 per week for rent. He tried to buy the house, but the housing Association was not selling the house, if the Housing Association ever decided to sell the house in the future, they would be able to buy it.

8.11.7　Conclusion:

In the year 1970, he became a British citizen. His primary intention was to come to Britain to earn some money and support his family who was living in Bangladesh. He never thought that he would consider bringing his family to the UK.

Bangladesh was in his mind; he was a patriotic person.

There was a good time when all men used to live in a house. There was a better relationship but now everything has gone. The people became so selfish since they brought their families to the UK. During the employment period, he used to help 10-15 people with writing letters to their loved ones. At that time main dominant communication method was writing letters and sending them by post. Those people, who were not educated, used to come to people who had some education to write letters on their behalf. They used to provide a voluntary service to those people. Now telephones and mobile phones have become the easiest way to communicate.

He considered himself a successful one as he worked hard to establish his family in the UK. Finally, he said to the people who have engaged themselves in the community or voluntary work, that they should work without looking for a position in the organisation with personal interest. In 1985 he performed his Hajj (Pilgrimage to Makkah). He has taken his wife and a son; he did the hajj for a second time. It shows that he is very obedient to his creator (Allah) and wealth is nothing to him.

He also felt that there was no one in his neighbourhood of similar age, where he could pass his retirement life by chatting with these people. But there was a time when he had many friends at his workplace. Sometimes he thinks to go to Bangladesh to pass his retirement life, but he is unable to do so, due to his family and children living in the UK. If there is a facility provided for the elderly people, then he would have to go there and pass some time.

8.12 Alhaj Shomsher Khan
(Interviewed on 13 July 2008)

8.12.1 Life in Bangladesh:

Mr. Shomsher Khan was born in 1940 in the village of Daorai, Jogonnatpur, Shunamgonj. His father's name is Mr Azim Khan. He has 4 brothers, and 3 sisters and Mr Khan is the youngest, he started his education at Local Jamar Gaon Primary School, and after that, he went to Kujkipur High School, which was 5 miles from his house, so he had to stay with someone else's house and study. He stayed there for 8 years; in 1958 he passed the S.S.C exam; he didn't get into college due to his marks in English. He started teaching in primary school as an assistant teacher; he used to get 60 Taka per month.

From 1960 to 1964 he did teaching. His father was in Britain from 1931 to 1949. They used to own 7-acre paddy fields, during that time they didn't have to buy fish or vegetables from the shop; sometimes they had to buy rice though. At that time, they used to grow their vegetables and catch fish from the river etc.

8.12.2 Journey to the UK & Immigration:

In 1964 he came to Britain by voucher, he used to teach at that time, then he found out about the form Voucher, and he sent one form to Britain for himself. Within 1 month they replied to him saying that he would soon receive the voucher. After a few days, they told him to get a Voucher from the Dhaka British High Commission, at that time in Dhaka British High Commission, they used to ask people for their date of birth and father's name. If they couldn't give the correct information, then they weren't given the voucher.

Then finally he got the Passport from the Sylhet Passport office, and he got the final decision from the Dhaka British High Commission. Then he got his ticket from the Aftab Ali office, during that time everybody used to get their ticket from that office, and everybody used to know it. For his ticket, it cost him 5 hundred and 50 Takas.

Everybody was very upset that day when he was leaving Bangladesh to go to Britain. His brother was waiting at Heathrow Airport to retrieve him, his brother thought that the flight would be delayed so he nipped out, but the flight had come through the Karachi and France route, so the flight arrived early.

At the airport gate, he remembers showing his address and name to the taxi driver and the driver dropped him off at his cousin's sister's husband's restaurant. The restaurant was called the East Bangle Restaurant. It was on Edgware Road in London. He didn't know how to open the door, so the taxi driver helped him to open the door, then he went to the kitchen and saw his brother.

Then he went to the "Light of Kashmir" restaurant to see his brother. He did not like the food in the restaurant because there was a fixed time for serving food, sometimes he used to feel very hungry, but he had to wait for a certain time that the restaurant would serve food. For this reason, he went to his other brother's house in Birmingham.

His brothers owned the house, and after a few days his brother went to Bangladesh; before he went his brother showed him everything. He showed him that for the time being they had to use the toilet outside of their house and that they didn't have any bath facilities inside their house.

8.12.3   Life in the UK:

He then told us about his first experience in Britain. Every week he used to go to the public bath to have a bath and he would pay half-crown for this. He used to use Cole to keep the house warm because it was too cold at that time. The toilet was outside of their house. He did not have any problem with his English Language, during the work he did not have to speak much English, at first, he had a bit of a problem but then he slowly improved and he also studied in Bangladesh, so he did not struggle with his English. Before his family came to Britain he had to cook and everything. At that time Shopping was not easy compared to this time. There were no Bangladeshi vegetables or things that he needed during that time.

There was one Pakistani man who used to live on George Arther Street, in Ashton; there was a Chicken farm backside of his shop, and they used to slaughter the chicken and take it to the house. The Raja Brothers in Trafalgar Square usually had all the meat. Also, there was a sweet bar shop that used to sell rice.

At that time there was a Pakistani Mosque in Birmingham, but they did not have any Mosque at that time in Ashton. They used to pray in a Church, and then in 1985 they bought the Church and built a Mosque there. In 1984 they opened the Bangladesh association in Ashton; in 1988-1991 he was Chairman of the Bangladesh association.

8.12.4   Employment:

His first job in Britain was in a tube mill as a labour worker, they used to make brush pipes within their mills. One day he was looking for a job and he saw that people were going in and coming out through the company door. He was looking at them and then he realized that someone was in charge, he went over and asked him "What do you want?"

He said he was looking for a job, the man in charge then asked him "Do you want to start today?" He said, "Not today but next Monday would be better". Then the man in charge accepted that he'd come to work on Monday. He came on Monday and started his new job, there were other people from Sylhet inside the factory, and Mr. Mashuk Miah from Balagonj told him what he had to do in the workplace. During the work they had to use a few English words, for example: anymore, not too much, not too much, etc. It made it easier for the workers who owned the factory to understand.

His weekly used to be 28-29 pounds; it was a hard job in a factory and long duty, they used to work till Saturday, and during the work, they had to use gloves. During this time, he used to work in a restaurant also and weekly he used to get 7 pounds, also his food and accommodation were free. After that he used to work in the gas board for good wages, there were 3 shifts of work, and he was happy to do that. The wages he earned were good. It was 10 pounds more than his first job's wages. When he had gotten offers for double shifts, he used to feel very happy to do them because he could then get more wages.

He has got experience looking for jobs, he mentioned that there was a factory that used to pay really good wages, but the manager didn't want to take anybody on for work. He went there and asked for a job, but the manager then told him that he wasn't going to give him a job. The next time he went back to the factory he had experience in looking for a job, he used to go to the factory every week for a job, and one day he finally got the job in that factory.

At the end of 1972, he came back to Britain, and in 1975 he went to Bangladesh a second time. That time when he came back to Britain, he did not find any jobs in the factory. That time his friend offered him a job at the Light of

Bangle restaurant in London. He started working there as a head waiter. Weekly he earned 70 pounds, he had worked there for 2 years. After that, he worked in The Curry House restaurant for another 2 years.

In 1982 he came to Manchester, Ashton with his family. Then he bought a restaurant called 'Ashton Tandoori' with his 50% share for 6 thousand pounds, he used to work in his restaurant as a waiter. Per week he used to earn 60-75 pounds. During that time, he owned a takeaway business, but the Chef was not very good, so he ended up selling the business.

8.12.5　Housing:

In 1972, during that time he used to live in a rented house with his family in London, Aldgate area, Colombia Road. In 1982, when he came to Manchester then he bought a house for 12 thousand 5 hundred pounds, unfortunately, the Council took the house to the Magistrate Court. In 1989 he bought another house for 85 thousand pounds and that is the house he is living in now.

8.12.6　Social & Family:

In 1972 he obtained his British Citizenship and went to Bangladesh, and he got married. In 1980 he brought his wife to Britain. He has got 5 daughters and 1 son; his children are all highly educated. Now he is a retired pensioner, in his free time he usually reads the newspaper, goes to the Mosque, goes to town and does plenty of exercises.

Sometimes he goes on holiday, and he usually goes to Bangladesh, in Bangladesh he has relatives and brothers and sisters and much more family. He sold everything in Bangladesh and used that money for important things in Britain, for example, business, house, etc.

For about 6-7 years he was involved with the association, when he first came to Ashton 5 Bangladesh families were living there and in 1989 15 Bangladeshi families were living in Ashton. During his involvement in the association, he had to face a few problems, for example, Bangladeshi people used to go to the Council and complain for no reason. He also said a few educated people were being involved in that.

8.12.7 Conclusion:

For the rest of his life, he wants to spend it with his family because it is not important to go to Bangladesh and leave his family in Britain. He also said it is impossible for him, he is a happy man, and he came to Britain because his children are all well educated, which wouldn't be possible if they were all brought up in Bangladesh. He also said if you have a 10-hectare field it is still very hard to maintain a family. He also notes that people have changed; they aren't as friendly and as respectful as they once were.

8.13 Alhaj Kari Abdul Baki
(Interviewed on 15 January 2008)

8.13.1 Life in Bangladesh:

Alhaj Kari Abdul Baki was born in 1938 in a traditional Muslim Talukdar family in the area of Nadampur, Nabigonj, Habigonj. His father's name is the late Mohammed Abdul Kamil & mother's name is the late Firuja Begum. His father was living in the United Kingdom; his father got him as a boy using a boy voucher, he was the only son, and he had one sister.

His first school was the "Mostofapur Primary School" and he spent his secondary education at the "Digolbagh High School". He studied up to the class of nine, he then moved to an Islamic institution to do religious study; he studied there for about 7/8 years and received the title of Kari.

His father was working on a British board ship; he maintained his family easily due to his income from the paddy field and there was income from his father's employment. His village people were very poor, and due to this, he has seen many people struggling to survive for their lives. He has also seen that the village people could not afford to pay for their children's tuition fees. For the economy, this was the reason why many children in his village were left uneducated. In his school life, he has seen more Muslim children than Hindu children.

In the British period, 37.5 kg of rice was only 5 Rupees and in the Pakistan period, the price went up to 10 Rupees. During the British & Pakistan period, the people relied upon income from agriculture. Many people used to work as a labourer, there were shortages of necessary goods. There are some goods, which used to sell at a cheaper price from the government agencies, even the kerosene oil. The people used to suffer a lot due to this. He went to Chittagong to search for a job. He spent six months there and returned to Habigonj without any success. In 1961, he went to Assam in India and found a job in the mosque to work as an Imam.

8.13.2 Journey to the UK & Immigration:

Mr. Baki's father retired from his job and returned to Bangladesh. At that time people could come to the UK through the voucher scheme. In 1964, he came to the UK.

Mr Baki flew by KLM Airlines from Dhaka Tej-ghaw Airport and arrived at London Heathrow Airport. His connecting flight was to Manchester but there was some delay from Heathrow Airport, and he requested the Airport Authority to arrange a train ticket for him. The airport authority arranged a train ticket for Mr. Baki.

He arrived at Manchester Piccadilly, took a taxi, and went to the restaurant. He found that the restaurant had been closed. The weather was very cold and foggy, he found a telephone booth, and he entered it to protect himself from cold weather. The people who were supposed to receive Mr Baki from the Piccadilly train station went to Victoria station by mistake. He waited outside the restaurant and a few minutes later, the people came back from Victoria Station.

8.13.3 Employment:

His UK working life had begun at a Restaurant, working as a waiter and living above the restaurant. Food and accommodation were free, and the weekly wages were £7.00. He used to work 12 hours a day, six days a week. He has some knowledge of English, and the employer provided some language support, he worked there for about 4 months and left the job.

He then found a new job in the factory with good pay (wages). He moved to Dunlop Textile in Rochdale and worked there as a labourer, the weekly wages were £18.00; also, if he worked on Saturday, he used to get another £4.00. That was a total of £22.00 per week, double the money, and better pay compared to the restaurant job.

During the above employment, he used to live at the flat just above the restaurant. While he was working in the factory, he worked during the weekend at the restaurant. Due to his part-time work, he used to get £4.00, and the accommodation and food were free.

He used to travel by bus from Manchester to Rochdale and the fare was 20 shillings, he worked in Rochdale for about a year and then moved to Oldham. At that time, there were many mills and factories in Oldham. He joined a woollen textile mill; he worked in the spinning and welding section. As for health and safety, the precaution was to wear masks, and ear covers for every worker who needed to be used whilst on duty. There was trade union support for all the workers.

If there was a demand to increase the wages, then the trade union advised the workers to strike against the employer, and the factory had to close many times due to strikes.

He did not have any language problems because he had English language skills. In his job, sometimes he used to do the interpreting for other workers and newcomers in the factory, he also used to provide help and support to the community by taking them to the Office and the Hospital. He also helped many people to fill out official forms and write letters.

8.13.4 Housing:

He bought a three-bedroom house in Oldham town centre; He paid £300.00 for a leasehold property. He was living there along with 7/8 other tenants. He used to receive the rent of £1.00 per person, then it was increased to £1.25, £1.50. There was no bathroom in his house, and he used to go to the public bath like others. The charge was 1 shilling to use the public bath. The toilet was outside the house.

The weather was very cold. He could feel it when he travelled to work. It was a very hard life in Britain and people had to suffer a lot.

In 1968, he bought a freehold house in Oldham town. The price was £500.00. The house consisted of 2 bedrooms. In this house, there was also a toilet. He bought another house; he carried out some improvement work in the cellar.

8.13.5 Social & Family:

In 1981, his wife & two daughters came to the UK. His second daughter sadly died years later in the United Kingdom. His eldest daughter is working as a teacher and his eldest son obtained a Chemistry degree from the University of Manchester and now working in Qatar as a teacher. His second son obtained an Economics & Finance degree from the same University of Manchester and now working in the Bank. The youngest daughter is working in the government sector.

The children have a connection with Bangladesh; they study the religion with their interest. His children often ask questions about Islamic history, for example, they ask where the handwritten script of the Holy Quran had been kept. From his knowledge, he replied to his children that a copy had been kept in the Taskand Museum, Russia, which was the first-handwritten script by a Hazrat Usman Gani (RA) [PBUH]. A copy has been kept in the British Museum; the written script was written by Hazrat Imam Hasan (RA) [PBUH].

One day, his son asked him a question about Hazrat Mohammed [PBUH], he asked why the prophet marry six years old Aysha Siddiqa (RA). Mr. Baki told his son that was an engagement; Mohammed married Aysha (RA) when she was 12 years old. He also added according to the Islamic Sharia, 12 years was acceptable at that time.

There were a few mosques in different towns and cities, compared with the present time. Many people used to do Salah in their own homes. There was one Bangladeshi and one Pakistani Mosque in the Oldham area, at that time if anyone died in the community, the people were involved and used to send the dead body to Bangladesh.

8.13.6 Independence of Bangladesh:

At the time of the liberation period, all Bangladeshi people who were living in the UK were supporting the war against West Pakistani aggression. The Bangladeshi people organised rallies and demonstrations in many places throughout the UK. He also joined the support of the independence of Bangladesh and attended many meetings.

Bangladeshi people organised fundraising & lobbying Campaigns. He has also taken the initiative to do a special prayer for liberation and to help bring peace to the people of Bangladesh.

Before he came to the UK, he had the feeling that West Pakistani authorities were depriving East Pakistani in many ways. That was the reason for him to support the independence of Bangladesh.

After the liberation, Mr. Baki went to Bangladesh to see the condition of the country in his own eyes. About 365 people hired a charter plane to visit the newly liberated country and he was amongst them. He was shocked to see the country's aftermath; he spent some time with his family, friends, and relatives.

He had been selected as the chairman of the relief committee to distribute goods amongst the poor people in his village.

8.13.7 Conclusion:

In his concluding remarks, he said when his children became 16 years old; he encouraged them to continue with their studies instead of working. That is why his children had the opportunity to obtain higher degrees from universities. He feels proud of his children's best achievements.

He is enjoying his retired life with his family; Mr Baki has been to Saudi Arabia four times to do the pilgrimage. He hopes that the Bangladesh people will make progress and peace for all the people. Mr. Baki is an educated, social activist involved with the local community and hoping to spend the rest of his life in the UK.

8.14 Alhaj Md. Dilwar Khan
(Interviewed on 20 June 2009)

8.14.1 Life in Bangladesh:

Alhaj Md. Dilwar Khan was born in 1942 in the village of Joinpur, Sylhet Bangladesh. His father's name is Md. Sultan Khan was a sub-inspector of the Police. His workplace was in the Sylhet Police Lane, Gulapgonj and Bianibazar, Sylhet. Since 1956 his father has served as a Police Inspector in different police stations in Comilla. Thereafter, while working in Bamparampur station he was retired.

He has six sisters and 7 brothers; among them, he is the eldest son. His 3 brothers are stepbrothers, and they are all living in America. One of his sisters lives in Britain and the other 5 sisters live in Bangladesh. Also, 2 of his brothers live in Britain.

He completed primary education at "Lauai Primary School" then he went to the south "Surma High School" and then "Raja GC High School". Then he went to "Nasirnogor High School" in Comilla. From 1958 to 1962 he studied at "Nasirnogor High School" and then he was admitted to "Rosomoy High School" in Sylhet and 1963 he took an S.S.C exam from "Rosomo High School" but he didn't know his result because he had to come to Britain. After the exam, he came to Britain, and he didn't a get chance to find out his result. He changed schools because his father used to work in different places.

In 1960 when he completed class 8 education from high school and was getting ready for class 9, he had gotten married. At that time no one was in Britain from his family, but his wife's elder brothers were in Britain. Through his wife's family, he came to Britain, and he thought that he was the eldest son in the family, and he had the responsibility to maintain his siblings. From that, he came to Britain.

8.14.2   Journey to the UK & Immigration:

In 1963, he came to Britain with an "Employment Voucher". At that time, they used to call them a "Labour Voucher". There was an Employment Exchange Office in Zindabazar, Sylhet, he collected a form from there, filled the form and sent it to the Ministry of Labour in Britain. In the form, it was mentioned that he would receive a reply within 42 days.

So, he told his local postman that if there is any reply from Britain then let him know as soon as possible. Then he got a reply on time, and he believed that he would get a voucher to go to Britain. In the letter, it was mentioned that within 1 month he would get a call letter, and then he needed to go to the British High Commission in Dhaka with the passport to get the main voucher. After that, he received the call letter, and then after 3-4 days delay, he got his passport then he went to BHC, Dhaka to get his main voucher.

For his ticket, it cost him 2 thousand Taka and his father paid for it. By aeroplane from Sylhet, he went to Dhaka, and then to Karachi, after 1 week of staying in Karachi on 9th July 1963, he came to Heathrow airport local time at 9 am. His relatives did not come to receive him at Heathrow Airport because Mr Ali did not get a chance to let them know that he was in Karachi for 1 week.

At that time the airfare was 2,000.00 rupees and his father bear the cost. He flew from Dhaka to Karachi and stayed in Pakistan for a week and then flew to London Heathrow. On 9th July 1963, he arrived at London Heathrow. He could not communicate with his relatives and tell them that there was a flight delay in Pakistan and therefore none of his relatives went to the airport to receive him.

There was another person on the same flight who was living in Britain. He discussed this matter and needed assistance from this person to sort out his travel arrangements. The person then told him he was going to Birmingham, but he did not have enough money with him to pay for an extra cost. Then he said, "Don't worry about money, I will pay the money for going to Birmingham". Then with 10 shillings, they came to Victoria by bus.

Then went to Euston, where his wife's eldest brother lives. Then he got some money from his brother-in-law's wife and paid the taxi driver to escort them there and gave some to the man who helped him get there.

He had £5.00 in his hand, which he brought from Bangladesh. At that time, it was not allowed to bring much currency from Bangladesh. That was the first time he came to a different country. When he arrived at London Heathrow, he was surprised to see that all the people were wearing ties, including the people who were sorting the trolleys out. He also said, "It does not matter what kind of job they are doing; the main thing is that they need a job".

8.14.3 Life in the UK

He studied in Bangladesh, but he had problems with speaking in English when he first came to Britain. He didn't have experience in speaking in English, but he knew how to speak a little and always found it difficult to remember.

He did not face any problems with his English at his workplace. For example, when he used to work in the tailoring factory, he didn't have to speak much English and there was a person from Bangladesh who was his colleague who used to work there, he didn't have to face any problems with English.

People who had migrated to England from Bangladesh didn't have much education due to their travelling to Britain. Mr. Khan used to write letters to their families and relatives in Bangladesh to help; also, he used to read letters that they received from their families and relatives in Bangladesh. He also used to fill up forms for example tax forms. From that, he got a chance to help the community.

He didn't have any problems with the food. He was attached to British food. For example, eggs and chips or bread and butter. He likes Britain's culture. He said, "If I didn't come to Britain then I am not able to say whether it would be better or worse living in Bangladesh".

But one thing he said very clearly is "If I didn't come to Britain then my children's education might not have been as good as their studies in Britain". All Bangladeshi parents encourage their children to study. Then he said, "It is good that we came to Britain, a better place to live".

The People from Bangladesh who came to Britain have benefited in many ways and the British have benefited too. They are contributing socially and economically. He said many things have developed and people are well-developed too.

He said, "20/30 years ago British society was very different than the present one; many things have been improved and developed". The standard of life has been improved; the communication has become easier. The young generation is enjoying the benefits of science and technology also.

8.14.4 Employment:

When he first came to Britain, he wondered how he was going to spend his time. He worried about this because the people he knew were all busy with their work. For the first few weeks, he didn't find any jobs and he stayed at home. He said, "What kind of country is this, how I am going to spend my time and where can I find a job".

For the first six weeks, he did not find any jobs. Then he found a job in London, and he started his first job in Britain in a tailoring shop. They used to make ladies' coats liner, as a learner he did 2 weeks training and then he learned how to do the work. After deducting the tax, he used to get £5.00- and 5-shillings wages per week. Then he moved to another tailoring factory in the London E1 area, and his weekly wages were £8.00. He worked there for 5 months.

During the work in that factory, he had stomach pains, so he had to take 2 weeks sick leave. After that, he did not go to the factory again and he was looking for another job. Then he found another job in a tailoring factory. He worked there for a long time and his wages were £18.00 per week.

His next tailoring job was in North London, and he moved to West London and worked as an attendant boy with "Royal Automobile Club (RAC)". That was a big company. Only members of the club were allowed to go inside the company. His wages were £10.00 per week but he used to get more tips, including tips he used to get £18.00 to £20.00 wages per week.

At that time one of his friends from the same village used to work in a Restaurant. With this reference, he was able to have accommodation in the staff quarter with the other staff and he used to pay £1.00 for a single bed and £1.00 for the food. Altogether, he paid £2.00 for food and accommodation.

He used to look for jobs by himself and he did not ask for anybody's help. After 2 years working in (RAC), his wife came to Britain (1965). He moved to east London, where his brother-in-law was residing. He stayed with them for about six months then he applied for a flat. He was able to get a one-bedroom flat with one reception room. The toilet was outside the house.

In 1980, he came to Manchester to open a restaurant business with his wife's brother's son and his sister's husband. His sister's husband used to live in Oldham, Manchester. The name of the Restaurant was "Akash Tandoori "and it was situated in the Manchester Stalybridge area. The restaurant had a 64-seating capacity, and they paid £25,000.00 for it. Most of this fund came from a loan.

He had no previous experience in working or running an Indian restaurant, but he relied upon his brother-in-law, who had experience in this field. His brother-in-law was a good waiter, so he managed the business and at the same time, they had to appoint a chef to do the cooking. The Business was good, they used to make 2-4 thousand pounds per week. Some weeks they used to make less money and sometimes they used to make more money. They used to do very well.

They used to pay £75.00 wages then they used to have £50.00 - £100 from the profit. He said every week the restaurant business used to be up and down. Starting the business, they used to live on the top floor of the restaurant then they moved to the next-door house (number 13).

He was involved with the business from 1980 to 2000. In 1997 he had heart bypass surgery; also, he had a few health issues. Since then, he has been retired from the business after 20 years. The other reason to quit the restaurant business was his sons did not have any interest in the restaurant business.

8.14.5   Housing:

When he was single, he used to live in shared accommodation. When his wife came to Britain, they stayed for the first six months with their relatives in the East London area. Then he applied for a flat and found a 1-bedroom flat including 1 living room and 1 kitchen, but they did not have a bathroom inside the flat because during that time they used to have bathrooms outside the house. He did not have to pay rent when he was in his wife's brother's house but in a Council house, they used to pay £1.00 and half a crown.

He bought a house in 1990 and that is where he is living now. He bought the house for 50 thousand pounds, and he spent extra to put a radiator inside the house, also the toilet and the bath are attached to the house. There was a 3-bedroom house in London from the Council attached a toilet bath and other facilities.

8.14.6   Social & Family:

When he came to Britain, he left 3 sons in Bangladesh but they all died. Now he has 5 children in Britain, his eldest daughter, and 2 sons are all highly educated, and his youngest 2 sons are studying. After he came to Britain, he did not get many chances to go to Bangladesh.

In 1972 he went to Bangladesh after the liberation war of Bangladesh. During that time, he stayed in Bangladesh for 10 months, and then he came back to Britain in 1973.

In 1984 he went to Bangladesh for a second time, and then in 1985 again he went to Bangladesh because his father died.

Then in 2007-2008, he went to Bangladesh on holiday to see his relatives. Now he has 1 brother and sisters living in Bangladesh. He has 1 sister in Britain.

He used to write a lot of letters, every day he used to write 5-6 letters. He used to write these letters to his father, mother, wife, and other relatives. He now doesn't write them anymore; he hasn't written one for 10 years.

During that time, they used to communicate with each other by letters. Now communication has improved a lot in Britain and Bangladesh. Now we have telephones, mobiles, and the internet at any time, anyone can contact their family and relatives in any country, which makes life a lot easier.

His personal life was hard when his wife and children did not come to Britain. After work, it was hard to do cooking and other stuff which would have been easy if his family was in Britain. He said now the kind of life he had was not like the one he had before.

8.14.7 Conclusion

He is an established person in Britain now and he is on pension. During his free time, he does personal things, and he goes to the Mosque to do Zuhr prayer. Sometimes he has hospital appointments. He has been the Chairman of the "Ashton Jameh Mosque" since 2002 and is still serving the committee and helping the Bangladeshi community. He was not officially involved with the "Ashton Bangladesh Welfare Association" but his younger brother was involved

officially.

He said that during the rest of his life, he wants to pray and fast. He prays to Allah that he stays well in health, and he can go to the Mosque and pray 5 times a day. Also, he prays to Allah that he helps him from having any problems and he does not want to stay at home with ill health. Then he said, "It is good that I came to Britain, my children are well educated". He does not know much English, but his children help him. He said, "All the parents in Britain should take care of their children and give them a proper education". For the rest of his life, he does not want to settle in Bangladesh he wants to remain in Britain.

8.15 Alhaj Abdul Aziz
(Interviewed on 13 July 2009)

8.15.1 Life in Bangladesh:

Alhaj Abdul Aziz was born in 1942 in a traditional Muslim family, in the village of Shaleswor Kuna, Bianibazar, Sylhet. His father's name is Late Mohammad Khurshed Ali; his father was a farmer and a businessman. His father used to have a grocery wholesaler shop, and it was situated in the local Boiragi Bazar. Goods used to come from all different parts of Bangladesh, for example, Rangpur, etc. His grandparents used to be very rich, but it was not much during that time. His father used to maintain the family very well from agricultural work and business money.

In 1947-1948, per 40 kilograms of rice's price was 5-7 Rupees. They used to do very well in agricultural work because their land was very close to the "Khushiara River". When the river overflowed with water it used to bring new soils in the paddy fields. So, there was a good production of rice.

Also, they used to get a lot of fish from the Khushiara River and small water ponds, on one hand, there was plenty of rice and on the other hand, there was plenty of fish. So, the local people used to maintain their families from agricultural work and fishing very well. In his childhood, he saw that the fisherman used to catch a lot of fish from the river. He has 3 brothers and 1 sister; his eldest two brothers have passed away. In his village, they used to have Hindu people, and everybody was very nice.

He passed his primary school in his village then he went to a famous school called "Ponchokhondo Horgobindo High School". The school was based in his hometown. From that school 1957-1958 he prepared for his Secondary School Certificate (SSC). Before that there was another famous school in Bianibazar, people used to call it "MA High School" but the actual name was "Dhukkini Muhon High School".

It was one of the famous Schools in the Asam province. The school also had another name which was "Surma Valley" because it had earned the name and fame by providing a good education. At that time, Teachers used to deliver good lessons to the classrooms, so the students did not have to employ any home teachers.

After completing the SSC exam, he wanted to start a job. A Lawyer he knew helped him to find a job; the job was working as a clerk at the Judge Court in Sylhet. At that time, he was only 17-18 years old. During his employment, he wanted to do law practice, but he did not get the chance to do that. For about 3 years (1960-1963) he practiced as a court clerk.

8.15.2 Journey to the UK & Immigration:

In 1963, while he was working as a court clerk in the Judge Court, Sylhet. He heard from people and the newspapers that there was a chance to go to Britain by "Employment Voucher". Like other people, he also completed a form and sent it to Britain. Four weeks later he received a reply from the labour ministry that an employment voucher would be forwarded to the British High Commission, Dhaka and he will receive another letter from the BHC. After a few days, he received a letter from the British High Commission to get his Voucher. He went to the Dhaka British High Commission to get an Employment Voucher. At that time, he also helped about 4-5 thousand people by filing the application forms and applying for Pakistani Passports.

He came to Britain in 1963 with an "Employment Voucher". He flew by Pakistani Airlines (PIA) and arrived at London Heathrow airport. The total cost of the processing of the paperwork, obtaining the Passport and airline ticket was 16,500.00 Rupees. On the same flight, one of his friends Fojlur Rahman Khan came to Britain.

Fojlur Rahman Khan was living in Luton at the time. He did not feel scared during the flight as it wasn't his first flight abroad. His relative came to receive him from Heathrow Airport, and then they went to London Cannon Street house. There was not much space for him to stay in that house, after 3-4 days he went to Birmingham Elizabeth Street to another relative's house. He stayed 5-6 months in that house, and then he went to the Small Heath area in Birmingham.

8.15.3 Life in the UK:

He said, "In the past, life in the UK was very hard and now everything is very easy". People who are coming to Britain now are in the golden age of Britain. During the 1960's there was no carpet, bath radiator, or heating compared to now. They used to use Coal to warm the house because it was too cold at that time. There were not any facilities to have baths either, they used to go to the public bath to have a bath. It was hard to sleep, etc because there was not much space. They even had to sleep under the bed; also, they had to share a single bed with other people.

8.15.4 Employment:

While he was living in Birmingham, he was looking for a job but there was a job crisis at that time. A few months later, he found a job in a factory. His first job in Britain was in a factory. The Factory's name was Harrison. He worked there for 4 weeks. He used to get £7.00 to £8.00 per week.

From Birmingham, he went to Bradford to his friend's house. He stayed there for 3-4 months but he did not find any jobs. His friends helped him to find a job in the Manchester Bolton area in a cotton mill. He worked there as a "Machine Operator" for 3-4 months. His wages were £7.00 to £7.50 per week.

He used to live on George Street in Bolton. He stayed there for 3 months, during this time his relative Syed Abdul Hannan who was from Liverpool opened a new restaurant and offered him a job work there. He started working there as a waiter and his weekly wages were £5.00.

He said, "The owner of the restaurant offered him free food and accommodation with the job but the Factory did not provide this facility". These are the reasons for him transferring to a job that paid less, so he could get accommodation. So, he thought it was good. He worked there for 7-8 months, and he used to live on the second floor of the Restaurant.

In 1965, there was a Restaurant called "Ojontha" in Ashton-Under-Lyne; he started to work there. He worked there for 1 year then in 1966 he bought a Restaurant in Ashton as a Partnership. They spent £10,000.00 and the name of the Restaurant was "Gate of India". At that time, it was one of the big Restaurants in Manchester. During that time, it was hard to maintain a business compared to this time. The business income was good but some of the customers were very rude, and they used to fight as well. Senior staff used to say to the new staff "Do you have insurance for your nose"; they used to say that as a joke.

They used to get extra people for the weekend because of the customers fighting, rude attitude and not paying their bill for the food. They used to prepare themselves for fighting. When he came to Britain it was hard for him to speak in English and understand what they were saying. He studied English when he was in Bangladesh and now that he was in Britain it was slowly getting better.

It was a good business. There were 4 partners including him, for the first few weeks they didn't get paid any wages because they had to make bill payments. After that, they used to take £5.00 per week for their wages. For about 38 years he was involved with this business. In 2004 he retired from that business due to his health problems and his children did not show any interest in getting involved with this kind of business.

8.15.5 Housing:

Since his arrival in Britain, he lived in Birmingham, Bradford, and Bolton. In 1965, he came to Hyde in Manchester. He used to stay in his relatives' house. He used to stay in a rented house with his friend. Per week he used to pay £1.50. In 1967 he bought a 4 bedrooms house in the Ashton-under-Lyne area in Manchester. For 1 year he paid 900 hundred pounds in a private mortgage. That was his first house in Britain. He managed to pay all the mortgages in time. In 1975 he bought another 3-bedroom house, which was built in 1963 and he paid £8,000.00 for it, also he bought a few houses, and he sold them after.

8.15.6 Social & Family:

In 1972, he went to Bangladesh, and he got married in his local area. In 1979 his family came to Britain. He has 4 sons and 2 daughters and they're all well educated. His eldest son obtained an undergraduate degree in Business Hotel Management and a master's degree in information systems management, and he is currently working for Balfour Beatty Workplace as a Planning Coordinator.

His eldest daughter obtained a BSC Degree in Computing and she is

working for Cisco Systems as a Senior Network Engineer. His 2nd son obtained a Degree in Business Studies and is working as a Branch Manager for Carphone Warehouse.

His 3rd son obtained a Degree in Product Design and now he is working for New Charter Housing Association as a Tenant Finance Officer. His 4th son completed his degree in Mechanical Engineering and is also a Qualified Mortgage Advisor and works for the Co-Operative Bank now he is also involved in selling vehicles and renovating residential properties and his youngest daughter just completed her Master's Degree in Architecture and works for an Architectural practice in Leeds.

8.15.7 Independence of Bangladesh:

In 1947 during the India partition, he used to study in a Primary school. During the War in Bangladesh, he was in Britain, and he helped a lot of people in Bangladesh. At that time the Restaurant Owner had to pay a large amount of money to help people in Bangladesh. After the Victory of Bangladesh in 1972, he went to Bangladesh.

8.15.8 Conclusion:

Now in his free time, he goes to Bangladesh to see his relatives, and, he helps his relatives. After he came to Britain, he managed to establish himself and now he is proud and happy about his children's education and jobs. He also said that the new generations will understand and maintain their Bengali heritage and

culture.

8.16 Alhaj Abdul Mannan
(Interviewed on 27 September 2010)

8.16.1 Life in Bangladesh

Alhaj Abdul Mannan was born in 1940 in Tengra, in Bishwanath, Sylhet. His father's name is Late Abdul Gofur. He completed his primary education at "Tengra Primary School" and "Lalabazar High School'. He studied till high school and after that, he migrated to the UK.

In the 1960's there were only a few people who owned their land. The people were engaged in the cultivation work, and they could support their families easily. He said he had seen that his father and uncles were cultivating the seeds in the paddy fields, digging the fields, and doing the fishing.

At the same time, they used to play in the village with joy and happiness, now you will see more buildings have been built and all the joy and happiness has gone away. He said when he thinks about those days it makes him emotional; he'd be close to crying even. With the closing of the old heritage and culture, he blames the social management system.

8.16.2 Journey to the UK & Immigration:

He was only 21 years old when he first arrived in the UK on 7th August 1961, his first intention was to work in the UK and earn some money. There were some close family members and relatives living in the UK, he was inspired by them, and he took the family visa to come to the UK.

His eldest brother and one of his cousins said they'd take care of the cost of coming to Britain. In 1958 he lost his father. He was deeply saddened by this, then to make things worse his mother passed away in 1960. Since after his mother's departure, he left the school and made up his mind to come to Britain.

8.16.3 Life in the UK:

When first arrived in the UK, many of his close family members gathered at Heathrow Airport. Many of his friends used to live there, so he went to Coventry. He stayed in Coventry for two days, and then he went to Birmingham. Then he moved to Middlesbrough. He did not like Middlesbrough due to its small community presence.

Then he went to Bradford, there were many of his relatives and people from his village who were living there. Since September 1961, he had begun to live with Monuwar Hussain at his house. His sister-in-law and her family were living in Bradford and that is the main reason for him to move into Bradford.

8.16.4 Employment:

In December 1961, he started his employment with the Hill Brothers Cotton Mill, Orme Road in Bridge House. He worked as a spinner with weekly wages of £7.40 and he used to do 40 hours a week. At that time there were plenty of job opportunities. Many of the people used to work in the factories. There were so many sections in the factory or mills, he was young therefore other workers used to show kindness and affection to him.

He used to ask the manager and the supervisor that if there is any vacancy then they should let him know. He helped many of the Bangladeshi people to get employment in the factories he worked for. He continuously worked in the same factory until 1966.

In February 1966, for the first time, he went to (East Pakistan) Bangladesh. He stayed there for about six months and got married. Upon his return to the UK, he rejoined with the same company. He worked there for another two years.

In 1968, he started employment with Hill Brothers. In the middle of 1969, he left the job. His friends Modoris Ali and Bashir Ali encouraged him to become a partner to do the grocery shop. The shop was known as the Bengal

Store in Bradford. Some other people were involved in running the business before they took over the business.

This business was very profitable, and he ran this business until 1975. As a businessman, he became well-known in the community. He received affection from the community, and he tried to provide services to the community.

In January 1974, he bought a grocery shop on Featherstall Road North, Oldham. The shop was known as Mannan Brothers. He was involved in running the business till 2000. As a businessman, he had the opportunity to get to know the local people very quickly. In 1978, Alhaj Moboshir Khan, Somuj Miah, Moksud Ali, and Mofozzul Hussain took a leading role in establishing the Bangladesh Association in Oldham.

In 1976, he started a restaurant business on Featherstall Road North, Oldham called "Mati Mahal". In the same year, he opened another restaurant on Union Street, Oldham called "Light of Bengal". Then he extended his first restaurant and changed the name. It was known as the Noorjahan Restaurant. He was successfully running this business till 2006. He also opened another restaurant in Hull town with the same trading name Nurjahan but unfortunately, he couldn't run this business due to management problems.

8.16.5 Housing:

He is now residing in the Coppice area of Oldham. Next to his house, there is a Mosque, known as Al Aksa Mosque. He does all his prayers as this Mosque is closer to his home.

8.16.6 Social & Family:

He has three brothers and three sisters amongst them he is the second oldest. His eldest brother died in 2002. His youngest brother and two sisters are living in the UK. One sister is living in Bangladesh. He travels to Bangladesh once a year to see his sister and other close relatives.

He wishes to spend his retirement time with his family and grandchildren. He is the father of two daughters and all of them got married. His eldest daughter is a solicitor living in Manchester and trading as TM Fortis. He said when his daughter completed the LLB degree; she was the first Bangladeshi lady to obtain this degree within the Bangladeshi community in the Northwest. His second daughter completed a degree in Chemistry, serving as a teacher and she is residing in Kidderminster.

He reflected on his whole life and made some of the valuable comments which are given as follows. He said, "I enjoyed my childhood with joy and happiness, the money and being busy with your job or doing business cannot bring real happiness".

He said, "Until I die, I wish to travel to Makkah every year and I would like to live there". In 1988, he went to Makkah to do the Hajj (Pilgrimage) along with his wife. Thereafter, he has been there 10 times to do the Umrah and Hajj.

While he was working with Monuwar Hussain, he was inspired to do community work. In 1962, on Manningham Lane in Bradford, a dancing hall was opened. The Bangladeshi and Asian people were not allowed to enter the Hall. Monuwar Hussain was the first person to protest this discrimination. He called a public meeting to discuss this issue and take necessary action including a demonstration. Abdul Mannan said, "It was my first appearance in politics in the UK."

At that time, there were many Bangladeshis with language difficulties. Now there are many bi-lingual workers employed by the council and other agencies. But during the 1960's there were no bi-lingual workers employed by the agencies. So, just for that reason, the people with language difficulties were relied on by people who had some education and were able to assist in filing forms and dealing with medical, housing, immigration, and tax matters. There were even people who used to come to write letters to their loved ones and read the letters as well.

Since the Association was established, they were able to provide advice and information services to the local community. Besides that, some people were confident with individual persons to get help and assistance from them.

In 1968, he became naturalised as a British Citizen. In 1978 he became General Secretary of Oldham Bangladesh Welfare Association. In 1988, he was elected as a Chairman of OBWA and since then he has been serving as a chairman. He recalled an incident of a woman, who was murdered and there was huge chaos of innocent people being arrested by the Police, and some deportation orders were made by the immigration authority. In protest of this, he had taken a positive step from the OBWA to form an "Azad Action Committee".

This movement was successful; the Police had to stop their harassment of ordinary Bangladeshi innocent people.

While he was involved with Mannan Brothers, he used to import vegetables from Bangladesh. Now he is involved with the money transfer business, known as First Solution Money Transfer. He was amongst the first person to raise some funds for the Oldham Central Mosque. He had given the receipts book to collect contributions from his customers. He was able to convince his customers to make contributions and he raised the highest amount. He was able to draw attention to all the senior community leaders.

During the years between 1974 and 1978, he was not able to say exactly how many Bangladeshis were residing in the Oldham area, but he had an estimate of 200 – 300 Bangladeshi households, and the total Bangladeshi population was around 500 – 700. Now the total Bangladeshi population has reached around 25,000. Before the liberation war in 1971, there was one Mosque at Church Hill Street for Pakistanis and Bangladeshis but now there are about 10 mosques that have been established by the Bangladeshi people.

He also had taken a leading role, to stop the deportation order made by the immigration. He was successful on those issues and many times he was able to convince the authorities that individual people should not be removed from the UK. He has also helped many families, to bring their loved ones from Bangladesh by assisting in preparing their paperwork to get the entry clearance from British High Commission, Dhaka.

The Oldham Bangladeshi Welfare Association had begun their activities from a small terrace house at 82 Featherstall Road North. Two advice workers were employed by the OBWA to provide advice and information services to the community. When the local council demolished the house, then they had to move to Sylvan Street.

In 1980, there was a demand for the local community to have a large accommodation. The local authority was given a grant of £60,000.00 and the OBWA was able to build the first community centre on Featherstall Road North. It was also known as the Bangladesh Cultural Centre in the Northwest. There were many activities run by the OBWA, such as Bangla and Arabic classes, wedding functions, social and cultural programmes, etc.

The centre was the stepping stone to develop other projects by the OBWA. The capacity of this centre was only 250 people. So it was not large enough to hold big programmes. They used to hire Queen Elizabeth Hall to hold any public meetings and other social events.

The OBWA had talks with many departments in the local authority to expand the centre. As a result of this, the local authority came up with positive responses and provided the necessary support to secure funding for the expansion of the existing building. With assistance from the multi agencies including the Millennium Trust, they were able to build a new building with a capacity of 1,000 – 1,500 people. This building is now known as OBA

Millennium Centre. This is a good example because it has been established by the OBA and is seen as a symbol of a success story.

There are some meeting rooms and there are many offices used by the council. The main hall has got the facility to play badminton, basketball, and football. There are also facilities for fitness rooms for the local community to use. The main hall has facilities with a large kitchen where the community people use it for holding weddings, public gatherings, and other social and cultural events.

They spent 3.8 billion pounds to build this center. This is a unique centre in this area and many people will benefit from this, he added. The Oldham Bangladesh Association also worked with many other groups, which include the elderly group, women, and young people. The facilities in the OBA Millennium Centre are not open only for the Bangladeshi people but it is open for the wider community to use this centre.

He played a vital role in developing the central Mosque. In 1996, they purchased the land from the local council and were able to set up the Central Mosque. In 1998, the OBA formed a convening committee for the development of the Central Mosque. He was appointed as a coordinator to serve on the convening committee.

The first budget was 3 million pounds but later they realised they may not be able to raise this amount of money. Therefore, they revised their original plan and brought it down to 1.5 million pounds. This fund has not been collected but he is hopeful that the Bangladeshi community is continuously contributing to the development work.

He also said that it's the house of Allah and Allah will help us complete this work. The people will come forward because this is a good piece of work. Being a chairman of OBA, he was involved with other organisations, but he provided his support to many of the activities organised by them.

8.16.7 Independence of Bangladesh:

In 1969, the liberation moment had started. He attended many meetings in support of the independence of Bangladesh and he enjoyed working with the community leaders. He was a member of the Bradford Action Committee in the liberation movement. Monuwar Hussain was the chairman of the Bradford Action Committee and Pakistan Peoples Association. At that time, there were only a few people who owned cars.

8.16.8 Conclusion:

He is a very active person and is still involved with the business. He never had free time due to his business commitments. He said that the culture of the British community has changed. The Bangladeshi community also has improved a lot but if there is no leadership then it can go downward. The Bangladeshi children are getting the highest qualifications but besides that, they do not get the religious study and right leadership, shortly they will lose their identity.

He also said that many of the Bangladeshi children after completing their university degree are working in the office with very good positions, but they are not showing any interest at all in getting involved with local community activities. The community leaders are responsible for not taking any initiative to encourage young people to get involved in community activities. The parents and the community leaders should work together to encourage the young people to make connections with the local community.

Although the young people are getting the qualifications, they are not getting the social teaching from their parents or any organisations. Therefore, there is a huge gap that has been created between the first generation and the new generation. Just for that reason, the young generation is not showing any interest in getting involved in community activities.

They get together for parties and other social gatherings, they used to be organised by community organisations. There was a good warm presence of parents and their children at the community events. There were opportunities for everyone to get to know each other. But nowadays organisations are unable to organise such parties due to a lack of funding support.

There is a need to continue this piece of good work, where the young people along with their parents would be able to participate in the community events. He said, "We need to encourage and motivate our young people to take part in the community events". Then the young generation might change, and they would take an interest in learning the social culture of the Bangladeshi community in Great Britain.

The new generation will recognise the importance of community values, social aspects, and practising culture. Finally, he urges all community leaders to forget about the differences and to be united in one flat form to develop our community even further.

8.17 Alhaj Muktar Ali
(Interviewed on 12 January 2008)

8.17.1 Life in Bangladesh

Alhaj Muktar Ali was born in a traditional Muslim family in the village of Shingerkas (Shekerghaw), Bishwanath, Sylhet. He was born in 1952. His father's name is late Haji Yunus Ali and his mother's name is late Haji Joygun Bibi. His father was living in the United Kingdom. He is the only son, and he has 4 sisters in his parent's family.

He went to the local Primary School and studied up to class three. At that time there were a Hindu and two Muslim teachers in the school and his village, there were two primary schools and about 4-5 thousand families were living there.

His father was involved with agriculture work; he had some paddy fields where he used to work, and income from this cultivating work made sure that his family was well maintained. His father had some primary education, but his two uncles were educated as Munshi. His grandfather had some education, and they had four houses in one boundary.

8.17.2 Journey to the UK & Immigration:

In 1957, his father obtained a Medical Voucher to enter the UK. On the next day, his father got the visa to go to the Hajj (Pilgrimage), so he went to Saudi Arabia to do Pilgrimage, when his father returned from the pilgrimage, he decided not to come to the UK but at a later stage in 1961, his father came to the UK.

In 1967, he came to Britain with a Boy Voucher as a license to enter the UK. He paid 12,000 Rupees for airline fare. The currency rate was £1.00 equal to 18 Rupees. He flew from Sylhet to Dhaka then flew from Dhaka to Karachi by PIA and arrived at London Heathrow on the 24th of September 1967. His father received him at Heathrow Airport and brought him to Walsall to live.

His father was living in Walsall, Birmingham and he started to live there. He was 15 years old when he first came to the UK. There was a very limited opportunity for him to study. Many Bangladeshi people did not give priority to studying, his main intention was to work and retire and go back to his home country.

The house where he used to live consisted of 9 rooms and about 40 people were sharing the accommodation. Some people used to live in a single room and some people used to share rooms. At that time there was a good relationship with people, people used to accept other people as their brothers.

The price of 45kg of rice was £2.50. Fish was not available at that time; he used to eat meat and chicken and usually dined at his own home. There was one grocery shop in Manchester where people could buy fish from. There were no Bangladeshi grocery shops in Oldham at that time.

8.17.3   Life in the UK:

The weather was very cold; people used coal to warm up the room. In the morning sometimes he used to eat rice and curry for breakfast. The snow and ice were common weather everywhere.

In 1968 there was heavy snowfall in the UK. The roads were closed due to this. The authority then had to clear the ice from the road and then people were able to use transport. This was repeated so many times, he added.

At that time, there was a Mosque in Oldham at Church Hill Street, which was established with help from Abdul Matin and others. The special Eid prayer used to be held there. The people had to apply to their workplace to get authorised leave for Eid day. If anyone attended Eid on a workday the manager or supervisor encouraged that person to take leave and celebrate their religious festival.

There was good understanding and co-operation amongst Bangladeshis, if there was a death in the community, the people came forward to raise funds to do the funeral. Sometimes they had to send the dead body to Bangladesh and sometimes they used the local graveyard to do the funeral held in the UK.

8.17.4   Employment:

When he was 16, he started to work in the UK in the metal Industry. His starting wage was £5.00, and he used to work 40 hours a week. Usually, a married person used to get more wages than a single person.

He used to live with his father therefore his father used to pay for the food and accommodation. The rent for the accommodation per head was 50 pence. At that time many people used to eat chicken curry for most of the week and once a week meat curry only due to the limitation of the grocery shop. There was one Bengali and Pakistani-owned grocery shop in the Walsall area.

In 1968, he came to Oldham. He started a job in a cotton mill as a labourer, at a later stage, he was promoted from labourer to machinist. In 1973 he became the staff supervisor of the mill. There was shift work involved with his job. His wages were £10.00 per week, and he used to work there for 40 hours a week. There were workers from the white community but most of them were women. There were some Bangladeshi people. In 1972 his wages were increased to £200 - £250 per week including overtime.

He would usually have his breakfast at home, there was a canteen in the factory, and he used to take his lunch there. From 1968 to 1986 he worked in the cotton mill. After that, the mill was closed.

8.17.5 Housing:

He bought his first house near Monor Mill. There were equal numbers of people present from the Bangladesh and Pakistan community.

At present times there are about 15 thousand Bangladeshi and 20 thousand Pakistani people living in Oldham. In the past, about 5/6 hundred people were living in the Oldham area. There were only 3/4 Bangladeshi families in Oldham. 15 to 20 people used to live in one house. Most of the Bangladeshis used to live near the Grange School in Oldham.

8.17.6 Social & Family:

In 1972, after the liberation, he went to Bangladesh and got married. He stayed there for about six months. In 1986 his wife and two daughters came to the UK. His father went to Bangladesh and never returned.

He has reflected on his memory and said that he can remember where he used to play kabady, football, and so on as a child. He sometimes asks himself "Why did I come to the UK?" He also mentioned that he was a young minority in the Bangladeshi community. Most of the people were older than him. He had the opportunity to learn spoken English while spending time with the Bangladeshi community.

He has three daughters and one son. One girl is working in the Hospital as a

nurse. Two other daughters are studying, and his son is working in Tesco.

The Bangladeshi community is doing better compared to the previous period. The children are now going to universities and obtaining degrees. He thinks that the parents and community both need to be more anxious and provide necessary guidance and support to their children. He said, "All parents should have the responsibility to maintain the family ties with Bangladeshi relatives, and taking children to Bangladesh is also important".

8.17.7 Independence of Bangladesh:

At the time of liberation, he was in the UK. On 19th March 1972, he went back to Bangladesh. He was one of the activists for the independence of Bangladesh. He also recalled his memory and said Bangladeshi people played a vital role in that period.

In Manchester, Mr Matin devoted his time to organizing meetings. He was the owner of Sylhet Travels. Mr Matin led the movement in and around the UK. He was the president of the Manchester region. Mr. Gous Khan was the leader from London, and he had originated from Biswanath, Sylhet.

At that time of liberation, there were Mr. Matin, Dr. Kabir, Somuj Ali, and Moksud Ali Khan worked together to achieve the goals of independence. Cornell Osmani and Abdus Samad Azad came to the UK to unite the Bangladeshi people. Justice Abu Sayeed came to the UK and appealed to all the Bangladeshi people to help the freedom fighters. He confirmed that they collected £20.00 per person as a donation to help the country. He also confirmed that the fund used to be sent to India and then transferred to Bangladesh.

At that time of the liberation, all the Bangladeshi people who were living in the UK supported the war against West Pakistani aggression. The Bangladeshi people organised a rally and demonstrations at Trafalgar Square, Hyde Park, and Downing Street in support of the independence. He said, "The Pakistani people often tried to get involved in an argument and tried to stop us from doing our Campaign in favour of our native country".

There were very limited telephones and televisions at that time. Somuj Miah, Abdul Matin, and Hushiar Ullah had the television set. The people used to gather at their houses to hear the news about the war. Some people got together and bought second-hand television sets to watch the news.

He said 3 million people sacrificed their lives for the independence of Bangladesh but due to corrupt and selfish leaders, Bangladesh is now going backward.

8.17.8 Conclusion:

In his conclusion, he said our community needs to focus more on education. He is working as a volunteer with the local councillors for the development of Bangladeshis living in Oldham. He wants to see our young people make further progress in education and employment.

He also said that his children have been educated because they are in the UK. If we did not have the opportunity to come to the UK, then it would have been more difficult for our children. The children who are living in the UK and missed the education due to negligence, are missing the opportunity which they will suffer for. He also added a proper administration can offer the community the best services which they deserve. He received an award from the local council for his tremendous voluntary community work.

8.18 Alhaj Muslim Ali
(Interviewed on 4 July 2010)

8.18.1 Life in Bangladesh:

Alhaj Muslim Ali was born in 1937 in the village of Alankari, Biswanath, Sylhet. His Father's name is Md. Israel Ali. He studied up to class 4 at his local "Alankari Primary School" and due to his Father's death, he could not continue his studies anymore. At that time, he was 11 years old. He has 2 brothers and 3 sisters; among them, he is the eldest. At that time eldest person of the family had to take care of the family so he used to do that. After his father's death, his uncles helped him to do the agricultural work.

Before his father's death, his uncles and his father used to take care of their family. When his father died, at that time village people were very poor compared to this time. There were not many rich people in their village; only two or three families were rich. They used to maintain their family from agricultural work.

8.18.2 Journey to the UK & Immigration:

In 1962 he came to Britain. East-West Pakistan was one country at that point. Mr. Anjob Ali from the village wanted his son to go to Britain; he came to know that people from Karachi in Pakistan are going to Britain by voucher.

Mr. Anjob Ali also came to know that Mr. Monir Khan from Moulvi Gaon used to live in Karachi and he used to help people with their Passports. He got the address from Mr. Khan's Father. The local school - teacher's son and 3 other people went to Karachi to Mr Khan because they wanted to come to Britain. He advised Mr. Anjob Ali that he needs 5000 Rupees to come to Britain.

He sold paddy fields and took some loans from other people, and he managed to collect 4000 Rupees, he attached a condition that the remaining balance would be paid when he could come up with the money. Then he went to Karachi, and another 3-4 people came to Karachi with him to come to Britain. In Karachi, they went to the teacher's house that came before and found out that people who came to Karachi with the teacher were all going to Britain.

After 2 months in Karachi, he came to Britain. When he came to Heathrow, it was his last day of coming to Britain. There were 7-8 people who came together. Mr. Monir Khan also came because if he missed this flight then he won't be able to come to Britain by the Voucher. From Heathrow, everybody went to their relative's house, and he went to his cousins' brother's house and people from his village in Bradford.

8.18.3 Life in the UK:

That time 3-4 people used to cook together. Everything was cheap at that time; they used to use shillings and pence. They used to spend 5-6 pounds every month. For example, the price of bread was one shilling or 50 pence, £1.00 or £1.50 rent for sit per person. They used to go to a public bath 1 day per week to have a bath.

They used to warm their house by using coals; there was chicken and lamb available at that time. Mainly Pakistani people opened Chicken and lamb businesses in Britain. From the shop, they used to get Chicken, Lamb, and vegetables. That time there weren't many vegetables and meat in the shops compared to this time. There were not many shops at that time. That time they did a lot of hard work.

8.18.4　Employment:

His first job was in Britain in Show Mill Oldham as a labour. He used to work 5 days a week for £5.00 and if he worked on a Saturday then he used to get £6.00. After 6 months working there, he found another job in a factory in Shaw. He used to get £17.00 - £18.00 per week. After 6-7 months he went to Bradford on holiday, and he found another job in a cotton mill.

He came to Shaw and told them that he found another job in Bradford. He used to do a twisting job there. His wages were £18.00 - £22.00 per week. When he used to work in Shaw, it was a hard job. After 1 and a half years working in Bradford, he found another job in the same area in a Carpet factory. He worked there for 15 years, and he used to go to Bangladesh and when he came back, he'd go back to the same job.

His starting wages were £25.00 - £28.00 per week. They used to increase his wages. In 1980 when he was about to quit the job, he used to get £60.00 - £80.00 per week including overtime. Without overtime, he used to get £45.00 - £60.00 per week. At that time almost everybody was single. At that time 15-16 people used to live in one house.

After he quit the job in 1980, he didn't get any other job. People started to retire, and he also retired at that time. He didn't do any job after his retirement.

8.18.5　Housing:

When he first came to Britain, he stayed with his cousin for 1 week. He did not have to pay for anything. People had started to come to Britain before or after 1961. His cousin's brother Mr. Toimus Ali had a coffee shop in Oldham. Then he came to Oldham, and he used to stay with his cousin's brother on the 2nd floor of the coffee shop. The coffee shop was in Oldham Mom Bridge. He stayed there for 1 and a half months. He did not have to pay any rent.

They used to warm water with a kettle or a cooking pot to have a bath at home. At that time, they didn't have radiators at home. They used to use coal to warm the house, some people used to have gas fires but not everybody. They used to buy coal and put it in a small room, and they used to get the coal using a bucket from the small room.

In 1975 his wife and 2-year-old son came to Britain. Before his family came to Britain, he bought a 6-bedroom house for £6000.00. When he quit his job in the carpet factory, he then sold the house and went to Bangladesh with his family.

He left his family in Bangladesh and came back to Britain. That time he bought another house for £3000.00 - £3500.00 in Manchester Oldham. Then they came to Oldham. After 4 years of living in this house in 1984, he got the house from the Council. Per week he used to pay £15.00 - £16.00 rent. In 1988 he bought the house from the Council.

8.18.6   Social & Family:

In 1969 after 7 and half years he went to Bangladesh and got married. He is the father of 5 children, 1 daughter, and 4 sons. His daughters have gotten married and are living with his 2nd son. The other 3 sons are living with their family in their own house. He has a lot of grandchildren. He has 3 granddaughters from his 2nd son, 1 grandson, 2 granddaughters from his eldest son, 2 granddaughters from his 3rd son, and 1 grandson from his 4th son.

He was involved with the Oldham Bangladesh Association, and he is still involved with that association. Also, he is involved with Oldham's Central Mosque, but he was more involved with the old Mosque, and he was (Mutwali) in charge for 2-3 years of the old Mosque.

In 1985 he went to Makkah to do the pilgrimage (Hajj), he also did Umra Hajj 4/5 times. He also said that he is planning to go to Makkah with his wife for Hajj. He wants to do Umrah Hajj with his wife during Ramadan and after the Hajj. His house in Bangladesh is locked up and 1 person takes care of it. He goes to Bangladesh to visit.

During the work in Britain, he used to get weekends off but sometimes he used to work On Saturdays. On his off day, he used to stay at home and chat with friends, playing games and they also used to go to the Cinema to watch movies. Now he feels bored with all his free time.

It is embarrassing to go and spend free time in someone else's house because everybody has their own family, daughters-in-law, etc. He also said that during that time everybody was single, and it was easy to go to someone's house. He thinks that there should be a centre for a get-together for old people to go and spend their free time. His children don't want to get involved in any businesses because they think a job is better than a business.

8.18.7   Conclusion:

He mentioned that he thinks the younger generations are going down the wrong path. He also said the young boys dress up and negatively talk to other people. Sometimes the community talks about it and says parents or guardians should look after their children and check on them. Mr. Muslim Ali is a happy man in our community. Also, he said the community should open **a new association for the new generation so that they can find the right path for their future.**

8.19 Alhaj Md Nasir Ali
(Interviewed on 26 June 2010)

8.19.1 Life in Bangladesh and Other Places:

Alhaj Md Nasir Ali was born in 1931, in the Kadipur village of Bishwanath, Sylhet. At that time Bangladesh was under the control of the Pakistani government and was known as East Pakistan. His father was called late Md Furkan Ullah, he was a farmer and earned his living by cultivating crops and was living a happy family life.

Mr. Ali completed his primary education from his local primary school which was called 'Shamspur Primary School' and in 1952 he migrated to Malaysia with the hope of earning a living. His uncle used to live in Malaysia, and he helped Nasir Ali with his immigration. He was accompanied by a friend of his uncle during his journey.

When he was living in Malaysia, he used to work at a mining factory, and according to him, life in Malaysia at that time was quite like life in Bangladesh. The weather in Malaysia was also like Bangladesh; the weather was amazing in Malaysia, and there were mostly sunny clear days throughout the whole year.

From 1952-1954, after living for nearly 6 years in Malaysia, he went to Singapore. He used to work with a ship's crew and after living for another 2 years in Singapore; he: went to Bangladesh for a holiday and then again returned to Singapore.

It was a very long time ago; people didn't have gas lines or gas cylinders as the source for cooking, people used to use dry wood as the source for their cooking and they had to bring packed lunch from home for work every day. In Singapore lunch for the ship's crew was cooked by the 'Special Chef' on board, they had him there so that the other staff and workers didn't have to bring their lunch.

As Nasir Ali was working with a ship's crew, he had the chance to see many countries; his role on board was as the assistant of the ship's chief engineer. There were small cabins on the ship, each cabin with two bam beds where the staff slept. Nasir Ali said that when he was working in Malaysia, he used to get wages of 150-200 ringgit (Malaysian currency) per month, and whilst he was working in Singapore as a part of the ship's crew, he used to get wages of 250-300 ringgit (Malaysian currency) per month and the food was also provided by the company for free. Therefore, he was able to save more money in Singapore.

8.19.2 Journey to the UK & Immigration:

He decided to move to the UK because of advice from relatives and friends, when he went to Bangladesh, he heard rumours that people were migrating to the UK for work. He also learned that the husbands of both his sisters had also migrated to the UK, in that time there wasn't a very good telecommunications system, and people didn't have telephones and mobiles as we have in our day.

It was said that only some of the richer people in Bangladesh had telephone systems in their houses, therefore sending and receiving letters by post was the only way to communicate with people who were living abroad, the husbands of his sister sent letters to him encouraging him to come to the UK, also mentioning that there were also good wages for work in the UK.

It is said that Nasir Ali wanted to migrate from Singapore to the UK in 1959, but in the meantime, Nasir Ali went to see his maternal cousin in Kuwalalampur which was 5-6 miles away from where he used to live. They offered the Maghrib prayer together and after prayer, they sat down for a little chat. His cousin was quite a religious person and told him that it is quite hard to live under the shade of Islam in the UK's varieties of culture, concerning his experience of living in the UK.

He shared his story with Nasir Ali, he told him about his embarrassing experience when he was living in the UK. During that time the workers in the UK were able to have a bath once a week as they had to go to the public bath. So basically, the only time he was able to wash would be on his day off, which was on Saturday.

He said that due to this, he sometimes couldn't take a shower even when he had wet dreams, which was embarrassing and uncomfortable. It is mandatory to take a shower if someone has a wet dream according to Islam. He gave much more advice to Nasir Ali. He took his maternal cousin's advice and decided that he would think about it later and that he wouldn't rush into any decisions.

Then in 1960, his brother-in-law suggested again that he should come to the UK. He was also told that there were many mosques built in the UK and many Muslims were also living in the UK, and hence he could also live his life under Islamic regulations. After hearing this news Nasir Ali decided to migrate to the UK. He sorted everything out that was necessary for immigration by 1961; he sorted out his passport and gained permission from the Pakistan High Commission for immigration. Many Bangladeshis who were working in Singapore were also migrating to the UK as there were rumours that there were good opportunities for work and good wages.

During that time, some rumours cleaning roads and cleaning toilets and bathrooms was the only work for Pakistanis who migrated to the UK it was said that cleaning was the only work for the Pakistani people (Both East and West Pakistan) but when he came to the UK, he saw that people were doing many good and respectful jobs.

He sent letters to his friends and said that those rumours were only made up by people and were said to criticise the people who were living in the UK. He also suggested to his friends that if they wish to come to the UK, then they should also come. About 80% of Pakistanis and Bangladeshis who were living in Singapore migrated to the UK but those who had a good job in Malaysia didn't wish to lose their job, so they didn't migrate to the UK.

He was travelling from Singapore to the UK by Ship. He described that it was a Huge Ship, with a football field, swimming pool, a cinema hall, and some shops as well. The ship passed through Sri Lanka, Mumbai, then Africa, then Suez Lake and then after a long journey of 23 days, the ship arrived at Marseille City in France.

The travel cost including the ship's ticket cost him about 260 ringgits (Malaysian Currency). From there it took 4 hours on the train and 8 hours on a small ship then another 8 hours on the train, he finally arrived at London Victoria Station. He was accompanied by Mr Surot Khan, who was a close neighbour of his. Mr Surot Khan's Brother lived in Brick Lane in London. They both went to Mr Surot Khan's Brother's house and stayed there.

The next day in the morning, while they were having breakfast, Surat Khan's brother asked Nasir Ali if there were any places that he wanted to see in London. Nasir Ali said that one of his nephews lives in South Hall and asked him if he could take him there, Mr Khan replied that if his nephew works during the day, then he may not find him at home, also if he lived in a rental house that belongs to 'Shikh' people, then it is most likely that they open the door if its someone they don't know.

At that time many Shikh people used to live in South Hall. Therefore, he asked if there were any other places he wanted to go. In reply, he asked if he could take him to Bradford, Mr. Khan agreed and took him to Bradford. Nasir Ali stayed there for two weeks and since he couldn't find any job, he moved to Blackburn. One month had passed and he still couldn't find a job. Then he decided to Move to Sheffield where one of his sisters was living with her husband. He still couldn't find any jobs there either.

8.19.3 Employment:

After two weeks he started to work in Leeds at an engineering factory as a learner. This was his first job in the UK. He worked 5 days a week and he used to get wages of £6.08 per week. He then rented which cost 10 shillings per person/ per week and expenses for food per week were 15 shillings. He saved the rest of the wages that were left, many Bangladeshi people were also working in the factory, but they were mostly English people.

Nasir Ali knew a little English; therefore, he didn't have any trouble working with his colleagues. His manager showed him his work; therefore, it wasn't necessary to know the English language properly. Two weeks later he went to Sheffield to visit his sister and luckily found a better job, wages of £10-£11 per week. In this Job, he worked six days per week.

The work was at a factory. After working there for 3 months, he had injured one of his toes and was unable to work. Since then, there was too much pressure from work in the factory, and since he was unable to work, he was replaced by another employee, therefore he lost his job. He then moved to Burnley. It was winter, and it was hard for Nasir Ali to work in this cold weather. Then after one month, he moved to 'Little Borough' in Rochdale and started working at a cotton mill.

He used to work at the 'spinning section' of the cotton mill. His wages per week were £7.50 per week including his 4 hours of extra work on Saturday. He worked there for about 3 months, and then with the help of a friend he was able to get a job at 'Tyre Company'. He changed his job because he was getting more wages at Tyre Company.

He worked during the night, 6 days a week and his wages were about 13 pounds per week. He worked there for 6 years continuously. Working there was very beneficial to Nasir Ali. With the help from his boss, he was able to bring his brother to the UK by Factory Boucher. After that, he was also able to bring his 2 nephews and his brother-in-law to the UK.

At that time Nasir Ali was working at 'Di Mill' in 'Show' in the welding section. His work was during the night, 5 days a week, and 12 hours every night. After that, He worked at several more factories.

In 1981, whilst he was working at

'Lees Road', the Mill was shut down and he couldn't find any more work, he also reached the age of pension, hence he retired from work. At the end of 1982, he was living with his wife in a town where there were about 250 more Bangladeshi families were also living.

8.19.4   Housing:

He started living with his wife in Oldham. With time, he then moves to Milton Street, and then to Waterloo Street. He bought a house at Marlboro Street and £350. Finally, he bought another house at Park Road in the Glodwick area of Oldham, where he is residing now.

8.19.5   Social & Family:

In 1969 he went to Bangladesh and got married and returned to the UK with his wife. Nasir Ali has two sons and two daughters. His eldest son graduated from the UK and is now working, and his younger son is studying at a high school. His eldest daughter has also graduated and is married, and his younger daughter is studying law in her final year at university.

There wasn't any mosque when he first came to Oldham. Then a mosque (Pakistani) was built at Churchill Street. At that time there were more Bangladeshi's compared to Pakistanis in Oldham. Mr. Majful Hussain of Manchester was an educated Bangladeshi man who was selected as the chairman of the Community, and Khoddus Bakt was his secretary.

In 1962 the 'Pakistani Community' was also created. Since the number of East Pakistanis was greater, the Bengali people claimed a 'Bangladeshi Community' as well. In 1971 after Bangladesh was an independent country, the Bangladeshi people hesitated to go to the old mosque which then belonged to the Pakistani people. After that, another mosque (Bengali) was built at Middleton Road.

As the number of Bangladeshi's started to increase another mosque was built at Orme Street in Glodwick, Oldham. This was mainly built to make it easy for young children to go to the mosque so that they could learn Arabic. At that time Mr. Abdul Latif was selected as the Chairman of the Mosque community.

Later, Mr Mofajjul Hussain joined the community. Nasir Ali said that he was the treasurer of the Mosque committee right from the beginning. When Syed Makhon Miah (Mutalli of the mosque) left Oldham and moved to London, Nasir Ali took the role of 'Mutalli' (caretaker of the mosque) and fulfilled his role for about 14 years for the benefit of the mosque and its community. This mosque was probably built in 1978 or 1979.

After that, he resigned from his job for personal reasons. He was elected as the president of 'Glodwick Bangladesh Society two times in a row (four years). The main duty of society was to help and serve the community. This included- immigration advice, benefits advice, and social advice. Besides if anyone needed help to complete an official form, help was given by the 'Glodwick Bangladesh Society'.

They also started a 'Bangla School'. It is said by Nasir Ali that the office was once a good running condition and there were also about 5 teachers, but now it has been closed for refurbishment for about 5 years. At present this old social worker is working in Tabliq to feed his desire to be involved in helping people and their community, and to invite people to offer Salah. **This religious and peaceful man first went to Hajj in 1984 and has performed Hajj 19 times in his lifetime.**

8.19.6   Conclusion:

He still misses his beautiful old days spent in Bangladesh. He loves his mother and his mother's country very much; he goes to Bangladesh for a holiday once a year to see his mother. After his mother passed away in 1996, he didn't feel like going there anymore. At present one of the elder brothers is living with his family in Bangladesh. His wish was to get his son married in Bangladesh.

As he is working for the community in the group – 'Tabliq' he is very respected for being one of the eldest and senior in the group. Whenever he went to Bangladesh to do his community work, he was often respected everywhere. There are poor people in the poor country of Bangladesh but their love for this social worker is priceless.

This successful man is now living his life in his own house in Oldham. He spends this retired time praying, working for the community and his Tabliq group by inviting people to offer Salah. In conclusion, Nasir Ali said that it was very beneficial to him to come to the UK, he had accomplished many things in his life, and it may not have been possible if he hadn't come to the UK.

8.20   Alhaj Mohammed Ali Annjab
(Interviewed on 27 January 2009)

8.20.1 Life in Bangladesh:

Alhaj Mohammed Ali Annjab was born in the village of Daud Pur, Bishwanath, Sylhet. His father's name is the late Mubashar Ali. Mr. Annjab has 4 brothers and 2 sisters. He completed his primary education at "Dirth Pur Khayakhir Primary School". After passing, Mr. Annjab enrolled in

"Ramsundar High School" where he studied there for a while.

8.20.2 Journey to the UK & Immigration:

His father came to Britain in and around 1937 and just before the Second World War his father (In 1944 or 1945) returned to Bangladesh. In 1958 his father came to Britain for the second time with a "Medical Voucher" and returned to Bangladesh [East Pakistan] in 1964.

In 1965, his youngest brother came to Britain with his father. He was inspired as his father and his brother already resided in the UK, so, in 1969, he came to Britain with a "Boy Voucher". It was also his father's wish that he should come to Britain.

The travel to Britain started from Dhaka Tejgaon Airport where he flew to Karachi Airport before departing to Heathrow Airport. There was a short wait in between the flights. His father and his brother were waiting to greet him at Heathrow Airport. At that time, the weather conditions were very severe as it was extremely cold, and it was snowing.

8.20.3   Life in the UK:

At that time, for six weeks the roads were covered in deep snow, and he never saw it like this ever again in Britain. His father lived in Halifax, and he stayed with his father. The house is comprised of two living rooms and three bedrooms. Around 14 people occupied the house; this included him, his father, and his brother. The Coal was used for heating purposes.

As his father was the owner of the house, sometimes he was responsible for making sure there was enough coal in stock, and he used to put the heating on by using Coal. During that time most of the kitchens were situated in the cellar and they used to do the cooking in the cold weather. Just before his father left the UK, he sold his house and moved to Oldham.

There was a halal grocery shop owned by a Bangladeshi and a Pakistani and they used to sell chickens, sheep and other grocery items. Mr. Annjab lived with his father for five to six months.

8.20.4   Employment:

His father used to work at "John Atkinson Textile Mill" in Halifax. When his brother reached the age of 15 years old, he also started the work one week before his arrival. He didn't have to search for work as it was prepared by his father and his brother. He got a job placement in the factory. This was the first job of his life. The factory workers didn't seem pleasing at first to him. The work was very hard and sometimes, he did not like to go to work. After working for 5/6 months, he got used to it.

In the first week, he received wages of £18.36, which he still remembers now, as it was his first wage in the UK. He used to give all his wages to his father as it was a social tradition that he followed.

Whilst living with his father and brother, he was not responsible for doing the shopping and cooking. His father and brother used to manage all this. At that time factory workers used to cook food by themselves.

Inside the factory, there was a heating facility, and he could do the work just by wearing a shirt. He worked day shifts at the factory and used to get a 45-minute break to have lunch. Food would be prepared from home to have for lunch. Some people used to buy food from the canteen.

He worked there for nine months and then in 1969, he moved to Oldham where a relative used to live. In the area of Shaw, he got a job in "Lily Mill" and started work for 8 hours shift. There was a night shift between 10 pm to 6 am and he decided to change his day shift to night shift.

Workers would have shift rotations, but the night shift was up to the workers' preference. He worked there till April 1970 before moving on to another factory which was well known in the West. This factory was called the "Null Spinning Company".

There was a shortage of workers, and due to this, the employer used to request the workers to do overtime (4 hours). So, altogether, the shift was 12 hours, and he said it was very hard to do the job by standing all the time. He did not have any previous experience but had to work in the factory. He said, "For the need to have money in my pocket, I considered working hard to achieve this goal".

At that time, it was not difficult to get a job. If anybody wanted to do work, it was easily available. The availability of workers was high. Sometimes factory supervisors would ask workers to bring any relatives or friends who were willing to work due to labour shortages.

Remembering the past he said, "At the beginning, sometimes I did not like to go to work, and my father became annoyed with me and booked a ticket for me to go back to Bangladesh". His friends and relatives became aware of this situation, and then they convinced his father not to send him back to Bangladesh, instead they advised his father to visit Bangladesh. Since then, his father never came back to Britain. In 1984, his father passed away.

In around 1972, he went to Bangladesh and upon his return, he re-engaged with his previous job in the factory. Since then, he has visited Bangladesh several times to see his close family members, relatives, and friends.

8.20.5 Housing:

When he moved to Oldham, he rented a single room for £2.00. In 1971, he bought a house in Glodwick, Oldham for £750.00. In 1975, he bought another house for £4500.00 with a mortgage. He was able to get a mortgage because he worked in a factory. The payment of the mortgage was £60.00 - £61.00 per month.

He then bought another house for £1800. All the houses were terraced. When visiting Bangladesh, he used to sell the houses to his friends and would buy houses again after returning. It was also difficult to find the tenant and if he found any tenants no one was keen to take official responsibility.

Thereafter, the house prices went up, from £12,000.00 to £20,000.00 then it doubled and tripled.

8.20.6   Social & Family:

In 1980, he went to Bangladesh and got married and in 1981 he brought his wife to the UK. He is the father of five sons and three daughters who have been educated; his eldest son has graduated with BA Honours and is working in a training programme for one year. The eldest daughter has gotten married and has one son and two daughters. The second son has studied up to his A-levels and is working part-time. His third son is in university and his daughter is undertaking a training programme at Oldham College.

He has twins who are currently studying whilst his fourth son is about to take his GCSE exams. He has been a successful father for being able to educate all of his children.

Having studied back at home aided him with an easier understanding of the English language. There were no language barriers whilst in England; he was able to communicate easily.

8.20.7   Independence of Bangladesh:

In the independence of Bangladesh, he was in the UK but he supported the independence movement and was involved in activities regarding this cause. The following people were involved in the same cause: Abdul Matin, Moffozzul Hussian, Muksod Ali, Mr. Shomuj Miah, and others from the Greater Manchester area.

On March 25[th,] 1971, Pakistani troops invaded Bangladesh [East Pakistan], the day after an action committee in Manchester was formed which was operated by Bangladeshi people. There were about 27/28 people from Oldham involved with this action committee.

Every Sunday, there were meetings organised by this committee and they used to take part in demonstrations in London Trafalgar Square to the demand for independence of Bangladesh. Two more leaders who should be included are Dr. Kobir Ahmed and Abu Syed who led this movement in the UK.

There were so many people engaged in this movement, but he was unable to remember the names of all the people. He acknowledged the contribution made by the British Bangladeshi. In the past, he used to remember his home country of Bangladesh. He had strong feelings for his birthplace and therefore he supported the independence of Bangladesh from the bottom of his heart.

With the outcome of independence, he said that the Bangladeshi people are no longer neglected by Pakistanis. He feels proud to be of Bangladeshi nationality. According to his wishes and advice from his father, he did not consider becoming a British citizen, which may face some problems.

8.20.8   Conclusion:

He said "compared with the other communities, the Bangladeshi children are still behind; due to parents who are not being educated enough to support their children with homework. Sometimes, it is quite impossible to provide support due to many other reasons".

In his personal life, he has been successful and is very happy with the achievements made by his children. His father's contribution has led to his success in life. He is very happy with his family and is having a peaceful life in the UK. He also said that no one can see success in life.

He is very grateful to Allah and his Father for his successes. He also said, "The social and state policy is very good in Britain; there are many people from different racial backgrounds, living in harmony and peace and getting many opportunities". Finally, he said, "The people in Bangladesh, who have not got anything, if I make comparison with them, then I think I am better off that I came to Britain and I am fortunate for that". Currently, he is spending his life happily in Manchester with his children.

8.21 Alhaj Mohammed Anis Ali
(Interviewed on 27 January 2009)

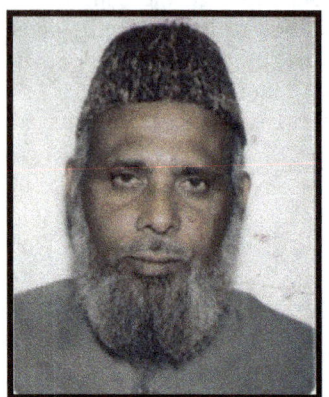

8.21.1 Life in Bangladesh:

Alhaj Mohammed Anis Ali was born in 1942 in the village of Bui Gaon, Chattok, Sunamgonj. His father's name is the late Alhaj Mohammed Azim Ullah. His father had some agricultural lands, where his father used to do the cultivation work and was able to maintain his family's expenses through the crops that were grown.

He went to the local village primary school and was not able to study much. The reason for not being able to study was that he had to help his father with farming work. He was the oldest of the two brothers. At that time school teaching was enough for a student and a private tutor was not required.

8.21.2 Journey to the UK & Immigration:

When he was twenty years old, he came to the UK through the 'voucher scheme'. At that time if anybody wished to come to the UK it was expected to fill out the form to get the voucher. Then the people usually received a reply from the labour ministry, and it was a procedure that people should obtain the passport and submit this to the British High Commission along with the voucher. Then the British High Commission, Dhaka invites people for an interview. He did the same thing, as many people did at that time.

The travelling costs to the UK were around 1650.00 Rupees. His flight started from Dhaka to Karachi by Pakistani Airlines (PIA) and then he stayed in Karachi for one day and then he travelled to Heathrow using British Airways. Another eight Bangladeshi people were with him throughout the journey. Everyone agreed that when they arrived in the UK, they would travel to the same place together.

However, upon arriving at Heathrow, all of them were taken for a medical check-up. The medical check-up lasted for an hour and a half, and the rest of the group had left without waiting for him. After a while, a Pakistani Taxi driver approached him and asked him where he wanted to go.

He showed him the destination address of a person living in the UK, which he received while he was in Bangladesh. The Pakistani taxi driver started his journey to the address. The Pakistani driver knew some Bengali and so they both spoke a bit of Bengali. The Pakistani driver took him to a different place in London. This was a Bangladeshi restaurant, and the owner was Surat Miah.

The owner of the restaurant paid the fare to a taxi driver. He contacted the people at the written address by telephone and a person came to greet him who was called Mr. Boshir Miah. At 6 pm on that day, they both travelled to the Euston Train Station in London where he caught a train to Halifax and was informed that Halifax is the last stop, so he does not need to worry about this.

When travelling on this train he knew that when the train stopped at its last stop then it would be Halifax. Mr Boshir Miah also tried by checking the whole train to find another Bangladeshi person travelling to Halifax but unfortunately, he did not find anyone on this train. Mr Boshir Miah gave him 2.5 shillings and a packet of cigarettes and paid for the train ticket.

The train reached Halifax at 1 am and he followed other people to find the exit. It was raining outside and was very cold. When people walked on the walkway then he saw couples holding their hands together. In the Muslim culture, this sort of action would be considered shameful. Mr. Ali felt shameful when asking for directions to places.

He was thinking and was a bit worried about how to reach the destination. At last, he showed the address to an English person and the person lit him a cigarette and carried his luggage before setting off. The English man took him to a Pakistani's house. The Pakistani people gave him food and then took him to another house where Bangladeshi people lived.

At 6 am he was taken to another house where people resided from his village. He felt pleased to see his villagers. A fellow Bangladeshi called Husiar Ali gave Mr Ali an overcoat and made him join the labour. In a week he would receive £2.50 as labour, and he would receive benefits for a few weeks.

8.21.3 Life in the UK:

Comparing Britain from the past to the present he believes that in the past living was harder and uncomfortable; now it is like staying in his father-in-law's house. In the past time, the UK's weather was very cold, and when people went to sleep a single person would use six to seven blankets to keep him warm.

He felt very cold inside the house. A kettle would have to be boiled to wash clothes. If there were too many people living in a house, then there would be two cookers otherwise there would only be one cooker. He said, "Cooking food was very difficult".

There were no shower facilities and therefore he would take a bath in a public bath once a week. He saw that English people and other foreign people use the public bath facility. The queue would take two and a half hours. Using the public bath would cost money. At that time people's living conditions were under extreme hardship.

He saw an English person making a cigarette by using a Rizzler and tobacco. After seeing this Mr. Ali asked Bangladeshi people why they did this, and the answer was that it is cheaper than buying cigarettes.

8.21.4   Employment:

A few weeks later, with help from some people, he received a job offer in a wool mill, in Halifax. The weekly pay was £7.00; the wages would be used to buy food and pay for accommodation, while some money would be sent back home.

He worked in the factory as a trainee. After two months of working, he learned to operate the machines. The weekly wages rose to £11.00, he worked there for around nine months. In the hopes of receiving more wages, he joined a job with Foundry. The wages would vary between £14.00 – £15.00 per week. He worked here for about four months.

The work in this factory was very hard because of being young this job did not suit him and that's why he left the job. He found another job in a cotton mill. Work used to start from 8 am till 10 pm. He worked there five days a week and the weekly wages were £13.00. The job with this factory did not appeal to him so he left work and got another job in a mill.

This mill had a two-hour overtime facility, and the weekly wages were £15.00 - £16.00. He worked there for one year and moved on to another factory. The wages in the factory including overtime ranged from £24.00 - £25.00. The work started at 8 am till 10 pm. On Saturdays, he would work overtime starting from 8 am to 4 pm. He worked at this factory for two and a half years. He had to leave the factory work due to his mother falling ill in 1968, he travelled to Bangladesh.

In 1969, he returned to the UK and enquired about his previous employer but unfortunately, there were no vacancies at that time. Through different people, he came to know that there were some vacancies in Mosley. He got a job in a Wool Mill, where he used to do night shifts, and the weekly wages were £25.00 - £26.00, he worked there for three weeks. After that, he found another job with high wages and moved on to the "Greenfield Null Spinning Mill", where he would operate the machines.

He worked there from 1969 to 1987. While working there, he was not entitled to any annual leave, so it was difficult to visit Bangladesh. The manager of the company used to say to him that upon his return if there was any vacancy he would be able to re-join. He left the job and visited Bangladesh several times, and upon his return to the UK, he was able to re-engage with his employment.

8.21.5   Housing:

In the past, he lived in different places and shared accommodation with other people. He described the condition of the houses as being awful, the toilet was located outside, coal was used to heat the house and there was no carpeting inside the house.

In 1973, upon arrival to the UK with his family and children, he went to his uncle's house and stayed there for two days. Then, he went to one of his relative's houses at Malborough Street, Glodwick, Oldham, where he stayed with them for a few days. Then he moved to another relative's house at Marlborough Street, Glodwick, Oldham, and shared this accommodation with them. For using one bedroom, he used to pay £5.00 per week as rent.

He bought a house for £1600 on Sickle Street, Glodwick, Oldham, because of the experiencing difficulties of sharing one house. The previous homeowner had an outstanding mortgage of £800.00 and he was to get the mortgage and pay the rest in cash. This property was a two-bedroom terrace house. This time, there was a bathroom inside the house. The current house where he is living now was purchased in 1983.

8.21.6 Social & Family:

In 1960 he got married before coming to the UK. In 1968, he went to Bangladesh due to his mother's illness and stayed there for nine months. In 1969 he came back to the UK and was not able to work in the same factory upon return.

In 1972, after the independence of Bangladesh, he went back to Bangladesh. He decided to bring his wife and children to the UK, but his mother did not agree to this. He said, "To convince my mother, I told her that I will leave my oldest son and oldest daughter with you". His mother accepted this and so in 1973, he brought his wife, two daughters, and one son to the UK.

During that time in Britain, a son was born. The hospital did not release the baby and the mother, because it was the procedure for the Hospital to keep them in their

observation for ten days. This meant he had to leave work to look after his kids.

His mother fell ill again so he visited Bangladesh again. After this, his mother made a recovery he returned to Britain. About a year later, he received a letter stating that his mother was ill again. This time he sold his house and went back to Bangladesh with his whole family. After his mother recovered, he returned to Britain on his own leaving his family in Bangladesh. His family stayed there for five years but he visited on occasion. Meanwhile, two sons were born in Bangladesh.

In 1980 his mother died and after that, his father passed away. All his children are educated in Britain. His two sons have been educated in Islamic qualifications. One of his sons can recite the whole Quran from memory. His son got a title (Muhadis) degree in Hadith from "The Faculty of Al-Azhar University in Mishar and now he is doing a PhD at a London University. One of his sons is an optician. Their mother has been a great help towards their education.

Mr. Ali was the Vice President of "Glodwick Bangladesh Society" and was the Chairman of the "Jalalabad Jameh Mosque" from 1994 to 2000. Due to diabetes, he had to resign from his post. In 1987, he left factory work because it was closing, and he became medically unfit. In 2007, he received a pension and now believes that the new generation of parents have affection for their children but also encourage their children to study hard.

8.21.7 Independence of Bangladesh:

In 1971 during the liberation moment of Bangladesh, Mofozzal Husain, Moksud Ali and Shomuj Miah organised a meeting in Oldham and requested everyone to donate their weekly wages to help towards Bangladesh's independence. They are also advised not to send any letters to Bangladesh. Everyone presents at that meeting made a promise that they would support the cause. He abided by these terms. He used to receive letters from his mother but was unable to write back and felt very upset.

8.21.8 Conclusion:

He urged all the parents to take care of their children and guide them, so they would be able to gain better qualifications, and it will improve their life careers. In his family, and personal and social life, he has been a successful person after arriving in Britain but also has feelings for Bangladesh. He has visited Bangladesh several times to see his close relatives and friends. He also said, "My children have respect for Bangladesh and still want to visit there". Now he is retired and is going to spend the rest of the time with his grandchildren and family.

8.22 Alhaj Mohammed Bashir Ali
(Interviewed on 25 June 2010)

8.22.1   Life in Bangladesh:

Alhaj Mohammed Bashir Ali was born in the Boratuka village in the area of Chattok, Sunamgonj. His father's name is Md. Amir Ali. The distance between Boraduka and Sylhet is about 18 miles and by transport, it takes about an hour.

His father was involved with the agricultural work. When he was in Bangladesh, he completed primary education at "Boraduka Primary School" then he went to Ramshundor High School and studied in class 6 then he came to Britain.

8.22.2   Journey to the UK & Immigration:

His father came to Britain in 1965. 5-6 years later he moved to Britain, he was 12 years old.

8.22.3 Life in the UK:

After arriving in Britain, he did not have any problems at work, concerning the language or anything else. He used to have friends, and he used to go out with them. He used to have a lot of friends, so he did not have any problems.

He also managed to adjust to the different cultures in Britain. When he was a teenager, he came to Britain and now he has been living in Britain for a very long time and he adjusted to the culture and the weather. He likes Britain but he also said in the past it was a hard life, things have changed and improved.

More specifically the environment, weather, and road communication have been improved. The standard of living has also developed over several years. Britain is now seen as the place to celebrate many cultures from different communities in the world.

All the communities can form their association and organize different activities including personal, social, cultural, and political. The community members are also contributing to this.

8.22.4 Employment:

He started to work at 13 years of age in Preston Bengal Restaurant as a kitchen porter. They used to make Indian food. His father used to work in a factory and used to live in the Mosley area. His father found a job for him. He worked for 3 years in that restaurant. His first weekly wages were 5 pounds which increased from £25.00 to £30.00. He was happy when he received his first wages for the first job in his life. Thereafter, he started work as a trainee waiter in the same restaurant.

After a few years of working in the kitchen, his employer allowed him to work at the front as a trainee waiter. His employer was confident that he would be able to do this job and that it wouldn't be any problem for him to speak and understand English because he studied in Bangladesh, and he has experience living in Britain.

During the waiter job, he used to go to a part-time language class to improve his communication skills by learning the English language. Attending the language class has benefited him personally in improving his English, he said.

From Preston, he came to Ashton-under-Line and worked in the "Ojantha Restaurant". He worked there for 3 and a half years, and then he went to Chester. He worked 2-3 years in Chester then in 1982 he opened his first business in Accrington which was known as the "Grand Mughal Restaurant". That was a partnership business with 3 partners.

He was involved with the business because he had experience and encouragement from friends and family. 3 partners paid 21 thousand pounds cash, and the rest of the money was used to pay mortgages. The restaurant was worth 80 thousand pounds which was a lot of money for the restaurant business at that time.

They used to get good wages. Every week they used to do receive £2,800.00 which was very good for the business. After 4-5 years he sold the business. Then he opened another restaurant with 4 partners in the Oldham area, it was known as the "Shagor Restaurant".

They bought the restaurant for 150 thousand pounds, 60 thousand pounds was paid in cash, and the rest of the money was on the mortgage. It was a good business. Every week they used to make 6-7 thousand pounds. Now the restaurant is still running but he had a personal problem with his eyes and other health issues, so in 1999 he sold his share.

8.22.5 Housing:

When he came to Britain he used to live with his parents in Mosley. His first job was in a restaurant in Preston, and he used to live there. During the restaurant business, he also bought a house in Accrington. Since 1991, he has been living in Oldham.

8.22.6 Social & Family:

He got married in 1976 and his wife came to Britain in 1985. He wanted to do something, so he bought a restaurant and house then his wife came to Britain.

He has 6 children, and his 2 sons have degrees in Business studies and now they are working. His daughter is a solicitor and another daughter is a teacher. His youngest 2 children are studying at the school. He has 4 siblings including himself, one sibling is in Britain and the other 2 siblings are in Bangladesh. After 1-2 years he goes to Bangladesh for a holiday to see his relatives and friends. Since he came to Britain, he went to Bangladesh 7-8 times and the first time he stayed 9 months in Bangladesh, after that he stayed 4-5 weeks in Bangladesh.

Along with family development, he contributed his time to the community's development. He is also involved with the Shahjalal Mosque, and he is a trustee of the Mosque. He said, "if there are any changes that need to be made, then the Mosque committee consult with the trustees". Also, he said, "During the process, they elect a new committee, and then the trustee board takes over the responsibility to run the Mosque for 90 days and elect a new committee". He is also involved with the "Bangladesh Neighbourhood Society".

8.22.7 Independence of Bangladesh:

During the liberation war in 1971, he was only 13-14 years old but still, he was involved and helped them in many ways. They used to collect money and send the money to help the freedom fighters to win the war. He was actively involved with action committees and attended many meetings and events which took place by this committee.

He is an established person in Britain; he is also a proud father and a loving husband. He is a hard-working person who dedicates his time to the community's development. In 2009, he and his wife went to Makkah to do (Pilgrimage) Hajj.

He is now retired, and during his free time, he goes to see his friends and goes to his relative's houses. On prayer time he goes to the Mosque to pray. Sometimes, he passes his leisure time by participating in social activities. On holidays he goes to Bangladesh. He goes to London to see his relatives 2-3 times a year, stays 4-5 days and enjoys himself.

8.22.8 Conclusion:

Finally, he made his remarks about the local community, and he said: "Everyone should be united and work together so that the new generation will concentrate on their education, and they will do good things in the future".

He urges the local community in Coppice including all the other communities living in Britain that working as a team brings better results and prosperity, so all the Bangladeshi community needs to sacrifice their differences and work as a team.

He also thinks that there should be a community centre for the local Bangladeshi elderly people, where they would be able to pass their time and do some activities. He believes that the Bangladeshi community will come forward to develop this project for elderly people.

If he hadn't come to Britain, would he have been able to have a family and personal life like this? He said it is difficult to say but if he didn't come to Britain then he would have been in a different situation.

He said, "if he was not able to make progress with his education then obviously the personal life in Bangladesh would have been different". He said, "I would have tried my best to obtain a better qualification, but it would depend on luck, whether or not I would be able to make a success".

Considering all aspects of his personal family life, he thinks that it has been beneficial to come to Britain. He was able to get a job and set up businesses to raise his family in the UK and all his children have obtained better qualifications and have good jobs.

8.23 Alhaz Ismail Hussain Shiraji (Jomir Ali)
(Interviewed on 25 June 2010)

8.23.1 Life in Bangladesh:

Alhaj Ismail Hussain Shiraji, also known as Jomir Ali was born in the village of 'Attaullah', in the area of Osmaninogor, Balagonj, Sylhet. His father's name was Alhaj Md Yakub Ullah. He has three brothers, and he is the third youngest among them.

He completed his primary education at a local primary school called 'Dowamir Primary School'. He took his SSC exam in 1969 from the 'Mongol Chondi High School' and was admitted into college. He completed college and earned a Higher Secondary Certificate (HSC) qualification in 1973 and earned a bachelor's degree from the "Modon Muhon Degree College" in 1976. Being a Graduate, he used to work at his Pharmacy in his spare time. Sometimes he had to work 24/7.

While he was a student, he was involved with politics and held the post of general secretary of the 'Balagonj Thana Student League'. Then he became the chairman of 'The Youth League' and was also chairman of 'Bongo Bondu Parishad' for a couple of years.

He says that his village and its neighbouring areas were in quite good condition and there weren't any financial problems. Their family was also running well with their earnings from cultivation and from the profit from the Pharmacy they owned. Besides, his father also used to live in the UK, therefore they lived a happy life and were able to complete his Higher Education, and hence he is a successful man.

8.23.2 Journey to the UK & Immigration:

He was asked why he moved to the UK whilst he was a well-educated person and was also from a rich background. In his reply, he said that his main intention for coming to the UK was for Higher Education. After coming to the UK, he started to carry on with Higher education. As he saw his father working in his old age, he asked himself if his father could work at his age.

By doing so he could help his father. His father wasn't very physically well, so he could replace his father in working. Therefore, he changed his mind and started work. Hence, he couldn't carry on with further education.

His father made all the arrangements for his migration to the UK. They used to live together in Bradford. The house they were living in was owned by his father. He saw his father working at a factory. He was finding the UK quite well because he knew some people who were working with his father and he also luckily met some of his old friends in the UK. Therefore, his life in the UK was going quite well.

8.23.3 Employment:

One day his cousin came to visit him, and his father was at their place and asked him to come and visit his restaurant in Manchester with him on the same day. He went to visit the restaurant and started to work as a waiter later. After that, he became the manager of the restaurant. His weekly wages were about £80.00 - £90.00.

His wages weren't satisfactory for the job he was doing. Since it was his cousin's restaurant, he was thinking and working at his restaurant, and sometimes he had to workday and night.

He left the restaurant job and moved to London to do a job in a garment factory. He didn't like the job there and therefore started working at a restaurant in Kent as a manager. He was satisfied with the wages he got. His wages were £180.00 per week. He was working in that restaurant till 1979.

In 1980, he was able to run his restaurant. He paid about £20,000.00 - £25,000.00 for the restaurant which was based in Birmingham. He wasn't earning much profit from the restaurant and hence he sold the restaurant.

After that, he started another Indian restaurant in Salford called "Curry Centre". He had a business partner this time who was also his cousin. The profit from the business wasn't that good but it was satisfactory for him and his cousin. They were running this business from 1980-1982.

After that, he started another restaurant in Oldham called "Prayri Indian Restaurant" This time he had two more partners, and the profit they were getting

from the business was also good. He was in partnership with this business till 1985.

While he was running this business, he bought another restaurant in Ashton-Under-Lyne and named it "Asian Tandoori". At that time his other two partners were maintaining the business very well. Those mentioned above were the only business he was running. He didn't start any new business.

8.23.4 Social & Family:

In 1992, he retired from the business due to his physical illness. He is a hardworking and successful businessman, and he has four sons and 2 daughters. His eldest son gained an Accounting Degree and is now involved in the business. His second eldest son graduated from Manchester University and is employed at present. His third son wanted to do Islamic education and, therefore admitted to 'Madrashah' and his fourth son is still studying.

Even though he started his business in Oldham in 1982, his relationship with the people in Oldham was from long ago. He was living in Oldham in his own house, where his parents also lived. Due to this, he joined the 'Glodwick Bangladesh Society'.

He was a very successful, active, and dedicated person and impressed everyone in the group by showing his hard work. As a result, he was elected as the Chairperson of the 'Glodwick Bangladesh Society'. He was involved with this social work and 20 years had passed and yet even with his physical illness he still wants to work for the community.

In 2002, he became a director of the Tigers International Association – TIA, and in 2009-10 he served as a chairperson. He was one of the most senior and respected people in the association who provided encouragement and motivation. Due to his ill health, he retired from the chairperson.

At present, he lives in Coppice, Oldham. While he was living in the coppice, he established an organisation called 'Coppice Bangladesh Society' with the help of his friends and it was running for about 3 years. At present due to lack of funding, they had to close the centre. The organisation is still famous at present.

He says that there are around 150 Bangladeshi families in the coppice, and the number of voters would be around 5000-7000. In the whole of Oldham, there are around 15,000

Bangladeshis'. He was able to set up a 'Bangla School' while he was living in 'Glodwick' where children can learn the Bangla language. Besides that, "The Glodwick Bangladesh Society" also provided advice on benefits, housing, immigration, and so on. They had to contact the local council and arrange meetings with councillors to resolve the housing issues. Even though they couldn't build a Housing Association, they were still able to help the community in many ways.

The Bangladeshi community is now beneficial considering the past times. Children benefited by educating in a developed country UK. There are mosques, therefore people can offer Salah and send their children for Islamic education. There are schools in every area, therefore, it's easy for students to travel from home to school. Therefore, everyone is getting lots of good facilities in the UK.

At present, he is a member of a political group called 'Bangladesh Awami League UK'. Even though he is working for a political group in Bangladesh, he is not involved with any British political party. Besides that, he was a School Governor in Oldham.

He visits Bangladesh whenever he gets the chance and likes to spend his holiday there. He has relatives, also two brothers in Bangladesh and his relationship with them is quite well.

His first performed Hajj was in 1993. This social worker and a religious person are now physically ill. This was also seen while he was being interviewed. In the past, he had heart, kidney, and lung disease and was in the hospital and once survived from being very close to death. He was in the intensive care unit for two weeks. He said, "The doctors lost hope that I am not going to survive, but due to the special payers from the many community members the creator (Allah) has given me a new life".

He needs the help of a cane to walk. His sons or daughters take him by car whenever he wants to go anywhere. Therefore, he spends most of his time at home. At present, he's waiting for his kidney replacement.

8.23.5 Conclusion:

Being a social worker, he says regarding the community that the education for the new generation, everyone must keep their eyes open so that they won't be caught behind on the educational grounds.

The parents need to make their children understand the importance of education, which will enlighten their lives. He also said, "The nation without any education cannot do any progressive work". He also said the phrase "education is the backbone of the nation". Therefore, they should keep on studying.

It is found that there is often at least one graduate in every Bangladeshi family, and this is also an honourable thing for the Bangladeshi community in Britain. Britain and other countries in the world are getting benefit from their contribution and he feels very proud of that. He is very thankful to the creator (Allah) for giving him this opportunity.

He is also hopeful that shortly this number will be increased if the parents give guidance to their children. The new generation may be negatively affected because of parents not keeping an eye on their children due to their busy lives. The parents should somehow find some time for their children's education.

Even with his current physical illness, he still sits with the elders to discuss

how to help develop the community, how to give religious education to our children, etc. At the moment he is not involved with British politics but still, he reads the newspaper to find out any news.

8.24 Alhaj Shah Husiar Ullah
(Interviewed on 12 January 2008)

8.24.1 Life in Bangladesh:

Alhaj Shah Husiar Ullah was born in 1955, in the village of North Dhormoda, Bishwanath, Sylhet, Bangladesh. His father's name is Alhaj Shah Latib Ullah. In 1960, he started primary education near his village known as Muhammedpur. At that time there was a pundit teacher whose name was Sifoth Ali, the pundit.

Two years later, he went to "Bishwanath Primary School. After he finished studying in primary school in 1966, he went to "Lalabazar High School". There was a school in Bishwanath called "Ramsundor High School" but he chose to go to "Lalabazar High School" due to his friends studying there.

When he was studying in class nine, the liberation movement had begun in 1969. There were public demonstrations and often the school was closed due to strikes. Since then he had gotten involved with student politics and he couldn't study.

His father was a businessman selling rice & crops. From his father's income from the paddy field and business; the family was well-maintained. His father had a partnership grocery business with his brother-in-law, where he was used to doing part-time help.

At that time, all goods used to cost less (reasonable prices). The people were very happy and enjoyed their life. For example, at that time the daily wages for a Person (labour) was one Rupee or one and a quarter Rupee.

8.24.2 Journey to the UK & Immigration:

In 1958, his uncle came to the UK and in 1961 his father followed. Before arrival to his uncle and father; his grandfather and grandfather's three brothers worked in a British board ship. So, he was aware of Britain through his family members.

In 1970 his father went back to Bangladesh and decided to bring his family to the UK. In the same year, he and his mother and two brothers came to the UK. He was only 15 years old at that time. His uncle and his father used to live in Bradford. He lived in Bradford for six weeks.

He wanted to go to school, and his father took him to school to get a place there but the school refused to accept him as a student and advised him to go for employment rather than education due to his age.

8.24.3 Employment:

There were plenty of jobs in the factories, but he first started work in a restaurant as a trainee waiter at the "Dilkush Restaurant" in Oldham. He used to get £7.00 a week but a head waiter would get £10.00, and the chef would get £12.00. After he worked there for about two months, he got a job in the factory, and he used to get £18.00 per week.

After working in the factory for two years he became a supervisor. He oversaw supervising 40 people. The workers used to bring food with them and there was a Canteen facility in the workplace.

There were people from English, West Indian, African, and Bangladeshi & Pakistani who used to work there. The factory had a friendly atmosphere between the staff but because of the Pakistan – Bangladesh war, there was some trouble with other Pakistani colleagues. He worked there till 1975 and then he went back to Bangladesh with his parents.

In 1984 he became a business partner at the "Kismot Restaurant" at Burry New Road. He paid £4,000.00 for a quarter of partnerships. His cousin's brother was also involved with this business. He had run this business for about 3 years. He started his takeaway with £17,000.00. He had run this business for about 12 years. Before he started his restaurant business, he used to have a partnership in a takeaway. His first takeaway did not earn enough money; there was a loss of £7000 due to fate.

He was involved in more businesses which included takeaways and a clothing shop. So, he did lots of business within this field of trade. Meanwhile, there were two more takeaways and one clothes shop. He has 7-8 houses that are on rent. Since he came to the UK, he bought 15 houses and set up 14 businesses. Now he has two takeaway businesses, one of which is managed by his brother.

He also has land & property in Bishwanath, Sylhet, Bangladesh. In 1991, he started a community centre in Bangladesh, and he owns a house in Bishwanath. Back home his cousins look after all the businesses and properties. He said "I have got a plan to do "Agriculture Farm" in his village.

8.24.4 Housing:

His uncle and aunty were living in Oldham and his family decided to settle there. It was the month of November; the weather was very cold with foggy skies and heavy snow. In 1979 He brought his wife to Britain and resided in Oldham town in his father's house. This house was purchased by his father in 1971.

He bought the first house for £700 at Belmont Street in Oldham. The house consisted of two bedrooms. There was no central heating but there was a coal heating facility. The bath was inside the house with a hot water facility, but the WC was outside. 15 years ago, he sold it for £30,000. Since he came to the UK, he bought 15 houses and now he has got 7-8 houses which are on rent.

In 1975 he had seen a lot of changes in Britain. The housing has been modernised with gas heaters and a central heating system. The climate has changed too.

8.24.5 Social & Family:

He was a football fan and was busy playing football and lived there for 22 months. His father then tried to get him married but he did not agree until 1976. He got married in Jalalpur, Sylhet. In 1979 He brought his wife to Britain and resided in Oldham town in his father's house.

He frequently visits them to check up on his business & properties. His youngest brother's youngest son goes with him to Bangladesh every year. He has planned to do an agriculture firm in his village.

In 1996 he went to do Umrah Hajj and in 2005 he went on a pilgrimage (Hajj) to Makkah with his whole family. He is happily married, and he has 3 sons and 4 daughters. The oldest son was married, and he has two children. The oldest son has studied in Britain and is working for a company. His two daughters got married. All the other children are studying.

He has been involved with the Bangladeshi community in Oldham. Oldham Bangladesh Association was formed on 17th July 1970. Since then, he has been involved with the Association and serving as a cultural secretary. He is also involved with Oldham Bangladesh Cultural Group, and he was a secretary.

He is also involved with the local Mosque and many other social and cultural organisations. He regularly donates money to help the poor people in Bangladesh. He is involved with Bangladesh politics.

He has kept in contact with all his family back home and takes care of them by giving them money. He recalls that there was a Bangla newspaper called "Janomot", he was a reader of this newspaper.

8.24.6 Independence of Bangladesh:

When he was a student in class nine, the liberation movement had just begun in 1969. There were public demonstrations and often the school was closed due to strikes. Since then he has been involved with student politics.

He can still remember the politics of Pakistan (East & West conflict). He clearly remembers Fatima Jinnah and Ayub Khan's election. Ayub Khan managed to get hold of some UP members, and some other corrupt people gave them money to do the Campaign for his party. Ayub Khan later gave a speech that if Fatima Jinnah wins the election, then the country will be in chaos and the public will be liable to pay tax. After Ayub Khan's campaign was ending, he ended up winning the election.

After the public movement in 1969, in 1970 Sheik Mujibur Rahman was released from jail. He remembered seeing Mujibur Rahman and he shook his hand and went with him to Lalabazar, where a public meeting was held.

He said Sheik Mijibur Rahman raised the issue of deprivation by the West Pakistan government. More particularly the goods were cheaper in West Pakistan than in East Pakistan. He said, "There were many things such as sugar, tea, rice, paper and jute used to be produced in East Pakistan, but the selling price was higher than in West Pakistan".

He said, "The government of Pakistan treated East Pakistani people differently and the people have realised that they have been deprived by the authority". There was no investment in the East but in the West, which was very clear discrimination with the nation, he added.

In 1970, there was a cyclone, a natural disaster in Bangladesh, and lots of houses were destroyed and many people died. The people heard it on television & radio, and everyone started to sympathise with the disaster. He said, "It was very sad that the West Pakistan government didn't visit East Pakistan and Bangladeshi people residing in the UK became upset".

Bangladeshi people started to think about the separation of Pakistan and becoming an independent country. The people started to give support to the national leader for the independence movement. There were meetings and demonstrations in support of independence. In 1971, East Pakistan became independent and now the country is called Bangladesh, and the British Bangladeshi people became very happy.

8.24.7 Conclusion:

He always wanted to be a successful businessman. He actively engages in politics and always helps poor people in Bangladesh. He has visited many historical places in the UK and has visited the Taj Mahal & Khaja Moinuddin Chisti in India, Dubai, Saudi Arabia, and so on.

He thinks that young

Bangladeshis have made progress in studying, employment & business. He also hopes that it is not far away to become a parliament member of the Bangladeshi community.

In 1988, he got his British citizenship, but he still has compassion for Bangladesh. He is well-established in the UK and he is very happy to see his children have made progress in the UK. It may not be possible to achieve all of these if he had to stay in Bangladesh. He thanked Allah for this.

He is working towards developing the Bangladeshi community. In Britain, he has a strong position and is happy with his family and achievements throughout his lifetime.

8.25 Mohammed Fozlu Miah
(Interviewed on 25 June 2010)

8.25.1 Life in Bangladesh:

Muhammed Fozlu Miah was born in the village of Projathpu, Haridorpur, in the area of Nabigonj Thana, Habigonj, Bangladesh. His father's name is Muhammed Sharjan Miah. He completed his primary education from his local primary school called 'Guplar Bazar Primary School' and was admitted at 'Awsh Khandi High School'. Due to a certain occurrence, he had to stop his education while he was studying in class 7. His main reason would be the lack of guardian's care.

He regrets not attempting to get a higher education even with his travels to Britain. At that time many people couldn't afford to go for higher education even if they wanted to, but he didn't have any financial problems, he was from a rich background, therefore, he could have graduated if he wanted to. He says that not doing higher education was his bad luck.

His father was a businessman, and he owned a cloth store in his local area called 'Guplar Bazar'. According to him, there weren't any financial problems in his family. The social condition of his village was also good. At that time Hindus and Muslims lived together friendly and peacefully. The relationships of one village with other villages were also strong.

8.25.2 Journey to the UK & Immigration:

During the Second World War, probably in 1942, his father left the business and started to work as a board ship's crew. Due to this job, he was in Australia for a long time. After that when he was living in London, he was able to go to Australia and come back to the UK whenever he wanted. At the beginning of 1964, Fozlu Miah's father settled down in Britain.

His father first brought him, his brother, and his mother to the UK on a family visa. His main reason for coming to the UK was merely his dream to travel by aeroplane for the first time and come to another country. When he arrived at Heathrow, he was glad to see his father after such a long time. This is the bond between a father and his son. He started living on Bridge Road in Uxbridge, where many other Bangladeshis also used to live.

8.25.3 Employment:

After coming to the UK, within 4 weeks, he first started to work in an Engineering factory where his father was also working. He used to work 40 hours per week and his weekly wages were £30.00 at the beginning. He worked there for about a year.

After leaving the factory, he started to work at a restaurant. The restaurant belonged to his maternal uncle and was based in the M3 area of Britain. At first, he found the job hard but luckily since he was the nephew of the owner of the restaurant, he didn't have to face hard tasks, therefore he was quite happy with his job.

That time there was a problem with the Bangladeshi chefs in the restaurants, it was that they couldn't read the bills as they didn't know English. That's why his main task was to translate the bills into Bangla, so the chefs could understand the order.

The waiters were to read out the bills in Bangla to the chef and the other staff working in the kitchen were to follow the instructions given by the waiters. **He made a deal with the chef of the restaurant that he'd read out the bills for him and in return, he would teach him how to cook.**

They both agreed and within a short time he was able to learn how to do the cooking within six months he moved to another restaurant with his work experience as a cook and the wages in that restaurant were higher than the one, he was working at currently. He used to get a maximum of £45.00 per week in his uncle's restaurant. Then his next job was at 'Sylhet Town Restaurant' where he worked for about 14 months and after that, he was able to start a restaurant on his own.

In 1981, his uncle was one of the business partners of a restaurant known as "Bilash Restaurant" in 'Leigh', the other partner wanted to sell his share. He heard this news through his uncle and later bought a share of the restaurant for himself and became a business partner with his uncle.

He was quite happy with the business. At that time, he used to live in the residential flat of the restaurant. He was involved in this business till 1984. After that, he started a tea house in Wigan, and the profit in the business was higher than the previous one. His uncle who was also his business partner left the business and moved to London because his other brothers had also moved to London. He bought his uncle's share.

He improved the restaurant a bit more and he was also getting more profit. Again, he was involved with this business till 1988. After that, he closed the restaurant for personal reasons and went back to Bangladesh.

After returning to the UK, he again started the business of an Indian restaurant. In 1993 he opened a new restaurant in Manchester, but he wasn't making much profit, so he left the business, But then again in 1997, he started another business in Wigan. It was also a high-profile business. At the same time, he bought another restaurant in the same area.

He was successful in managing both businesses. In 2003 due to some personal reasons, he had to sell both businesses. At present, he isn't involved with any business. He spends most of his spare time with his kids.

8.25.4 Social & Family:

He used to visit Oldham when he was living in Leigh. Then in 1989 after bringing his wife to the UK, he started to live in Coppice. When he first came to Oldham there were only about 20-25 Bangladeshi, who helped open an institution for children to learn religious studies called 'Shahjalal Moktob' and he also with time became involved with helping the institution.

He tried to give as much time as he could for the improvement and benefits of the institution even though he had a business to take care of. In 1993 everyone in the community decided to build a new mosque because they felt uneasy in the Pakistani Mosque.

The elders in coppice also supported them and for their hard work, they were able to buy two houses and convert them to a mosque. He tried his best to build the Mosque. The mosque was named 'Shahjalal Mosque and Islamic Centre' and is based on Stewart Street of Coppice, and it consisted of 44 members.

At present due to the extension and modification of the mosque now about 400 people can offer Salah but still, it is sometimes overcrowded. Another house is bought for further extension of the mosque so that more people can offer Salah. At present Many Bangladeshis live in Coppice and the number of houses in Bangladesh's dwelling would be around 1000. There are 209 house members of the Shahjalal Mosque.

Besides offering Salah, many other religious events take place, for example, Islamic Lectures, and Arabic education classes for children 5 days a week, 2 hours per day. He also said that there was also a Bangla School which was held in Coppice Community Centre.

He isn't sure but according to him the 'Bangla School' is closed now due to a lack of funding. He also said there might be another reason, for example, there may be poor attendance of students or almost no students in the 'Bangla School' and therefore the school may be closed down.

For the elderly, there is nowhere where they can go to pass their retirement time or participate in any activities. The only place the people can go is the Mosque. There is no place for senior people to do exercise or to participate in leisure activities. He said considering this need, the community can do something about it.

There was a Bangladeshi Community Association in Coppice, and its main organiser was Alhaj Jomir Ali who was the chairman of the 'Bangladesh Society' in Glodwick. It was based on 179 Leigh Street, and due to the hard work of the people, the organisation administrated one community centre for about 3 years. Many people benefited because of this. Sometimes, the elders used to visit the centre and discuss how to arrange the marriage of their son or daughter.

It was hard to find people from the Bangladeshi community who could fill up official forms. The centre was created to help people with such matters and to give them advice and discuss other important issues, but the centre has been closed due to lack of funding.

He said that if everyone in the community works together, then they will be able to accomplish great things for the good of society. He encourages people to work with the community for the benefit of the people.

The feelings for the community of people are breaking down day by day at these busy days of people in the coppice, while it was friendly and filled with love 15-20 years ago. The people in the Bangladeshi community are arguing with each other regarding their local culture. Everyone from the local Sylhet district denies accepting this. Some are 'Bishwanathi', 'Bianibazari', 'Nabigonji', 'Moulobibazari', etc. This localism politics is letting the society down; because of this, the community is behind the other minority communities.

He said, "The Bangladeshi people in Coppice should work together as a team". He also gave an example: two mosques were built when there were less than a hundred Bangladeshi in coppice whereas the second mosque wasn't necessary considering the number of Muslims.

One Mosque was sufficient and the bond and friendly behaviour between people would have been good. Even though the Bangladeshi community is ahead on education grounds, it's quite behind when compared with the neighbouring communities. He believes that if all the people in coppice work together, they can bring benefit to the community.

He says that although he doesn't have any relatives in Bangladesh, he still loves and misses his birthplace. After coming to the UK, he went to visit Bangladesh about 20 times. His last visit to Bangladesh was in April 2010. He stays there for 2-3 months, sometimes 6 months. He didn't go to any other country from Britain for a holiday except Bangladesh, but he did go to other countries for his reasons, not for a holiday. Also, he went to many places in Britain with his family for holidays, for example, the seaside, etc.

At present, he spends most of his spare time with his wife and his kids. Besides he also stays busy with a project called 'Ashroy Kendro Nirman Prokolpo' which is to help orphan and handicapped children. He also sometimes must go to Bangladesh to maintain the project.

The project is based in his village 'Projatpur' in Nabigonj, Habigonj. His father and his grandfather left some property for them. He and his mother donated some of this to help run the project. Within this project, there will be a School, a Madrashah Mosque, a Training Centre, Hostel, etc in a complex way for the orphan and handicapped children.

The project will be run as a registered charity in Bangladesh, and he also hopes that the charity will be registered in Britain as well. No one from his family is involved with this organisation, indeed it is run by a committee of 31 members, and Mr. A.K.M. Faruk, UP Chairman of his village is selected as the Chairperson for this project. The project was named in 2003 and it was named after his beloved son as-'Ruman Welfare Trust' which was registered in 2009.

8.25.5 Conclusion:

With his experience in the UK, he says that he benefited from coming to the UK. This was his destiny and the blessings of the Almighty Allah. He may have stayed in a better social condition as his father was in Britain, there weren't any financial problems, and their family was also running well. Therefore, he believes he may have been living a better life if he didn't come to the UK.

At last, he requests all the Bangladeshi people who are living in the UK especially the 'Sylhet' people to forget about the arguments they were having regarding their local region and live together in a different country. This will bring benefits to society and its community. We should leave behind a peaceful and beautiful society for the new generation, for their good fortune and he asks to support him to become successful in his welfare trust project by praying for him and by wishing him luck.

8.26 Alhaj Mohammad Azmal Khan
(Interviewed on 18 November 2007)

8.26.1 Life in Bangladesh:

Alhaj Mohammad Azmal Khan was born in 1939, in the village of Doulothpur, Bishwanath. His father's name is the late Wajidul Haque Khan and his mother's name is Nazmunnessa Khatun. He is the 3rd out of 4 brothers.

His father used to take him to the Mosque. His father used to say to him that this world is for a limited time only and the reason I am taking you to the Mosque is that we are Muslims. As Muslims, we should follow our religion, and we should pray five times a day. When he used to go home after the Mosque, his mum used to ask him what he had learned today. During his religious study, he used to go to school as well.

He used to go to "Doulothpur Primary School". He studied in that school for a few months, and then he went to his eldest sister's house in Sylhet. His father thought that Sylhet School was much better than the village schools, so his father sent him to a Sylhet School for better study.

He completed his primary education at "Khalpar Primary School", and then he started his secondary education at "Lalabazar Junior High School". During that time his father died, which caused him to stop studying. After 1 year his mother wanted him to study again. He started his secondary education at the same school "Lalabazar High School".

In 1959 he passed the Secondary School Certificate (SSC). Then he studied at Sylhet M.C College. During that he found a job in the Chittagong Agrabad, He started work in Agrabad Air Aviation. Bangladesh is famous for agricultural work, most of the villagers used to do cultivation on the paddy fields and maintain themselves by selling crops. The income they received from the cultivation of paddy from the paddy fields was enough to maintain their families. At the time there were plenty of fishes in the ponds, small lakes, canals, and rivers; they used to catch fish from there all the time.

There was no need to buy fish from the shop; there was plenty of fish that would be exported from India for them. There were varieties of fruit trees available in every house. When he used to go to school on a rainy day, he used to go to people's houses because of rain and they used to give him mangos, etc.

During that time Muslims and Hindus were very friendly, Muslim people used to go to Hindu houses and they used to feel very happy and welcome. Even Muslim people used to invite Hindu people to their parties. He said on his eldest sister's wedding day Hindu people also came to the party. On the language movement day in 1952, he used to study in secondary school. That time he used to go to meetings etc. He said at that time Muslim Hindu teachers were very good and they used to give good advice to the students for their future.

8.26.2 Journey to the UK & Immigration:

He prepared himself to come to the UK; a travel agent helped him to sort out everything. He started his journey from Narayongonj and then by streamer he came to Gualond. From there he came to Calcutta by train. In the Calcutta train station, he met his cousin's brother; His cousin's brother lived in Calcutta.

When he said that he was going to the UK, his cousin's brother wanted him to stay a few days in Calcutta which he agreed to do so. His cousin had taken him to a few places in Calcutta and he wanted him to stay in Calcutta permanently. He also said, "Why would you want to go to the cold country which is the UK?"

He didn't want to stay in Calcutta. From Calcutta Airport he came to Tehran airport, there was a stoppage for 1 and a half hours, then he came to Britain through Paris. From Heathrow Airport, by train, he went to his relative's house in London. He stayed there for 3 days, and then he went to his eldest brother's house in Blackburn.

8.26.3 Employment & Business:

The Landlord opened a new grocery shop called "Ever Green" and his first job was in that shop. Before that, he was on benefits, and he used to get 2.50 pounds per week. From the shop he used to get 3 pounds per week, he used to work from 9 am to 10 pm shifts within the shop. For halal food, they used to get sheep from the farm, and they used to slaughter the sheep. Every week they had to get 2 sheep for the shop, during that time things were cheap; the price of 4 Chickens was a pound, and for a whole sheep it was 7-8 pounds. He worked in that shop for 9 months.

He found out about another job in a textile spinning mill from the newspaper, he went to the mill, and he saw the rainwater inside the mill. They asked him whether he would be able to bring some people and clear the rainwater from the factory. He asked them if they provided a pump to clear the water which they did have. Then he started to clear the water with the pump, with some other people. Within 3 to 4 days, they cleared the water. They paid them for the job and also they gave him a job in the factory.

He used to work 8 hours a day and had a 30-minute lunch break. He used to get 5 pounds per week. He worked for 1 and a half years in that factory. During the work, there was wool in the factory, so they had to wear masks during work.

In 1963, he had hoped that he would get better wages in Rochdale, so he moved there. He found a job in a factory in the Shaw area. In that factory, there was a provision that helped him to learn how to use the machines. From this training, he learned how to use a waiving machine. He used to get 9 pounds per week. After that, he went to the "John Bright Mill". He worked there for 23 years.

About two and half thousand people used to work in 3 shifts. In Rochdale, there were 7 mills from the same company. In 1979 he went to Bangladesh. In 1980 the mills and the factories started to close. Also, he was involved with a business during his work life in Britain. First, he opened an Indian takeaway, but he sold the takeaway and opened a clothes shop.

8.26.4   Housing:

The house where he resided in Blackburn consisted of 2 bedrooms, toilets, and 1 bathroom within the house but there was no boiler, so they had to warm the water in the kettle for a shower, etc. Also on the weekend, they used to go to the public bath to have a shower. They used to use Coal to warm the house.

While he was living in Haslingden, there were no Mosques to pray in; therefore, he used to pray at home. There weren't radiators around at that time; it was too cold, so they used to use cold water or warm water from the kettle to wash their faces, hands, etc for praying. On Friday they used to pray at home, for Eid prayer they used to book a hall. It was hard in those times due to the cold weather and the heavy snow.

For a single bed, they had to pay 1 pound, about 40 people used to live in one house. The landlord used to change the bed sheets once a week. He used to live with his brother and the Landlords were 4 Bangladeshis. In Rochdale where he used to stay, there were not any hot water facilities, no central heating and the toilet was outside of the house. They used to warm water with a kettle. For a single bed, he used to pay 1 pound, and sharing the bed was 10 shillings. He used to cook food by himself.

When he was in Haslingden he used to know Rochdale very well. He used to live in a rented house, and then he bought a 4-bedroom house for 300 pounds.

8.26.5   Social & Family:

In 1967 he went to Bangladesh and got married and in 1976 his family came to Britain. He established himself in Britain and his children were educated, he feels very happy and very proud.

During his life in Britain, he was involved with the community. In 1962 he became a member of the "Haslingden Welfare Association". They built a Mosque, and he became the founder of the Mosque. He was the secretary of the "Haslingden Welfare Association" after he came to Rochdale.

When he came to Rochdale there were about 25-30 Bangladeshi people. Haji Mokbul's brother used to own a Grocery shop on Drake Street, there was another shop on Yorkshire Street. When there was a Pakistan Welfare Association in Rochdale, he was the Secretary-General. A Few days later, he left his General Secretary position at the "Pakistan Welfare Association".

He said "We thought we needed to organize `Bangladeshi Welfare Association` in Rochdale. In Rochdale, they organized a public meeting to organize this. From Manchester, the Bangladesh Association Chairmen MA Matin and the Pakistani High Commissioner Agar Shahi came to the meeting. It

was his first visit to Rochdale.

After the meeting, he proposed to establish a Bangladesh Association in Rochdale, but MA Matin did not agree with the proposal, and he stated that there is no need to establish a separate association and this can be done at a later stage.

In 1964, they opened a new Mosque in Rochdale called (Sonali Mosque). He was involved with the opening of the Mosque. After that, he organized a

meeting with the Bangladeshi people. The reason for this meeting was to establish a Bangladeshi Association. Mr Koramoth Ali, Dr Qadir, Abdul Motlib, Lala Miah, Wajib Ali, Gazi Monuhor Ali, and more people attend the meeting. Before the Bangladesh victory, he tried to organize a Bangladeshi Association.

In 1972 he came back from Bangladesh and found out that the local community in Rochdale organized a Bangladeshi Association & Community Project to provide support to the liberation war in 1971. Lala Miah, MA Goni, Mannan Talukdar, Shofiqe Mirza, Khuwaj Ali, Aiyubur Raja Chowdhury, Ator Miah Chowdhury, Abdul Rashid Master, and many more people were involved in this committee.

After that, they established an Islamic Centre. Through the election, he became the Chairman of the Islamic Centre. Then it became a Mosque. They were able to set up a project and the local Government authorized the project and gave some funding. He worked there for 2 and a half years.

When he was doing voluntary work on the weekend; he used to read & write letters, fill up tax forms, and do other official work. People who came from Bangladesh usually struggled to speak English. On his days off he used to go to his friends' and relatives' houses.

In Britain, it used to snow heavily. He said till 1976, there was heavy snowfall when snowed it was too cold and it was hard to walk on the road, it used to stick to their feet in the snow and it would hurt.

8.26.6 Independence of Bangladesh:

The liberation war started when the East Pakistani people were deprived and discriminated against by the West Pakistani authority. When Sheikh Mujibur Rahman won the election, the West Pakistani people did not hand over the power. The independence movement began. East Pakistan (Bangladesh) was invaded by the West Pakistani Military, and they killed 300,000 people. At that time, he was in Bangladesh and witnessed many incidents which had taken place in Sylhet during the war.

At the time of the general election, he actively participated in the election Campaign. He supported the movement and voted for the party, which won the election. During the war, one night the Pakistani military entered their village, and he had to escape by hiding somewhere safe and sound. At that time, one of his cousins and nephews was arrested by the Pakistan Military and was taken to the Bishwanath Police Station. With help from the local chairman, they were released later.

One of his friend's relatives used to work at the Bishwanath Police Station and he used to take passes from Officer in Charge (OC) and visit Sylhet Town frequently. He witnessed the mass killing in the Shahjalal Mosque in Sylhet. He used to share information and give regular updates to all the Bangladeshi people living in Britain at that time.

Whilst he was staying in Bangladesh, during the liberation period, his passport had expired, and he had to go to the British High Commission and wait for Dhaka to reply for entry clearance to come to the UK.

He said, with hope and aspiration Bangladesh became independent but people still did not get the full benefit. He also said "If the British Bangladeshi people take some responsibility to develop the country, then it would be possible to see the benefits because the new generation British Bangladeshis have been educated in the UK and will be able to bring new changes to develop it even further.

He also said "The government of Bangladesh needs to take the initiative to facilitate the new generation of the British Bangladeshi people to contribute their knowledge and skills to bring the changes for the better. He believes that the young generation will take some interest in this kind of development for any society.

He also commented that the corrupt people should be punished, and then the country will make progress.

8.26.7 Conclusion:

Alhaj Azmal Khan is living in Rochdale, but he loves his country very much. Also, he said he would like to go to Bangladesh and stay there for a long time if the country's conditions get better.

8.27 Alhaj Hafiz Ekhlasur Rahman Chowdhury
(Interviewed on 2 December 2007)

8.27.1 Life in Bangladesh:

Alhaj Hafiz Ekhlasur Rahman was born in 1938 in the village of Chandborang in the area of Bishwanath, Sylhet. His father's name was Shunahor Ali Chowdhury. His father died when he was 2 and a half years old. His father was a farmer, and he used to cultivate paddy. His father was able to maintain his family easily due to the income from the cultivation.

When he reached the age to study, one of his uncles (father's cousin) guided him and he was able to become a "Quran-E- Hafiz" (memorized the holy Quran). His uncle's family used to love him very much.

He became the Quran-E- Hafiz from the "Oliarpara Madrasha". At that time, while he was learning Arabic he used to go to primary school, and he completed his primary education too.

The Madrasah (Islamic Institution) and Primary School were in Jagannathpur Thana, but it was miles from his village. At that time, he stayed with a family. When he was only 15 years old, he completed his Islamic qualification (Hafiz). When he became a qualified Hafiz he worked at the "Budrai Mosque" and performed the prayer during the month of Ramadan, also known as (Kotme Terabi) a complete recitation of the Quran through special prayer, he also did the same thing twice at "Shiramishi Mosque" and then he came to England.

8.27.2   Journey to the UK & Immigration:

In 1963 when he was only 20 years old, he came to England by voucher. From his initiative, he collected the form to apply for the Voucher. One of his relatives also gave him some advice and told him that if he sends his completed form to the British High Commission, Dhaka then they will process his application and send him the Voucher.

One of his relatives completed the form and sent it to the British High Commission, Dhaka. He received a reply from the Labour Ministry of Great Britain, and it was mentioned that within 6 months he would receive his Voucher from the British High Commission in Dhaka. Accordingly, he received the Voucher on time.

One of his nephews "Mujibur Rahman Chowdhury" helped him to obtain the Passport. He was a student of the "MC Collage" Sylhet. At that time, he did not inform anything to his family because everyone would think that a Hafiz of

Madrashah should not go to England because in England there were no Mosques to pray in at that time. Soon after, he received his passport; he contacted the British High Commission and obtained the Voucher. Then he came back to his house, collected the money for his air expenses, and left the home.

He came by train to Dhaka, and he brought his uncle along with him to get guidance before he caught the flight. He flew from Dhaka by PIA Airlines, and he paid 1800.00 Rupees to come to England. His father-in-law paid the full amount when he confirmed that all the necessary paperwork had been sorted, and he was ready to go. Before coming to Britain, just about a year ago he got married to his cousin (uncle's daughter), the uncle who guided him to do the study. He was then only 19 years old.

After he came to Heathrow his uncle's son who is now his brother-in-law came to receive him from the airport and took him to Uxbridge, where he used to live. Other people used to live there too at that time. He had seen that the people who used to work at night would sleep during the daytime and vice versa and he saw two people sharing the same bed.

Due to the lack of living space for him, after two days he decided to leave this place. So, his brother-in-law took him to London to Abdul Muttalib Chowdhury's "Dilshad Restaurant" who was his brother-in-law's uncle. He was passing his time by living and eating there. His relative told him that he was a respected person, he did the "Hafizi", so he should not be working in the restaurant. His uncle used to like him very much due to his religious qualifications. His relatives also told him that if he finds another kind of job then he would be able to do it but until then he should live there as a guest.

8.27.3   Life in the UK:

There was no telephone in most houses, so the main communication was to write letters to his loved ones to stay in touch with them. In the past the weather conditions were very poor, it was very cold, nowadays even some people cannot imagine.

8.27.4   Employment & Business:

His uncle proudly introduced him to other people, and he used to say to them "My nephew is a Quran-E-Hafiz". After living there for three months, he left the restaurant and went to live with his uncle's son in Haslingden. He did not find any jobs for himself after trying so; he went on benefits for the first time, he used to get 50p per week.

Then he used to get £1.00 or £2.00, he cannot remember exactly. He was unemployed for about 4 months, and then he finally got a job in a cotton mill in Haslingden. The name of the mill was "Smith Nephew & Co". In the beginning, he used to get £3.50 every week as a trainee worker. He used to work there for 7 and a half hours. His job was to change the springs and rings in the factory machines.

After working there for a few days, his work pattern had been changed and he used to get £5.00 every week. He used to talk to English people by body language and it was going well, he didn't have any problem at that point. Whilst working with the English people, he was able to grasp the technical English language. There were some Bangladeshis who were able to speak good English; he tried to learn some of the English languages from them. In this way, he was able to learn the essential English language.

Due to a lack of bath facilities at the time, he was not able to perform the Salah and read the Quran regularly. He worked there for 10 years (1964 – 1974). His latest wages were £80.00 per week. While he was working in the factory, he sponsored his uncle's son with a factory voucher and brought him to England. After a while, when he gained experience, he became a supervisor.

In 1974, he got a job at Mars Textiles Limited in Rochdale and his weekly wages were £90.00. He worked there until 1976. After that, he had another job in Rochdale, but the wages were higher than before. He used to work from 7 am until 5 pm dayshift and the wages were £100.00 a week.

Whilst he was working in that factory, he opened a grocery shop in Rochdale, and it was known as "Surma Food Store" based on Entwisle Road. There were four partners, and they paid £10,000.00 to set up this business, so each of them paid 2 and half thousand pounds. They used to sell fish, chicken, meat, Beatle nuts, and many more grocery items.

He used to get the supplies from London and Birmingham. He used to take orders from local shops in Rochdale and the surrounding area and he used to do deliveries. Three partners used to work at the shop, and they used to take £80.00 every week. After receiving the wages, they used to get £20.00 to £25.00 as profit from the business. They run this business until 1980.

After that, he opened a partnership restaurant in Todmorden, and the name of the restaurant was "Tajmohol Restaurant". That was the first restaurant that opened in Todmorden. The business was going very well and had a seating capacity of 40 people. In 1982, he opened another restaurant by himself and in 1983 he sold his share in the first partnership, and in 1985 he sold his second restaurant.

He didn't like the idea of his eldest son getting involved with the business, but he encouraged him to study. He retired for about 1 year at that time, his older son got into Leeds University, and he moved from Rochdale to Leeds as his son requested him to move there. In 1987, he did not have any chance of doing a job or business, so he moved back to Rochdale. In Rochdale, he had a Fish & Chips shop, and the shop was rented by a Chinese person. The lease had expired and the shop became empty, so he decided to live in the flat and buy a house later.

At that time, he was planning to go to London. He opened another grocery shop in Leeds, and he spent £16,000.00 to open this shop, it was called "Evening News Shop". He used to sell grocery items along with Manchester Evening News. He had run this business for two years.

8.27.5 Housing:

At that time, he used to live with some other people; he had to pay 10 shillings for the food and 10 Shillings for the accommodation. The toilet was outside the house, so he used to take the water with him if he needed to use the toilet. He used to have a bath every Saturday in the public bath because he did not have a bath facility inside the house.

He used to take bread from home for his lunch. Even though he did not know English very much, he did not hesitate to mix with English people. He used to visit different factories for jobs; the people used to tell him about no vacancies with their hands. He said, "When I used to go past any factories, then I used to say "I want a job" after learning some of the English languages. He worked there for about 8 months.

Whilst he was working in Haslingden, he used to visit Rochdale frequently to meet some of his friends. When he first visited Rochdale, he came with one of his friends, and then he was able to visit on his own. Sometimes he visited Rochdale to make inquiries for a job because, at that time, there were plenty of mills and factories in Rochdale. He used to get one day off from work and if someone missed a day, their wages used to be reduced by deduction of missed hours.

He managed to get a job in Heywood and the weekly wages were £10.00. His job was to work on the Dope Machine. The wages were good, so he moved to Rochdale. He used to live in a rented 2-bedroom house, 10 people shared the cost between them. The toilet was outside of the house and for hot water; he used to boil a kettle and had a bath once a week at the public bath.

8.27.6 Social & Family:

In 1972, he brought his wife, son, and daughter to England. After that in Rochdale, he bought a two-bedroom house for £3000.00, and it had a bath and toilet.

In 1986, his son completed his graduation and got a job at the same University. He wanted to get his son married in Bangladesh, so on 8 November he bought a house for his son, he went to Bangladesh, and then he took his son to Bangladesh and got him married. In 1987, he returned to the UK. Whilst he was in Bangladesh, he bought a house in Subidbazar, Sylhet area.

In 1987, he did not have any chance of doing a job or business, so he moved back to Rochdale. Now he is a father of 6 daughters and 2 sons. His eldest sons passed their degrees and are now working in the UK, all the other children have been studying, and now they are busy with their own lives.

Since 1979 he has been involved with the Bangladesh Association in Rochdale. **Bangladesh Association first started in 1973 at its premises above the grocery shop "Surma Food Store".** He was a member of the Association and then he became the treasurer and then the vice Chairman. He was involved with them from 1973 until 1977. From 1997 to 2006 he was the Chairman of "Jalaliya Jameh Mosque".

8.27.3 Conclusion:

He went to Bangladesh several times with his family. He has two houses in

Sylhet town and owns some lands in Bangladesh.

His wishes and dreams have come true in England. All his children have been educated and are earning a good salary. He feels proud of his children. The community in Rochdale is doing very well in education and business. At present, he is spending his retirement time with his family and likes to spend some time in Bangladesh but he is unable to do so, due to his ill health.

8.28 Alhaj Keramoth Ali Ahmed
(Interviewed on 15 December 2008)

8.28.1 Life in Bangladesh:

Alhaj Keramoth Ali Ahmed was born in 1941, in the village of Pirerchock, Biyanibazar, Sylhet. His father's name was the late Moboshir Ali, and his mother's name was Mofura Bibi. His father was a landowner and used to stay home and look after his property. He has 4 brothers and 1 sister, and he is the youngest of all his siblings.

At that time, his village's condition was not good. In the rainy season, his village used to drown down under the water for a few months. At that time, they used to use boats as the main transport to travel from one place to another. Now the road communication has been improved and all the motor transport can go into their village.

When he was a child, he began his primary education from home, and then he was admitted to the local primary school, which was about a quarter mile away from his home. He used to walk to school. He studied there for about 2 or more years. In the rainy season, it was hard for him to go to school because he had to use a boat to go to school, and sometimes people used to sink his boat for fun. Remembering the past, especially in the rainy season, when he used to go to school that makes him very cheerful even today.

He moved to Chittagong because one of his relatives was living there. He was admitted to "Collegiate School" in Chittagong and completed his Secondary School Certificate (SSC) form there. Then he moved to Dhaka and went to "Jagannath Degree Collage" where he completed his Higher Secondary Certificate (HSC) and BA degree.

At that time, he was thinking of coming to England to study for about two years and going back to Bangladesh.

8.28.2 Journey to the UK & Immigration:

One of his siblings insisted that he should come to Britain. He went to Karachi with his friend and sorted out all the paperwork. He spent about 2,000 Rupees including the flights. Before he left home, he took some money with him and his friend gave him some money, so it was enough money for him to come to England.

In May 1961, he came to Heathrow from Karachi by PIA airlines. At that time, he felt that the weather was really cold in England. Before he left home, he brought one of his relative's addresses with him, when he came to London. He went to this address in Aldgate, London. From London, he came to Birmingham, and then he went to Preston.

8.28.3 Life in the UK:

At that time, it was very difficult to do Salah and fasting during the month of Ramadan. He said, "When I came to Rochdale, I have seen that people are performing Salah and fasting as well in the month of Ramadan". There was a Mosque in Rochdale known as the "Sonali Mosque" and every Friday he used to go to this Mosque to do the prayer.

He also said, "While I was living in Leicester, I never seen anyone performing Salah and pasting during Ramadan and celebrating Eid". It was a very difficult time, in the past. The children are getting higher education from universities and doing good business and employment. The new generation is far more advanced than the previous generations and is contributing to British society politically, socially, and economically. Since the arrival of Muslim Bangladeshi people, the community has been developed.

He has been living in the UK for the last 40 years and has seen and learned many things. **He said, "We have faced a lot of discrimination; many foreigners are suffering in silence".** Apart from the Doctors and Engineers, other degree holders did not get the recognition. When someone obtained a Diploma Course or Degree in the UK, they would be hassled if they had gotten a good job.

For them reasons, many highly educated people used to work in factories or restaurants.

8.28.4 Employment & Business:

He had a job in a Restaurant which was in Preston, and he worked there as a waiter. Besides his employment, he started an English language course near his workplace. After working there for a few days, he was bored so he went to Leicester. He found a job on the Birmingham Railways and worked there as a guard.

A few days later, he transferred his job to Leicester, where he was residing. He was admitted to college to do further study. He used to work overtime as well, he used to work about 42 hours every week and his weekly wages were £10.00 - £12.00. He found that after working, it was really hard to maintain college at the same time. So, he decided to leave his job and continue studying at college.

He left the Railway job and found a job in the factory. The name of the factory was "Tizer Brooks". His weekly wages were £15.00, and he worked there for 3 years. At that time his brother was very ill, and he went to Bangladesh in 1966. His brother died and he decided to stay there for a few more days. He had gotten married and left his wife in Bangladesh and came back to England.

After coming back from Bangladesh, he re-joined the Railway. He took his holidays and came to Oldham to buy a house because houses were cheap in Oldham. At that time, he used to live with his friend and got a job in a cotton mill. After working there for a few weeks, he found a bus contractor job in Rochdale, and he moved there.

He used to work 70-80 hours a week including overtime, and he used to get £30.00 - £40.00. At that time, it was 9 pence per person to come from Rochdale to Oldham by bus. He worked on the bus for 4 years and bought a house in Rochdale for £400.00.

In 1970 he left the bus job and bought 4 machines and started garments manufacturing. In 1978, when the industry declined in the UK, he had no choice but to close his business. In 1979, he established a restaurant in Oldham, known as the "Himalaya Restaurant". This was a partnership business, and he ran this business until 1990.

8.28.5 Social & Family:

In 1966 he got married and in 1967, he brought his wife to England, at that time three more Bengali families were living in Rochdale. One of them was known as Abdul Karim, he had a grocery shop in Rochdale.

He is a very hard-working person and did not do just employment or business, in his spare time he was dedicated to the community. As a result of his active involvement with the community, in 2000, he became the first Bangladeshi origin Councillor in Rochdale MBC to serve the local community.

8.28.6 Independence of Bangladesh:

In 1971, Sheik Mujibur Rahman declared the movement for Bangladesh's independence. The Bangladesh Association in Rochdale was formed at that time, and he became the General Secretary. While he was in Leicester, he was also involved with the Association run by Bangladeshi and Pakistani people. In 1970, in Rochdale, there were about 350 Bangladeshi.

After achieving the independence of Bangladesh, he did not think it has been benefited the public. He said many of the Bangladeshi people hoped that it would be better if Bangladesh became independent but unfortunately, only 10% may be achieved by becoming an independent country, as he doubted.

Bangladeshis are behind because they brought their families in the late '70s & '80s, so a new community emerged in Great Britain. **The first-generation Bangladeshi, when they brought their families to the UK, their children immediately entered employment to support their elderly parents. So, you cannot blame the second generation for not concentrating on education, simply, they did not have any choice.**

8.28.7 Conclusion:

He said, "The new generation claimed to be westernised or semi-westernised and therefore losing the identity of Bangladeshi". The parents should teach their children to be patriotic for their motherland. At the same time, the Bangladesh government can play a vital role in facilitating these young people to get involved in developing the nation of Bangladesh, and then they will take some interest.

He is a father of 2 sons and 2 daughters. All his children have graduated from the UK. He has 8 grandchildren. He wants to stay a few days in Bangladesh and a few days in the UK, due to his family commitment in the UK.

8.29 Alhaj Khondokar Abdul Musabbir MBE
(Interviewed on 16 January 2008)

8.29.1 Life in Bangladesh:

Alhaj Khondokar Abdul Musabbir was born in 1939 in the village of Hajipur, in the area of Balagonj, Sylhet. His father's name is the late Komor Ali. His father was a religious Imam and worked in the local Mosque in his village. He has 4 brothers and 4 sisters; amongst them, he is the youngest. He completed his primary education at "Tajpur Primary School" and went to "Mongolchondi Nishikanto High School".

Although his father did not have much land his family members were happy. When he was young his father passed away. Remembering his father's death, he feels a lot of grief, which he cannot tolerate. Due to his father's death, he was unable to complete his secondary education. Then he started a cloth business in his village. He was responsible for maintaining his parent's family, whilst his eldest brother was in the Police force, the second brother was responsible for looking after the home; the third brother was an Alim (Islamic Qualification).

He was involved in this business for 6-7 years. When he was young, he enjoyed his loving life, at that time the village was much better. Everyone in the village cared about each other, they trusted each other, and if there were any problems or arguments everybody used to solve the problem together. When he started the business, he was a secretary and if there were any problems the Bazar committee would help solve the problem and so would the village, it was such a good time.

8.29.2 Journey to the UK & Immigration:

In 1963, he came to the UK with a "Labour Voucher". He heard the news from one of his schoolmates that people were going to Britain through the "Labour Voucher". He then went to the Employment Office in Sylhet and collected the Application Form there. He also took some forms for his friends and relatives too. He completed all his forms and posted them to the Employment Ministry. He also kept a copy of the forms in his file, so they did not have any problems later.

Three months later, he received an acknowledgement letter, which confirmed that within 6 months, he would receive another letter, which would enable him to get the Voucher. When he received a call letter, he then went to the Passport Office in Sylhet and obtained his Passport from there. After collecting the Passport, he went to the British High Commission, Dhaka to get his Voucher from there. At that time, there were about 10 of his friends who went to Dhaka at the same time.

Before going to the British High Commission, Dhaka, they went to the local restaurant to have some breakfast. There were some other people, who saw this group of people as planning to go abroad. These people asked where they were planning to go, and they obtained the paperwork. In response to their question, they said "We are going to the UK with our Employment Vouchers, and it is costing us about 1,600.00 Rupees". These people were surprised to hear that the amount of money, they were spending too much money on going to Britain. That is because, with the amount of money, anyone can do business at that time.

After collecting the voucher, he returned to Sylhet and went to the travel agency in Sylhet. He sent a telegram to his brothers, who were living in the UK. He mentioned in the telegram that one of their relatives is coming to the UK; they need to go to the Airport to receive them. He did it purposely to give them a surprise, so he did not mention that he is coming to the UK.

In 1963, he arrived at London Heathrow Airport and his eldest brother went there to receive him from the Airport. His brother was surprised to see him at the Airport because the telegram message was completely different, there was no

mention of him coming to Britain.

8.29.3 Life in the UK:

Now in Rochdale, about 6/7 thousand Bangladeshi people are living there. In 1963 when he first came to Rochdale to live, at that time no Bangladeshi families were living in Rochdale. Everybody was single at that time. 5-7 people or 15-20 people used to live in one property. Many of these people used to work in factories. The people used to prepare their meals by themselves.

They used to cook curry on Monday for the whole week and used to cook rice every day due to lack of time. The people who used to work in the restaurant did not have to prepare their meals as there was free accommodation and food was included by the employer.

When he brought his family in 1973 there were 5-6 families in total living in Rochdale.

In 1963 there was no Halal Grocery Shop in Rochdale but after that, the first grocery shop was opened by a Pakistani and then Bangladeshi came forward to open shop in this area. At that time, there was only one Mosque in Rochdale called the "Sonali (Golden) Mosque".

He could not come to the Mosque on Friday due to his work, but he used to go to the Mosque when he had holidays. In the past, there were plenty of job opportunities in the factories; therefore, many people came to Rochdale including Bangladeshis. The weather conditions were bad; he used to feel cold during the summer, which is the current temperature in the winter.

8.29.4 Employment & Business:

He came to Rochdale, where his brother used to live. About two weeks later, his brother took him to a factory, where he was working. His brother took permission from the manager and showed him around the factory. On the next day, his brother told him that he had spoken to the factory manager and got him to offer him a job for you and the job had been arranged, if he wanted to start work immediately then he would be able to do so. He said, "Can you find any other jobs, as I am not interested in

working in the factory".

Then his brother took him to one of his friend's restaurants in Manchester. The name of the restaurant was "Everest Restaurant". He had a job as a "Trainee Waiter" and his starting wages were £5.00 a week and he used to get weekly tips of £3.00 and altogether he used to get £8.00 a week at that time. He shared this information with other people, and they said it is good wages compared with the factory wages.

He used to keep some money for his pocket expenses and deposited all his money to his brother. At that time, the wages of the head waiter were £10.00 per week. He worked there for about two years and then he went to Brighton with his brother. He got involved with his first restaurant business in the UK. The restaurant was situated on the seaside, so the business was good only for 4 months and remaining the 8 months were always quiet.

They decided to close the business, and they came back to Rochdale again and started working in the factory. After that one of his brother's friends Yousuf Miah forced him to take employment in his restaurant in "Ashton-under–Lyne. After working there for a few days, he became a partner with him.

In 1972, he took three months' leave from the business and went to Bangladesh but due to some family business, he had to stay there for 15 months. During that time his partner messed up the business and he left the partnership. He got married in 1961 before he came to England, and he brought his wife with him to England in 1973.

After working in the factory for quite some time, he left the factory job and in 1978 got involved with the restaurant business. This business is known as the "Star of Bengal". He paid £25,000.00 for this business, £12,000.00 cash, and the

rest of it from a business loan. This business still exists, he has now retired, and his son is running the business. He reflected on his past employment life and he said, "Father Gallon Hervey was 3 miles away from Rochdale", where he used to work as a learner and his weekly wages were £15.00. He also worked at "Turner Brothers" and "Great Mill".

8.29.5   Housing:

During that time, he and his wife were living with his brother in Rochdale. Later, he bought a 3-bedroom house in Rochdale for £600.00 and started working in the factory again. At that time the price of two bedrooms house was around £200.00 to £250.00.

In the past, people had a hard life, as there was no central heating, no baths or toilets inside the house. The people used to go to the public bath to have a shower. They used to use coal to make the room warmer and with the kettle, they used to get hot water. The toilet was outside the house, many Bangladeshi houses did not have a television or telephone.

8.29.6   Social & Family:

Everyone who came to Britain had to leave their loved ones including parents, siblings, friends, relatives, and other social ties. In the past, most people came to Britain from Sylhet. When they saw that many people getting rich very

quickly and their lifestyle was beautiful, that had inspired many Sylhet people to follow in their footsteps.

At that time, people in Bangladesh [East Pakistan] were very happy, even though people were not rich at that time. There was peace within the community and amongst the villagers. Most of the people were involved with agriculture work and now it is the opposite. There was plenty of rice, fish, vegetables, and other resources available at that time. There was no jealousy or competition, and all the people used to follow a very simple lifestyle.

There were fewer court cases, and if there were any problems then local senior people used to resolve the problem, this local group is also known as "Panchayet (a local mediator group)". Therefore, the people did not need to go to the Police or the Court.

At that time, the standard of education was very good in Schools and Colleges. There was a strict rule in the school to build up bright futures for the students. The schools were free from politics. Now the result is the opposite. The culture in the schools was very good, the teachers used to get a lot of respect from the students. The teachers used to be seen as respected people in the community. Every time he visited Bangladesh, if he met with any of the teachers, he had shown respect by touching their feet. It was a culture at that time, he added. This culture is now lost.

He was upset, while he was thinking that he would have to leave all his

family and social ties and go abroad. Eventually, he had to leave all his ties, and he came to Britain finally. He said, "Sometimes I could not hold my tears as I am leaving my country and going abroad".

Till now, whilst he is passing his retirement age, he likes to continuously do community work. He was involved with the "Bangladesh Association" and the "Mosque Committee" and served there as chairman of this establishment.

The new generations of Bangladeshis are doing better. In the past, it was impossible to think. Technology has now offered more facilities, like mobiles, the internet, satellite televisions, newspapers and so on. He said, "We are now receiving instant messages from the other side of the world".

At that time, not many people knew much English or Bangla. Therefore, the people with some educations were respected by them. He used to help those people, who were in need to fill the forms, read and write letters, make appointments with doctors, and so on. Since then, he has become a community worker and received an award of MBE from the Queen.

8.29.7   Conclusion:

He is a successful businessman and a hard-working person. He is a father of 2 sons and 1 daughter. His eldest son and daughter have obtained a degree from university and the youngest son is involved with the restaurant business. Now he is retired, and he goes to the restaurant sometimes to oversee the business. He said, "The Bangladeshi community is doing well, and the new generation will bring some more success in life". He is very optimistic about this.

In the past, there was good a connection with Bangladesh but now these connections have been lost. He wishes to spend his valuable time with his family and friends living in the UK. He has also established his Trust known as "Musabbir Trust" and he wishes to use this fund shortly for a good cause.

8.30 Alhaj Ayubur Raja Chowdhury
(Interviewed on 16 January 2008)

8.30.1 Life in Bangladesh

Alhaj Ayubur Raja Chowdhury was born in 1938, in the village of Asharkandi in the area of Jagannathpur, Sunamgonj. His father's name is Alhaj Abdur Rob Chowdhury. His father was the local school - teacher then he went to India in Jomshed pur and found another job in the "Tata Cable Company". After that, he worked for the "Sunshine Cable Company" in Chittagong, Bangladesh. After that, he used to work as a Primary School Teacher in his local area. At that time, his father was S.S.C. passed.

Most of the people used to walk on foot during that time, as there was no proper road for transport. Most of the people were poor at that time. In the past, people used to wear pieces of cloth to cover their bodies. The women used to wear simple clothes. The young people never used to look at girls. At that time, boys were very shy. In the past, when young men reached the age of 40 years old, then their parents used to talk about their marriage. At that time, they did not have any choice compared to this time. They were very shy.

In the past, the village people were very innocent and simple. Things were very cheap at that time. For 1 Taka they used to buy quite a lot of things which is impossible at this time. Teachers used to get 10 Taka per month. That was enough wages for a teacher to maintain their family. They never used to buy fish and vegetables from the shops because most of the people used to grow their vegetables in their village homes. Also, they used to catch fish from the rivers, ponds, etc. At that time Paddy fields prices were 20-25 taka, which was very cheap.

The people who were rich at that time used to have the nicest houses and plenty of land. They were also known as "Jomidar (Big Landlord)". The poor people used to work for them. There were some people, who did not like them but in his own opinion, he did not see anything wrong with holding plenty of lands.

He studied at "Asharkandi Jakir Mohammad Moddobongo Primary School". After that, he went to "Digol Bhag High School" in Nabigonj. He studied up to class eight. The school was too far from his village. Then he went to Bishwanath and started his education from class nine at "Ram Shundor High School". He did not like to study in that school, he went to "Rosomoy High School" in Sylhet instead. He used to stay in a rented house with other students. Then he went to "Mongolchondi Nishikanth High School" in Balagonj.

At that time, "Mongolchondi Nishikanth High School" was very good for education. He passed his Secondary School Certificate (SSC) from this school in 1960. He passed his SSC after a few years because of changing schools. He used to stay in a rented house. After that, he went to "Modan Mohon College" in Sylhet.

He has 4 brothers; amongst them he is second. He did not have any sisters. He enjoyed his education during childhood. During his college education, he did not come to Britain. After that, he came to Britain by Voucher. His father and his brother came to the UK one month before his arrival. His father and brother also used vouchers.

8.30.2 Journey to the UK & Immigration:

During his studies, he used to work as a Travel Agent. One of his relatives used to live in Britain and he arranged everything for him to come to Britain to Study. He was very happy to come to Britain. Then he went to Dhaka to get his Passport and Visa. He told his teacher about coming to Britain. He gave his Passport to his Teacher to see. His teacher told him that you don't need to go to the UK, and he took his Passport. Also, he said if you still want to go to the UK then I will give you the Passport.

After that, his friend wanted to know about his Passport. Then he said, "The passport is in my teacher's house". His friend told him to check if the Visa expiration date had gone, if so then he couldn't go to the UK. Then he checked his Passport and the Visa was expired. That time he did not come to the U.K.

In October 1963, he came to Britain. Including his ticket, the total cost was 1,600 Rupees. He flew from Dhaka and arrived at London Heathrow. Although his father and his brother were living in Britain at that time he could not go to Airport. His relatives came to Heathrow airport to receive him. Then he came to St. Albans in London where his father used to live. It was too cold in Britain. He has seen that it snowed for nine months.

8.30.3 Life in the UK

At that time there were not many Mosques in Britain compared to this time. They used to pray at home, there were not many Telephones or Televisions at home; they did not have radiators at home either. They used to have Coals to warm the house, they did not have a duvet, they used to have a blanket instead. They used to have 5-6 blankets at bedtime because of the cold. For Halal food, they used to get Chicken from the shop and slaughter it. Also, they used to get fish, rice, and vegetables from the shop.

8.30.4 Employment:

After 3 months he came to Manchester. He did not find any job in St. Albans, and then he found a job in Manchester. Mr. Hussain from his village helped him to find a job in a Waiving Mill. Mr. Hussain used to work in that mill. Ladies used to work the day shift. He did not want to work with the Ladies because he thinks as a Muslim he was not allowed to work with ladies. So he used to work in night shift. 8 hours shift. Not many people used to work in night shift. The Manager and other English people never worked in night shift. One person used to be in charge. They used to get 30 minutes break.

Bangladeshi, Pakistani, and other country people used to work in that mill. "Father Gillen and Harvey" was the name of the mill. They used to do cotton and fabric work. They used to get rice and curry from home for their lunch. They didn't get food from the shops because they didn't know which one was Halal or Haram.

There was Health and safety procedure in the mill. There wasn't any dust in that mill. First, he used to get £7.00 per week. Since he came to Britain he has been working in that mill. His highest wages were £150.00 per week. They used to provide their food and accommodation. They used to get chicken from the shop or go to the farm and slaughter them by themselves for Halal food. At that time there was no Bangladeshi fish or vegetables at the shop. There was fish at the shop from other countries that they used to have.

8.30.5 Housing:

He bought a freehold 3-bedroom house for £200.00. He used to stay in that house and other people used to stay in that house. They used to pay rent 50 Pence per person. He used to wash their bed covers and the landlord had to provide blankets for them. He used to share with them, but they used to cook. Whoever used to cook and clean the house for him didn't have to pay rent.

2.30.6 Social & Family:

In 1965 he became secretary of the "Pakistan Welfare Association" and started to do community work. He was involved with other things, and he used to help people.

He is married and in 1982 his wife came to Britain. He has got 3 sons and 2 daughters. His eldest son has studied B.S.C from Manchester University. He is working in the Rochdale Council. His second son is studying at college and his 2 daughters are studying at the University in their final year.

8.30.7 Independence of Bangladesh:

Before the War Pakistani people used to like Bangladeshi people. When the War had begun between West and East Pakistan then they used to hate the Bangladeshi people. During the War in Bangladesh, they used to do meetings, etc in Britain. He was involved with the meetings. He used to collect money from the Bangladeshi people and send it to people in Bangladesh. In 1971 he went to Bangladesh to see the Victory.

8.30.8 Conclusion:

He is very proud that his children are educated; also, he said it may not be possible if they were in Bangladesh. He is retired now, and he is enjoying his time with his friends and family.

8.31 Alhaj Atar Miah Chowdhury
(Interviewed on 2 December 2007)

8.31.1 Life in Bangladesh:

Alhaj Atar Miah Chowdhury was born in 1935, in the village of Gabdev, Nabigonj, Habigonj, Bangladesh. His father's name is the late Suruj Miah Chowdhury and his mother's name is Khudija Bibi. Mr Chowdhury studied at the "Muraura Primary School" then he went to "Gojonaipur Primary School" and then he studied in the local high school up to class nine.

All the students used to go to school on foot; school was far away from home. He has one brother and one sister. After finishing his education, he started a business in his village, the village people were very ordinary, and the way of life was very simple. The people were dependent upon agriculture.

There were huge fish in the ponds and river, and the people used to catch the fish from the ponds and it was enough food for their family. Even in the market, the fish was very cheap. The price for 37.5 kg of rice was 5-7 Takas. The price of everyday goods was available at very cheap prices also. The people were very happy and there were not many rich people in the village, there was no competition.

8.31.2 Journey to the UK & Immigration:

His nephew and cousin were in the UK, and he had the information from them. There were some people from the village also who told him about the UK. He came to know that there were plenty of jobs available and people could earn and save money from this employment.

In 1962 he came to the UK, at that time he was only 27 years old. When he had the passport, he made the journey in two weeks. His nephew also came with him. His nephew was educated therefore he did not have any problem coming to the UK. He departed from Tejgaon Airport and flew by PIA.

He arrived at Heathrow Airport; he then took a taxi from Heathrow Airport and went to a restaurant in London called the Karachi Restaurant. When he was coming from Heathrow airport to London, he remembers seeing the roadside and he saw that there were no leaves on the trees, and he thought all the trees were dead. Later, he came to know that due to the cold weather, all the leaves had fallen from the tree. The taxi fare was paid for by the restaurant owner. The owner of the restaurant also arranged transport to come to Manchester.

He went to the Euston train station, and He paid £11.00 for the train fare. When he arrived at Manchester Piccadilly, it was in the morning. Mr Chowdhury and his nephew went to the Bombay restaurant.

8.31.3 Life in the UK:

In the house where he lived, there was a toilet outside the house and the kitchen was in the cellar. The rent was £1 per seat, sharing the bed was 10 shillings. His cousin and his brother arranged the accommodation for him.

8.31.4 Employment:

After about a week his cousin and brother took him to Nottingham to see a restaurant and introduce him to the owner. He started the job at the restaurant as a trainee waiter at the starting wage of £5 per week. Usually, all the workers get free meals and accommodation. His cousin opened a restaurant in Blackburn known as the "Anglo Asia Restaurant".

He left the other job and worked there as a kitchen porter. His cousin was encouraging him to become a chef, his cousin also told him that working as a chef is respectable and appreciated by many professionals. After working for about six months, he was able to become a cook, he used to learn skills from the chef and observed other people even on his days off. For this learning effort, he spent 72 hours working in the restaurant. He worked there for about 2 years.

His cousin sold his restaurant therefore the job had ended, and he found a new job in the "Lucas Factory" in Burnley. He used to get £14 per week. There was a canteen facility, but he used to take his meals to work with him. He used to work the night shift (10 pm – 5 am), He worked there for a year.

He found another job at "Bayfield Cotton Mill" in Burnley. He would have the weekend off. He worked in the restaurant on the weekend and earned £5 for two nights. After that, he joined a new factory where he worked there for about 12 years (1967 – 1981). That factory was very big, about 2,000 people were working there in 3 shifts.

Following the closing of all the mills and factories, he became unemployed and started to claim unemployment benefits. Mr Chowdhury said although the wages were low in the restaurant work the food and accommodation were free which helped a lot. If he wanted to become a chef, he needed to work as a kitchen porter and if he wanted to become a waiter, he needed to know how to make coffee.

There were some dishes such as chicken curry, meat curry, Bombay duck, and Bombay chicken; there were some English dishes available at that time.

8.31.5   Housing:

During his employment at the factories, food and accommodation were his responsibility. He used to share accommodation and food with other people. Most of the housing conditions were very poor, with no inside toilets, no central heating or hot water facility, and the kitchen was in the cellar. For heating, the room people used the coal fire. It was so cold, and the beds were not warm enough to go to sleep straight away, so it was a very hard time for all the people.

On his day off, he used to go to the public bath because there were no bath facilities inside the house. 22 people were living in one house. They would also get live chickens roaming around the house which would be used for food.

8.31.6   Social & Family:

He married in Bangladesh and his wife came to the UK in 1970. He has 3 sons and 2 daughters. All the children have been educated and are working. He has many relatives living in Bangladesh; therefore, he has travelled there many times.

He was one of the supporters of the Bangladesh independence movement. He is a founding member of the Bangladesh Association & Community Project in Rochdale. He also served as a treasurer. Throughout the BACP they were able to establish a Bangla School in Rochdale.

In 1983 the Bangladeshi mosque was established. Before establishing this mosque, there was also a small mosque. The mosque was able to accommodate only 15-20 people. In the Sonali Mosque, the Bangladeshi and Pakistanis used to pray Friday prayers together, but due to the 1971 war, the Bangladeshi community felt unsecured to go to the same mosque. The new mosque can accommodate 1,000 people.

8.31.7 Conclusion:

Mr. Chowdhury became a British citizen, but he still is very compassionate about Bangladesh. He is very happy to see his children have made progress in the UK. It may not have been possible to achieve all of these if he lived in Bangladesh. He thanked Allah for this. He is serving the community as a volunteer and helping the Bangladeshi community in Rochdale.

8.32 Alhaj Surab Ali
(Interviewed on 12 May 2008)

8.32.1 Life in Bangladesh:

Alhaj Surab Ali was born in 1936 in the village of Doshghor Nowagaon, Bishwanath. His father's name is Mr. Alhaj Mafij Ali. He has two brothers and one sister and amongst them, he is the oldest. His father owned 28.80 Acres of cultivated land, and he lived in England. He went to "Doshghor Primary School" and went to "Ramsundor High School" in Bishwanath. He studied up to class seven.

8.32.2   Journey to the UK & Immigration:

In 1959 his wish was to come to the UK, so his father gave him a factory voucher. As soon as he received the "Voucher" he went to the "Sylhet Passport Office" to apply for his Passport. One of his friends helped him to fill out his form after he got the passport; he arranged everything including the flights. The cost of a ticket was 2,200 Rupees; his father paid all the expenses for him to come to the UK.

The date was confirmed for him to come to the UK, and his uncle took him to the "Sylhet Train Station" and said goodbye to him. He was travelling by train from Sylhet to Dhaka and flew from Dhaka to London Heathrow. At the time, there was another man who had the same flight, he was known as Mubarak Ali, and they both were from the same village.

In 1963, Surab Ali arrived in England, and he was only 23 years old at that time. He used to live in England before, so it was easier for him to fly to England with someone who knew that country already. So, from Heathrow, they went to Victoria and then they passed through Manchester and from there they got a bus and came to Haslingden to his father.

8.32.3   Life in the UK:

They all used to eat together. They used to buy live chickens from the farm and slaughter them to make it into halal. There was a grocery shop in Rochdale, and they used to have lamb meat and vegetables at this shop. At the time vegetables were available at English Markets but there were no Bangladeshi vegetables available. He remembers how he used to cook and he said, "he used to cook Mondays and Wednesdays and eat the same food for a whole week".

He said, "We did not have any bath facilities, and due to this I used to have a bath every Saturday in the public baths". At the time, he had a toilet inside his house but there wasn't any central heating system to warm his house. There were no carpets inside the house, but the floors were covered with a liner instead.

8.32.4 Employment & Business:

Since his arrival to the UK, two days later his father got him a job in the same factory where he was working. The factory was known as "Brian Fabric's Printers Limited". He used to work there from 8 pm to 8 am and he used to work overtime on Saturdays and Sundays from 8 am to 6 pm.

After deducting the tax, he used to get £22.00 - £23.00 every week. He used to get half an hour to eat at night and he used to get his lunch from his house, and he used to warm it up at the factory.

There was a Bangladeshi man who oversaw the factory, so he didn't have any problems with communication. 200 people were working in that factory and 30 of them were Bangladeshis and some English women used to work there as well.

He described his first experience of working in the factory and he said that on the first night, he destroyed many of the fabrics due to him being new to the job. In the first two nights, he learned how to do the job properly, and then he didn't have any problems. His main job was to insert the cloth from one side of the machine, and it used to come out of the other side of the machine. He worked in that factory for about 2 years and then went back to Bangladesh.

In 1966, he worked two weeks at "East Enders Cotton Mill" in Rochdale and then went to "Manor Mill" in Oldham. He used to do the night shift from 10 pm till 6 am and he used to do 4 hours overtime on Saturday and used to get £22.00 every week.

After working there for 6 months, he went back to "Marsh Mill" at Rochdale, and he was doing the night shift. He used to start at 8 pm and till 7.15 am and even in this mill, he used to do 4 hours overtime every Saturday. And he used to get £28.00 every week. He worked in the factory for 16 years. He worked in the "Aero Cotton Mill" in Rochdale for about 8 years and did overtime; the wages were £160.00 - £200.00 per week.

He was able to set up a restaurant, which was known as the "Everest Restaurant" in Rochdale. There were 3 partners involved with the business and they all paid £30,000. The capacity of the restaurant had 70 seats, and they used to make £2,000.00 every week, but afterwards, it went down to them making £1500.00 - £1600.00 every week. After running the business for 15 years, they sold the restaurant.

8.32.5 Housing:

At that time, he used to share the house, he used to live with some other Bangladeshis people, and he used to pay £1.00 every week for his seat. At that time, 8 people used to share a house between them.

In 1967, he bought a house with a partnership with his cousin and they both paid £150.00 each and paid £300.00 in total. In 1976, he bought the other half from his cousin. In 1982, he spent £38,000.00 and did the extension of his house. After the improvement work, the accommodation now consisted of 5 bedrooms and 2 reception rooms, 2 dining rooms, and 2 storerooms.

8.32.6 Social & Family:

In 1965 he got married in Bangladesh and stayed there for 6 months, he then left his wife in Bangladesh and came back to England (1966). In 1986 he brought his two daughters, two sons, and his wife to the UK. At that time his older son had completed his SSC in Bangladesh. In his own opinion, he thinks that many Bangladeshi people started to bring their families in 1976.

When he first came to Rochdale, 27 Bangladeshi people were residing in Rochdale and only one person had his family with him and everyone else was on their own. In 1971 he became a British citizen, and he learned so many things by living in Britain. During the war with Pakistan, they used to have arguments with Pakistanis regarding the independence movement.

He went to Bangladesh 16 times and twice he took his wife with him but the other times he went alone. He went to Bangladesh recently to see his 95-year-old mother. Since he came to the UK, he worked all the time and in 1989 he retired from work due to his ill health.

He is the father of 2 sons and 3 daughters. All his children are in the UK, and they are all married. He said, "I took the advantage since I came to Britain, and my children have been educated in the UK, if I would not come, then it would not turn out the same".

Since the formation of the "Bangladesh Association" in Rochdale, he has been involved with the Association. The Association's main aim was to employ someone, to provide help and assistance to the local people by reading and writing letters and filling out forms. This project work was over well warming and other communities benefited from this project.

At present, the "Bangladesh Association" is running a "Bangla School" every weekend. There are also provisions for elderly people; 2 days for men and 1 day for women. He said "I am a religious person and went to Makkah with my wife to do pilgrimage (Hajj). He is enjoying a happy life with his family.

8.32.7   First in the Town:

To his knowledge, he confirmed that "Haris Miah" was the first Bangladeshi who came to Rochdale to live the first restaurant was called the "Kohinoor Restaurant", the owner was "Dr. Khadir" and the second restaurant was known as the "Omar Kaiyum Restaurant". In 1966, there was a tailoring shop owned by "Keramot Ali". They used to make cardigans, coats, and English clothes. There was a grocery shop owned by "Abdul Karim Chowdhury" and he had Bengali food in his shop.

8.32.8   Independence of Bangladesh:

In the past, there weren't many Mosques in Rochdale, and he had to pray in his house but at a later stage, a Mosque was built, and it was known as the "Sonali Mosque". At that time more Pakistani people used to live in that area, so they built this Mosque.

After the liberation war, the Bangladeshi community built up a Mosque in Rochdale. Shiraj Miah initially helped them to buy a house in Rochdale and build a mosque there. There were about 30-35 people who could pray together. Afterwards, the local MP Smith helped them to buy land from the council and they built up a new Mosque. The Mosque has the capacity of more than 1000 people who could pray together.

8.32.9   Conclusion:

At that time, he was selected as a treasurer of the Mosque Committee and served there for 12 years. The Mosque has facilitated not only Salah but also to deliver Islamic teaching (Arabic) to the young people.

He said, "I wish all the people have success and progress in life".

8.33 Alhaj Mohammed Rafique Uddin
(Interviewed on 12 May 2008)

8.33.1 Life in Bangladesh:

In 1943, Alhaj Mohammed Rafique Uddin (son of Mr Arshad Ali) was born in the village of Doshghor Nowagaon, Bishwanath, Sylhet. He has 3 brothers and 1 sister; amongst them, he is the second son. When he was 6 years old, his father died, and his grandfather looked after him.

His father's family originated from Binna Kandi, Khadimpur, Balagonj, Sylhet. His grandfather then moved to Bishwanath. During his childhood, his family used to own a huge amount of land, so that would be where they received their income, and they were happily maintained. At that time, they had 13 lakes and 191.52 acres of land, they were very rich at that time, but the Pakistani government changed the laws, and they lost most of the lands and lakes. They still have huge amounts of land owned by their family.

When he was a child, he finished his primary school education and didn't get a chance to study at the High School. He used to walk to school and the condition of the school was very good. There were two Hindu teachers and two Muslim teachers: sometimes the teachers used to swap classes. After having the lessons at the school, there wasn't any need to employ a teacher at home.

Before he came to the UK, he was involved with the family business. He used to purchase goods from India and used to sell them in the local market. He was 18 years old. He had a well-known person in the military in his family and he was advised to join the Military. He went for the test, passed it and got the job. When he came home and told his mother, she did not allow him to go to Karachi for military training. He then submitted a medical report, confirming that he was not well, and he quit the job with the military.

8.33.2 Journey to the UK & Immigration:

In 1957, he tried to come to Britain. The people who had houses and businesses were able to sponsor people from different countries. His uncle gave him a voucher and then he obtained his passport and arranged his ticket, he flew from Dhaka by PIA and went to Karachi. He stayed there for 11 days and after that, he went to the London Heathrow Airport with his uncle who gave him the voucher.

He didn't have any problems in the UK because he had his uncle with him. So, after completing the immigration procedures at London Heathrow Airport, he took a bus and went to London Victoria. From there, with help from an Italian, he took a taxi and went to Uxbridge to one of his friend's houses.

He lived there for two weeks and moved to Bradford to his uncle's house. From London to Bradford, he had to catch a train to go there, and he paid 5 shillings.

8.33.3 Employment & Business:

He lived with his uncle for 4 months and went on benefits because he did not have a job at that time. After a while, a man who he knew arranged a job for him in a cotton mill in Bacup, Rawtenstall. His wages were £15.00 a week.

One of his relatives Mr Siddek Ali told him that he would get better wages if he came and worked in Rochdale. He started working in the factory in Rochdale and his weekly wages were £22.00.

After that, he moved to a new job in the "Shaw Mill" in the little borough. The wages were quite good, and he used to work 78 hours every week and used to get £40.00 - £45.00. At that time, it was hard for Bangladeshis to get this amount of salary. He worked there for 1 and a half years.

He started a job in Cheltenham but afterwards, he came to know that if anyone working in a factory in Oldham was able to get vouchers, they could bring people from Bangladesh. So, he came to Oldham and got a job in a factory.

In 1969, the factory announced that they had stopped giving out vouchers. After that, he left the job and went back to Bangladesh. At that time, he started a flying business in Bangladesh.

In 1971 when the war started in Bangladesh, many businesses were affected and suffered a total loss. In 1972, he got married again and the main reason for the second marriage was his first wife couldn't have any children.

In 1973, he came back to England and started an IP business. He was involved with this business from 1973-1975 and then went back to Bangladesh again. In 1979 he came back to England and started a job in the "Turner Mill" and he was in charge of that factory. Suddenly, one day he fainted and after the medical check-up, he became unfit. That was his last job.

He did not like to stay at home all day, so he started a restaurant business. He opened about 4 restaurants with partnerships with other people. One of the restaurants was in Aberdeen Shire, Scotland and it was known as the "Star of

India", which was his third restaurant. After 2 years he sold that restaurant and went to Makkah to do pilgrimage (Hajj). In 1988, he opened another restaurant but at that time there was some trouble with the customers, and he decided to sell the business.

8.33.4 Social & Family:

In 1966, he went to Bangladesh and got married. After his marriage, he left his wife in Bangladesh and came back to England in 1967. In 1982, he brought his wife to England and stayed in a rented house with his wife. In 1984, the house he is living in now was bought and he bought it for £800.00 from the council.

He is the father of 4 sons and 3 daughters. His eldest son has been studying in the UK and now he is working in a security company as an assistant director, and he is married. His eldest daughter passed her A levels, and she is married too, and all his other children are studying.

In 1970, the first mosque was built by Bangladeshis, at that time he was in Bangladesh, so he didn't get a chance to get involved with them, but he was able to get involved with them at a later stage when he returned to the UK. He became one of the trustees of the Mosque.

He was involved with the Bangladesh community. He said "the Bangladesh Association" in Rochdale first started the community centre, afterward they rented a house and bought a house and started working and it's still working now. Mr Gulam Rasul from Sheffield told the Bangladeshi community in Rochdale that there is an opportunity to get funding for the projects from the government.

Through his involvement, the Bangladesh Association was able to obtain funding and set up a project to help the community. In 1985 he went to Makkah to do pilgrimage (Hajj). When he came to Rochdale for the first time, he heard that 180,000 people used to live there but now there are about 220,000 people who live there and amongst them 8,000 Bangladeshis.

When he came to England, he was very pleased working with English people. At the time, when he was coming from Victoria by taxi, an Italian guy helped him to get a taxi. After that when he showed the address, that guy told everything to the taxi driver, and he put his luggage in the taxi for him and told him that the taxi driver would take him to the right place by body language.

If he had any problems whilst he was walking on the streets the English people used to help him, especially English women, they used to love helping people out. In the past, the weather in Britain was very cold. He said, "I used to think that we would never have daytime because we didn't see the moon or the sun, and the new generation would not believe this".

8.33.5 First in the Town:

To the best of his knowledge, the first Bengali in Rochdale was Mr. Harris, and the first grocery shop owner was Mr. Syed and his English wife. The first restaurant was the "Omar Kayum" and the owner was Dr. Ahmed and his Pakistani partner. The second restaurant was known as the "Kohinoor Restaurant".

8.33.6 Conclusion:

He still loves Bangladesh very much and therefore visits Bangladesh. He still misses his friends and relatives. He could not maintain communication with people back home as he used to do in the past.

He is enjoying the time with his family, and he is trying his very best to give them the right education that will enable them to go ahead in life. He urges the community to guide their children and encourage them to do more study to be successful in life. He is retired and is living a happy life with his wife and children.

8.34 Alhaj Mohammed Wajib Ali

(Interviewed on 11 May 2008)

8.34.1 Life in Bangladesh:

Alhaj Mohammed Wajib Ali was born in 1934 in the village of Chorchondi, Bishwanath, Sylhet, Bangladesh. His father's name is Alhaj Mohammad Montaj Ali. His father died when he was 4 years old. He studied at "Habra Bazar Primary School". High school was too far away, about 2 & a half miles away from his house. It was based in Bishwanath. Due to the distance of the school and transport system, not many students were able to do higher education.

At that time, it was a British colony [East Pakistan]. There weren't many schools compared to this time. There were not many facilities for teachers. Primary school teachers used to get 12 Rupees for monthly wages. It was hard to maintain a family with the wages. His childhood was good.

At that time things were very cheap, it was affordable to every family. The people were enjoying a very simple lifestyle. There were affections amongst villagers but nowadays you will see the opposite. The overall social system was very good. He said, "if there was a problem, local seniors used to come forward to resolve the problem".

Everyone used to respect each other. On the Eid days, in the Eidgah and the Mosque, after the Salah, people used to embrace each other. Everyone used to invite each other to visit their houses and to have special food on these occasions. Everybody used to get holidays from their work. There were no business activities on this day, everything was closed.

8.34.2 Journey to the UK & Immigration:

The reason he wanted to come to Britain was to establish himself. He wanted to come to Britain, save some money and then go back to Bangladesh. In 1963 he came to Britain, and he was 33 years old. In 1961 he got married before he came to Britain. His eldest son was 12 days old before he came to Britain. There were another 2 people from his village who came to Britain with him. He arrived at London Heathrow Airport then he stayed 1 night in London. Then he went to his cousin's brother's house in Bradford.

8.34.3 Employment:

He got his first job in a Wool Mill. After a few days of working there, he learned how to use the machine. They used to make thread from wool. He used to get £10.50 per week. He worked there for 2 and a half years. After that, he came to Rochdale. More Bangladeshi people used to live in Rochdale. With their help, he found another job at the "March Mill".

After working there for 2 weeks, he had the opportunity to work on the machine. His wages were £12.50 per week. After working there for 6 months, he went to Oldham and worked at the "Manor Mill". He worked there for about 4 years. He used to get £26.00 per week. After that, he went to Bangladesh in 1969. He stayed in Bangladesh for 4 years.

After the War, he came to Britain. He found another job in Rochdale in a "Cotton Mill". After working there for 6 months, he found another job at the "Turners Mill". He worked there for about 7 years. In 1982, he retired from the job because of his ill health condition. That was his last job. When he was working at the factory, the factory in charge was responsible for giving training to the new workers.

The colleagues, if they had the opportunity, then they used to help the new workers. He did not have any language difficulties whilst working with English and other people. The people who were able to understand the language of foremen used to get the job. 80% of people used to use their body language to make them understand.

He used to take his lunch with him because they didn't have any halal food in the canteen. All the white people were not English, to avoid any conflict; he used to work frankly with them. His family was in his mind while working in the factory. On the weekend he used to go to the public bath to have a shower and he had to pay for this.

There were time limits; 30 minutes maximum time was allowed to do the shower. On the weekend he used to socialize with friends and family. On Sunday he went to go Cinema to watch movies. Also, he used to Write letters and send money to Bangladesh over the weekend.

8.34.4 Housing:

He used to stay with his cousin's brother at his house and he used to pay rent, 50 pence per week. When he came to Rochdale, he did not have a bath or toilet inside the house because at that time they used to have baths & toilets outside of their houses. It was very difficult to use the toilet at night. He bought a house to bring his wife and children. His eldest son sent money to him from America for the improvement work of the house. It cost him about £5000.00 to buy furniture and to complete the work.

8.34.5 Social & Family:

In 1986 his wife and children came to Britain. He is the father of 3 sons and 2 daughters. His eldest son passed his BA when he was in Bangladesh then he went to America and stayed there for 7 years, then came to Britain.

Now his son is involved with a Business. His eldest daughter studied, and she was working. After that, she got married and she quit the job to look after her children. His youngest daughter got a degree and now she is working as a School Teacher. His youngest son is a Chemical Engineer.

He established his family in the UK and, he is very happy about his children's education. At that time, there was a Mosque called "Jalalia Jameh Mosque" in Rochdale. He used to pray in that Mosque. After 2 and half years,

102 Bangladeshi people opened a second new mosque called "Al Amin" and he was involved with this Mosque.

He went to Makkah to do the pilgrimage. In his free time, he prays, reads the Quran, reads books, reads newspapers, and talks with friends. Sometimes he goes to town in a taxi. Also, he talks to his relatives in Bangladesh over the phone. He is very happy with his family in Britain.

8.34.6 Independence of Bangladesh:

In 1969, he went to Bangladesh and stayed there for 4 years. He had seen the liberation movement and war when he was in Bangladesh. In the war people who were from Britain had to be very careful because they used to kill people who were from abroad, and due to this they used to stay outside at night.

During the time of war, there were night guards, patrolling their village to make sure, no one could enter their village. He maintained a good relationship with these people. He said, "During the war period it was very difficult for people because anyone could be killed by the invading Military".

8.34.7 Conclusion:

He said community members need to work together to develop the community even further. Without cooperation, the nation cannot succeed. He said, "The people came to this world for a short time; everyone will have to leave this world". He also said, "To get a better life after death, he suggested doing payers in this world".

He also said, "We have to obey the rules and guidance from Allah, and helping other people is a great prayer". The people will be benefited in this world and hereafter.

8.35 Faruk Ali
(Interviewed on 29 June 2010)

8.35.1 Life in Bangladesh

Mr. Faruk Ali was born in 1955 in the village of Nurpur, Fenchugonj, Sylhet. He is the third born out of four siblings (Two boys and two daughters). He is 14 years different from his youngest sister which is amazing. He completed primary education at the local "Fenchugonj Dorgapur Primary School". Then he was admitted to the local Kasim Ali High School. After the class 7 exam, he came to Britain.

8.35.2 Journey to the UK & Immigration:

In 1969 he came to Britain with his mother, at that time he was 12 years old. At that time his father used to work in British Army. Mr. Ali used to work in Manchester in 1963 then he moved to Rochdale and started working at Dunlop.

8.35.3 Life in the UK:

After that, he came to Britain and was admitted to "Bradfield Primary School". In 1973 he completed GCSE from "Green Hill Senior High School". Then he did a Textile Engineer course for 2 years from the college.

He has been living in Rochdale since he came to Britain. He also said that his father used to live in Rochdale, and his children and his grandchildren also live there. When he first came to Rochdale, he did not like it because there were not many Bangladeshi people around that time. At that time about 2/3 of Bangladeshi people used to live in Rochdale. **His mother was one of the first Bengali female spouses in Rochdale.**

At that time 4 Bangladeshi children used to go to school with 2 boys and 2 girls. In 1970 there were not any Bangladeshi boys who were the same age as him, first, he used to face problems with his English, and he used to have English and European friends. He has been in Britain for over 40 years, and he gives thanks to his parents for their support for his Bangla language.

He came to Britain when he was very young, and he used to have English friends, but he still managed to speak Bangla to them. In 1970 Bangladeshi people started to come to Rochdale.

At that time there were not many facilities compared to this time. He said Britain has changed, he also said about Rochdale that it is a lot different from what it used to be like. In 1970-1980 there were jobs you could apply for, but their answer was sorry no vacancies. He said that there was discrimination, or they did not want to give out jobs to Asian people. He said between 1970 and 1980 it was a very hard time. They used to treat people the way they wanted, and it wasn't nice treatment.

In 1980 a lot of Bangladeshi families used to live in Rochdale, which was 200-300 hundred families and 4-5 thousand Bangladeshi living in Rochdale and contributing to Britain's economy. He used to like that people from Bangladesh were living in Rochdale because he enjoyed seeing people who shared the same race around him and, he enjoyed helping the community with these people.

During that time, they never used to give jobs to people who were Asian, when they used to apply for a job, they would say sorry no vacancies. He also said that he could get job satisfaction, he was an intelligent man and had an education as did many of the Asian people living in Britain, but they'd still turn them away due to their race.

Now in Britain, every Bangladeshi family has a student graduate. He said graduating is a big achievement. One example is when he was a school student his 2 years junior was Mr Anwar Chowdhury, later, who became a British High Commissioner for Bangladesh. He is one of the prime examples of Bangladeshi students who studied in Britain, and he is working as a British Government representative. He said from that Insha'Allah we can hope Bangladeshi students can achieve more.

He thinks that the next generation will involve themselves in that. He also said we must learn how we can sacrifice to become a good Muslim; you must be a good person first. The Rochdale Association & Community Project offers advice and guidance to elderly people regarding health issues, they have a dinner party for men 3 days and 2 days for women every week. They also have gym facilities for everybody and children's activities for example Kabadi, football, etc.

In the Bangladeshi community, to become a good learner you must be a good person, without knowledge and education money doesn't work in the right way, we must be honest and do a good job. You are Muslim but you must prove it through community activities and help people in your community etc. In 1960 in Rochdale, there was Kohinoor Restaurant and a Bangladeshi Grocery shop.

8.35.4 Employment:

He started his first job as a Textile Engineer. After completing his studies, he started a job in a mill as an Engineer. When the textile mill started to close, he had to choose the alternative which was a restaurant business.

In 1977, he opened the "Rajmohal Restaurant" with his partner. The restaurant is one of the most famous catering businesses in Britain. He had to choose this route because the textile mill was closing. He was involved with the business till 1981. He also said that during times life was quite difficult, mainly with Asian people who didn't have a good job, it was also sad because most of the time they weren't given a job due to their race.

During work in a factory, they used to get 30-minute tea breaks but after 10 minutes they used to tell the workers to start work. In the factory young people like him who studied in Britain, grew up and learned how to speak English used to question the people in charge due to them treating the workers badly, they didn't use to like that and because of that, they would fire people.

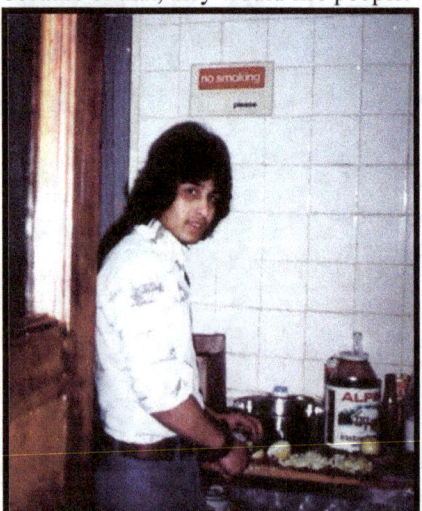

He said that the restaurant business was right. There was not much competition compared to this time. In 1981 he left the factory job and started his business, and the factory people asked for him back. They wanted to know if he would he come to work for them again. Then he went back to the textile mill, he got promoted to Health & Safety Inspector. He said that was a really good job & he worked there till 1995. His last wages were around about 300 hundred pounds per week.

In 1995 after the last factory job, he started the restaurant business again. That time he opens a takeaway. First, his business's name was Sarga but after that, he changed it to his granddaughter's name Maria. At that time everybody knew it as "Maria Takeaway". He is involved with the overall management and administration. He also said that he likes it and he doesn't have any problem with it.

The older generation said that there were jobs available in Britain, for example: If they lost a job in the morning then on the same day they could manage to get a job in the evening, He said that was 100% true. He said from his experience when he used to work in the textile mill if they had given you an order which is not good, you'd argue you would be put into a "bad book".

When the older generation came to Britain, they did not know any English, and because of that the people in charge of the factories used to make them work anyway. When a job was asked to be done the workers made sure it was done as soon as possible with good intentions.

When he used to work in a factory they used to get 30 minutes tea break. English people used to have a full 30-minute break, but the Indian, Pakistani and Bangladeshi people after 10 minutes would be told that they have to start working again. Then Mr. Ali gave notice to them and said I opposed the white people. This was due to him noticing that Asian people were not getting treatment right at work.

Then he was involved with the GMB trade Union and appealed to Asian people for their unfair dismissal, he was Successful. He said that he had proved that white people were in the wrong.

8.35.5   Housing:

When he was young living with his parents in Rochdale, he said the majority or 100 percent of people didn't have baths or toilets inside the house. They used to have toilets outside of their houses. The people used to go to the Rochdale Central public bath to have their bath. There weren't any radiators inside the houses also. They used to use Cole to warm the house. Single people

(10-12 persons) used to stay together. They used to cook for each other. He said now everything is so easy.

8.35.6   Social & Family:

In 1977 he got married and afterwards, his wife and children came to Britain. At that time in Rochdale, older people opened a school for the Bangla language and his wife used to teach Bangla in that school. Sometimes he used to go and teach Bangla also, he was involved with the school community.

Mr. Ali has 2 brothers and 2 sisters, his eldest brother and sister are in Bangladesh with their family. Occasionally he goes to Bangladesh. Since he came to Britain he's been to Bangladesh 2 times, he went to Bangladesh after the Victory against Pakistan in 1972, and the last time he went to Bangladesh was in 2008. On holiday in Britain, he goes to Blackpool, Brighton and Wales. Also, he likes spending time with the community people. He also said when he gets retired, he thinks he will spend time with his family.

During the praying in the Mosque, he was getting involved. He used to collect money for the Mosque and helped the senior people. When the senior people started the Bangladeshi Association in Rochdale then he used to help senior people with their tax credit forms etc. That time if he had any problems then the senior people used to help him. In 1974-1975 he was more involved with the community. When he started a full-time job, he did not get a chance to give time to the community but in 1977 he was more involved with the community.

In 1980 he became a member of the Bangladesh Association and in 1990 he became the Secretary-General, and he worked there for 4 years. Later, he became project chairman for the Bangladesh Association & Community Project. Now young people are involved with the association, and he thinks it is good. Also, he thinks that keeping youngsters involved with the community is good.

Now Mr. Ali is involved with the association, Mosques, and verities cultural projects. In 1998, he became a member of Sylhet Tigers Club, UK and in 2001 he became the founding director and general Secretary of the Tigers International Association – TIA; to date, he is still serving the charity. Also, he is involved with Bangladeshi and British politics. He is a member of the British Labour Party and a supporter. He thinks it is good to give time and support British politics.

He was living in Rochdale for 40 years and he said when people first came into Britain their biggest problem was learning the language. When they started to bring their families into Britain, some people studied in Britain and some people studied in Bangladesh. He said that the new Bangladesh generation came to Britain in 1980; they started to get involved in British politics.

8.35.7   Independence of Bangladesh:

During the war in Bangladesh, Mr. Ali used to go to high school, and he was 15 years old. In 1971 during the war in Bangladesh, Pakistani students didn't talk or sit near Bangladeshi students at school. He used to stay with his English friends. He also said during the liberation war; at workplaces, Bangladeshi had been hurt by the Pakistani rather than the English.

During that time Bangladeshi people in Britain helped with people demonstrations & other things for the war in Bangladesh. He also mentioned that we can never forget the Bangladeshi people in Britain for their wonderful support.

He also said the Bangladeshi older generation had to work at night and in

the morning, they used to watch Bangladesh news on TV plus when they used to get wages on the weekend, they would donate all their wages for the independence of Bangladesh. Mr Ali used to go to different programmes and demonstrations with senior people. He also helped the senior people with their support.

After he came to Rochdale he was involved with the community. In 1971 there was a Pakistani Mosque called Sonali Mosque in Rochdale. After the victory in Bangladesh, Pakistani people did not allow Bangladeshi people to pray in that Mosque. In 1983-1984 Bangladeshi people bought a house and started to pray there. Now 12-13 hundred people can pray together in that Mosque.

8.35.8 Conclusion

Now he is living in a house that his father bought. He also is glad that he came to Britain. He also mentioned that his friends have respectful jobs now such as doctors, lawyers, etc. If he was in Bangladesh, then he would have been in the same position as his classmates. In Britain when he was young, he used to watch English Hindi movies and sometimes he would read the Bangla newspaper.

When he used to go to school, people used to say to his father that they'd rather his son study in Bangladesh. His parents allow him to study in Britain and he also said education is the most important for the community. His 3 sons have graduated. He gave thanks to the older generation for their help and for involving him with the community. He also said to the new generation that they should be honest, be a good example and be a good British person.

8.36 Phul Bhanu Ali
(Interviewed on 29 June 2010)

8.36.1 Life in Bangladesh

Phul Bhanu Ali was born in Lokkipasha, Rakhalgonj Bangladesh. She got married to her sister's husband's cousin, her brother-in-law arranged everything for her marriage. Now her village is in Bramman in Bangladesh.

8.36.2 Journey to the UK & Immigration:

She came to Britain over 41 years ago; she came to Britain with her son to her husband. At first, she did not like Britain, but when she came to Britain, she left 1 of her sons & 1 one of her daughters in Bangladesh.

Her husband & his brother's son came to Heathrow Airport to collect her, then they went to Rochdale where her husband lived.

8.36.3 Employment:

When she first came to Rochdale, her husband used to work in a factory. First, he used to work in Dunlop Factory, and then he started to work in another factory. Her husband was in the British Army fighting in Bangladesh. He worked there for 3 years in Bangladesh, during that time people used to fight a lot, for the safety policy; they used to hide themselves to protect themselves from the opposite group. She did not have any children when her husband was in the Army. After that, he used to work in Bongshal Company in Fenchugonj, Sylhet.

The Company moved to Chittagong then her husband moved there as well. During the work in Chittagong, people who used to work in the Army; would

185

have the chance to go to Britain, he came to Britain at that time. When Mrs Ali came to Britain; there were not many Bangladeshi people in Rochdale compared to this time. At that time, she didn't know any English but at the moment she understands a little bit of English and she also said that time educated people used to help a lot.

When she first came to Britain her husband was working in a Dunlop factory. After that he worked in another factory then he became a pensioner. Her husband managed to do Hajj but she didn't because at that time her daughter was studying.

8.36.4   Housing:

It was a rented house, after 5-6 months she told her husband that she did not like it and she wanted to go back to Bangladesh. They soon rented a different house.

During that time there were not many things compared to this time, there was no pan or Shupari, which is very common to our Bangladeshi people. Now everything is available. At that time, they used to get fish & vegetables from Manchester. At that time people used to get slaughtered chickens from the shop.

First, she did not like Britain but now she likes Britain because she's been living there for over 41 years. She also said that she doesn't want to go to Bangladesh, she wants to spend the rest of her life in Britain because everywhere is blessed by Allah. She also said that time there was an illness called Cholera, a lot of people died from the illness, and a lot of her relatives died from that illness.

8.36.5   Social & Family:

She had also wanted her son to get married to a Bangladeshi girl & she was proud of him. Then she came back to Britain because her youngest daughter was ill. Now her younger daughter is married, and she is happy with her husband & family; also, she did a study in Britain. Mrs. Ali has 4 grandsons & 1 granddaughters. Her son who came to Britain with her has 5 sons. Now they are all married & living with their family. She loves her country very much. Her son's daughter is in Bangladesh and her son is in Britain with his son, he got married to his cousin's sister and now they have 1 daughter. She allows her son to study in Britain now that he is established and has his own business. Her son-in-law is also involved with a business.

Her children are educated and happy with their family and she is happy also. She also said that time there were not many Bangladeshi families in Britain. Now people are increasing everywhere. Now she stays at home because of her stroke she's been at home for 9 years and she cannot go outside even if she wants to. Even if she doesn't go to her daughter's house her daughter comes to see her.

When she needs to go to the doctor her son Mr. Faruk Ali takes her in a car. If he is busy, then his wife takes her to the doctor in a taxi. Now she spends a lot of her time at home. Before the stroke she used to go to her daughter's house mainly when her daughter was pregnant, also she used to go to relatives' houses, or she used to go to town shopping.

During that time her daughter was born, and then her husband bought a house. At that time the war had started in Bangladesh between Bangladesh & Pakistan, after the victory in Bangladesh she went to Bangladesh with her 2-year-old daughter. Then her eldest son got married in Bangladesh, when she first came, she had a Pakistani passport but when she went to Bangladesh back from Britain for the first time she had a Bangladeshi passport.

After her son's wedding, her husband came to Britain & she stayed with her younger daughter. After 1 year she came back to Britain because her younger daughter was ill, and after 3 & half years she went back to Bangladesh with her son who was in Britain. Her sons got married in Bangladesh and she gave thanks to Allah.

8.36.6 Conclusion

For the rest of her life, she wants to spend in Britain. Before she wanted to go to Bangladesh but now, she does not want to go there because she thinks all the close family members are in the UK. She also said from her father's side no one's alive. Her son and daughter want her to go to Bangladesh, but she doesn't

want to because of her health issues.

If she wants to go then someone must look after her every time and in Bangladesh, there are no good facilities for her. She wanted to do Hajj but now she cannot go because of her health issue. She wants her life to end in Britain because every place in the world is Allah's. She is a religious person, and she wants everybody to have a good and happy life.

8.37 Nazrul Islam
(Interviewed on 28 March 2008)

8.37.1 Life in Bangladesh

Alhaj Nazrul Islam was born in 1952 in the village of Bhugshail, Bishwanath, Sylhet. His father's name is late Khurshid Ali and his mother's name is late Nojiba Khatun. His father was a school-teacher at "Bhugshail Primary School". He has 5 brothers and 2 sisters; amongst them, he is the third oldest.

He started his education at "Bhugshail Primary School". When he finished his primary education, he went to Madrasha and studied there for 1 year. He went to the "Ramsundor High School" and studied up to class seven. He went to Sunamgonj with his cousin and was admitted to "Sunamgonj Government High School". He studied there for 2 years and came back to Bishwanath. He continued his study up to class 10.

He described the old days as flourishing with rice & crops, and plenty of fish in the ponds and rivers. There was no distinction between the rich and the poor. The people lived in a bonding society. During the period of harvesting the paddy, the village people worked together and had celebration parties in every house with joy and happiness.

There were many fruit trees in their homes, mango, jackfruit and so many other different kinds of fruits were available in most of the houses. There were cows, goats, hens, and domestic animals which were available in every house. There was a different taste altogether.

The villagers' life was very simple and straightforward, nowadays it is very expensive. His father was working as a teacher and his monthly salary was 40 Rupees/taka. Receiving income from the paddy field and salary received from a teaching job, his father's family was well maintained. There was no hardship in maintaining the family.

There was limited transportation, the people used to walk a lot. There were no rickshaws or bicycles available in the village at that time, he used to go to school on foot and the school was about a mile away from home.

There was a loving relationship amongst village people. On Eid day there was a lot of happiness due to visiting families and eating verities homemade food. There was a culture of inviting people to visit their homes. Now we are losing this culture. People are very busy; they have no time for their family and friends. The environment in the school was very good. The junior students used to respect the senior student as an elder brother. Similarly, the elders used to get respect from juniors.

8.37.2 Journey to the UK & Immigration:

He came to the UK in 1962. There was a rule at that time, if you knew someone in the UK and could show that he would be your granter, this meant you could come to the UK, simply by submitting the passport to the British High Commission and getting permission.

At present, the Immigration law is very tight; it was not like it before. There was a relative from his in-law's side, who used to live in the UK before. Through his help, he came to the UK. He first stayed with his relative from the in-law's site. From there he came to Hyde to live.

8.37.3 Life in the UK:

Many people used to live in one house as everyone was single. Some people used to live in single rooms and some people used to share rooms. He used to pay 10 shillings for accommodation and 10 shillings for food every week. The price of goods and costs of living were very cheap at that time.

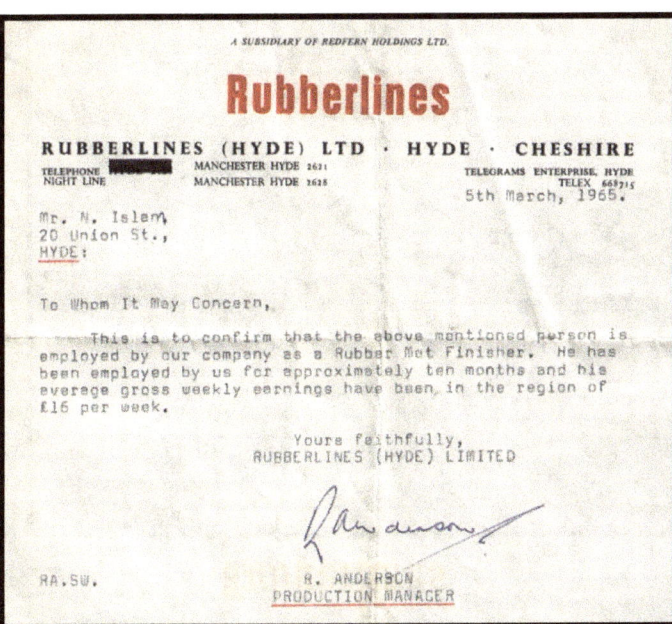

Life in the UK was very hard, but it was

not that difficult. The English men and women used to help anyone who had a problem. If someone couldn't find a location, then they used to hold the hand of that person and they used to show the destination address. Even at the workplace, English people used to help the Bangladeshis people and others. At that time there was a popular proverb **"Bangladeshis are peace-loving people"**. The senior people can verify this truth.

8.37.4   Employment & Business:

Whilst he was in Bangladesh, he used to work in the land registry office in Sylhet. When he first came to the UK, the weather was very cold and there was snowfall. He met some people in Hyde. He took 2 of his friends and went to a factory called "Dixon Simon Limited" at New Bridge Lane to find a job. They had been given job applications.

They could not understand the English language, which was written on the job application form. He wrote their name and addresses on a plain piece of paper instead of filling out the forms. The manager was pleased to see the English writing and they offered the job.

The starting weekly wages were £24.00. In some weeks with the overtime, he used to get £30.00-£40.00 per week. While working in this factory he found another job with good facilities. If anyone worked for about 2-3 hours, his full day was counted by the manager. He had no experience in working in the factory

when came to the UK but he has learned this skill by engaging with the job, like many others.

There was help and support from the management. When a worker started a job in the factory, training was given by the management. By working and gaining experience, people can move from one job to another and used to get good pay. In his second job, the people in charge of the factory had given out keys to him and some other workers to lock up the factory when they finished work. There were plenty of biscuits and tea available for the workers.

He got involved in the property business after his first house was knocked down by the council. He bought an old house, made some improvements to it and sold it with some profit. He was also involved with the restaurant business. He was involved with this business for quite a while. He became a partner with his father-in-law in a grocery shop. In 1984, he retired from work.

8.37.5 Housing:

When he first arrived in Hyde, there were only 7/8 houses. Later, many people arrived from Bangladesh and the immigrant community began to emerge. Just in a year, the total in houses had increased to 60.

The toilet was outside the house. There was no bathing facility inside the house; he used to go to the public bath once a week. It was very difficult to use the outside toilet, during cold weather. The new generation would not believe this. At that time there was a good relationship with people. People used to accept other people as their brothers and sisters.

When he quit his second job, he bought his first house for £100.00. He paid £50.00 in advance and £50.00 was paid later by instalment. At that time, buying a house was so simple, that on the same day, anyone was able to purchase the house using one solicitor.

This house was demolished under the Compulsory Purchase Order (CPO) by the local government. He received £200.00 including compensation. With this amount of money, he bought two houses. Since then, he started the property business. He used to buy an old house make some improvements and sell it with some profit. He was involved with this business for quite a while.

8.37.6 Social & Family:

In the past, most of the people who came to Britain with no education or some education, and the lack of English language was the main barrier for many Bangladeshis. He used to provide voluntary services to those people who required such assistance. He said people used to come up with taxes, passports, and other official letters, including filling out forms and writing letters. Some people used to go to his workplace to get this assistance.

When the management took notice that many people were coming at work time, which caused some sort of disruption, they made a rule that no more than 10 people every day could come to the factory to see him. Then it was reduced to

5 people. He generously if help to the needy. He used to prepare his meals. The price of chicken was 10 Shillings. The fish and vegetables were also available. There were no difficulties in eating food.

In 1963, he passed his driving test. He never hesitated to use his transport to take people to different offices. The new house, which he bought, had become a private office by the local people. Later, the house was on the demolition programme and was eventually knocked down. He received £200.00 including compensation. With this amount of money, he bought two houses. Since then, he started the property business.

He was planning to go to Bangladesh and made some savings of £1,600.00

The Lord Chamberlain is
commanded by Her Majesty to invite

Mr. Nasrul Islam

to an Afternoon Party in the Garden of Buckingham Palace
on Tuesday, the 24th July 1973, from 4 to 6 p.m.

Morning Dress or Uniform or Lounge Suit

but unfortunately, the independence of Bangladesh, and the liberation movement affected his plans, and he could not go. In 1959, he got married before he came to Britain and after the liberation, he went to Bangladesh in 1972 and brought his family. When his wife came to the UK, by that time, the housing conditions had improved a lot but there wasn't a central heating system.

He is a father of four daughters; all of them are educated and married. He was actively involved with Hyde's Bangladesh Welfare Association and became a founding member of the Association. His father-in-law was the first person to facilitate the place of worship for the Muslim people in Hyde. He is also a trustee of the Shahjalal Mosque in Manchester.

The Bangladeshi community is doing better compared with the previous period. The children are now going to universities and obtaining degrees. He thinks that the parents and the community both need to be more anxious and provide necessary guidance and support to their children. All parents should have the responsibility to maintain family ties with Bangladeshi relatives and taking children to Bangladesh is also important.

He has one elder brother and one younger brother living in Bangladesh. He regularly contacts his brother's family. He visited several times Bangladesh for holidays and to see his loved ones.

He said it is important that everyone should learn the English language to make effective communication. He was involved in setting up an Adult Learning English language school and many people took part in learning the Basic English language. Many other literate people helped him with this project.

He was amongst other people to read a Bengali newspaper called "Jagoron". He also likes to write poems in his spare time.

8.37.7 Liberation of Bangladesh:

He is one of the active members of the liberation movement in the UK. At that time, he was planning to go to Bangladesh for a personal visit but due to this conflict, he could not go. He said the time was very crucial for the Bangladeshi living in the UK, to show support for the independence movement.

He felt strongly that it was very important for Bangladeshi living in the UK to show the world, why the Bangladeshi need a separate independent country. He said many people donated the necessary funds for the victims of the war. Due to this conflict, the Pakistan Welfare Association was divided in every town and city including Tameside.

He was serving as the last general secretary of the Association. As an alternative to the association and for immediate action, the Bangladeshi people came together and formed a group called "Lancashire and Adjoining County Committee". That committee later developed as a Greater Manchester Bangladesh Association.

He also recalled his memory and said "I can remember some of the names who devoted their valuable time to establishing this organization, such as Nazir Uddin, Moksud Bokth, Abdul Matin, Lal Miah, Shamsuddin Ahmed, Bosharoth Ali and so on. Mr. Matin lead this organization as chairman of the first committee.

At that time of liberation, they worked hard during the day and night to make communication with people living in different towns and cities. Their role was to convince the British government to support Bangladeshi independence. They were also responsible for collecting funds for the people who were on the ground and fighting for the country.

He recalled from his memory that there was a trustee board formed with 3 Britain and 1 Bangladeshi to look at possibilities to provide help to those who were victims of the war. There were different channels they did this; they used to monitor the funds that had been transferred in the right direction. He worked with these people until the country was liberated on the 16th of December 1971.

8.37.4 Conclusion:

In his conclusion he says, **"My first intention was to come to Britain for employment and make some savings and go back"** But after living in the UK for 5/6 years, he decided to stay in the UK, therefore he became a British citizen. He thinks that it has benefited in many ways in his personal, social, and economic life by deciding to stay in the UK.

In his spare time, he goes to the mosque and contacts his Bangladeshi and English friends. The generation should have a good education and there should be equally respected Britain and Bangladeshis. The future generation Bangladeshi community will be educated and will be able to make a positive contribution towards community work.

8.38 Amir Miah
(Interviewed on 3 November 2007)

8.38.1 Life in Bangladesh

Amir Miah was born in 1954 in the village of Singerkas, Bishwanath, Sylhet. His father's name is the late Akoddus Ali, and his mother's name is the late Jomila Begum. He has five brothers and one sister; among them, he is the eldest. All his siblings are residing in the UK. His primary education was from Singerkas Primary School and his secondary education was from Aklim Miah Junior High School. He studied up to the class of eight.

He spent his childhood time with joy and happiness. He left Bangladesh when he was only 13 and a half years of age. He did not get the opportunity to do more education because he arrived in the UK at a very young age and started to work in the restaurant, but he feels proud that at least he managed to provide education to all his children. He said five of his children are graduates and are in good professions.

His father was a farmer; he had plenty of agricultural land. He used to manage the family farming. His father was not interested in coming to the UK, but he visited the UK. He said his children are educated because they are in the UK, if he did not have this opportunity then it may not have happened. There could have been different circumstances altogether.

8.38.2 Immigration:

In April 1967, he received a "Boy Voucher" from his father. He contacted his cousin Monir Miah, who was living in Dargah Mahalla, Sylhet. His cousin's brother helped him to obtain the Passport and get the visa from the British High Commission, Dhaka. Once the visa was received, he purchased the airline ticket.

The costs of processing the passport and airline ticket were paid for by his father. In September 1967, he flew from Sylhet and went to Dhaka, from Dhaka, he flew by PIA and arrived at Manchester Airport. At that time, he was only 13 and a half years old. His father went to Manchester Airport to receive him.

On the same flight, his cousin Mahbub Ali joined him in going to Britain. Firstly, they went to Burnley, where his father used to live. He stayed with his father for six weeks, and then he went to Preston. Since he came to Britain, he was able to bring his three brothers to the UK. His sister married a British Bangladeshi, so she came to Britain as well.

8.38.3 Employment:

Since his arrival in the UK, he started to work at the "Kismot Restaurant" in Preston. He worked as a kitchen porter at a weekly wage of £6.50. The working hours were 10 am to 3 pm and 9 pm to 3 am. There was a flat just above the restaurant, which was for the staff. The food was also free of charge for the staff.

From 1967 to 1972 he worked in restaurants in different towns and cities. Although he initially worked as a kitchen porter, he, later, worked as a waiter. At that time, his wages weekly was £12.00. He then moved to Cheltenham and worked there as a waiter at the weekly wage of £18.00. After that, he moved to Gloucester, Burnley, Warrington, Southport, Manchester, Lincoln, South Wales, London, Bury, Chester, and North Wales.

In 1973, Mr. Miah became an experienced worker and started a Restaurant business in north Wales, the restaurant was known as the "Tajmahal Restaurant". He became very successful with the business and with the savings he bought about eight houses in the UK. He made more profit by purchasing properties. He ran his business for about 18 years.

Mr. Miah told us that he became a partner of the Restaurant where he was working. The owner of "Tajmahal Restaurant" offered the partnership and he paid £12.50 every week by way of instalment payments. All together for a quarter of the share, he paid £4,000.00. The weekly business turnover was about £300.00 - £350.00. When he became involved with the business, the sales were increased to £800.00 - £900.00 per week.

In 1975, he became a third partner with his brother-in-law and got involved in the restaurant business in Lincoln. He paid £2,300.00 for his share. That business was also known as the "Tajmahal Restaurant". After three years he sold his share and received £7,000.00 for surrendering his partnership.

In 1977, he entered a half-partnership business in Caernarfon, North Wales. He paid £2,500.00 for his share. He was involved with this business for about 4 years. He sold his partnership for £15,000.00. In 1978, he entered a sleeping partnership with half a share and opened a restaurant business in Redding. He paid £4,000.00 for his share. After three years he sold his share for the same amount, which he originally invested.

In 1980, he entered a new partnership and opened a restaurant in Bangor, which was known as the "Oriental Restaurant". He was one of the third owners and he paid £2,333.33 for his share. He ran this business for two years and sold his share for the same price. In 1980, he bought the share from his partner, and he paid £35,000.00 to pay out his partner. He became the single owner of the first restaurant, which was known as "Tajmahal Restaurant". In 1989, he sold this restaurant business for £143,000.00.

In 1984, he joined the third partnership and opened a restaurant in Holyhead, which was known as the "Holyhead Restaurant". He paid £15,000.00 for his share. He sold this business after 15 months due to the management. In 1989, he started a restaurant in Bangor, which was known as the "Tandoori Night". He invested £140,000.00 and bought the freehold building plus business. In 2004, he sold the "Tandoori Night" and retired from the business due to his ill health.

Mr Miah expresses his view in terms of UK life; generally, he enjoyed UK life. He liked to work in the restaurants where he enjoyed his time the most. His first job was at the "Kismot Restaurant" which reminds him of his old memories. The owner of the restaurant was a very good person, more specifically his behaviour and personal support to all the staff were amazing.

There was more flexibility and a good choice for food; it was a good condition, and the staff quarter had heating and TV facilities. He did not have any intention of staying in the UK for an indefinite period but due to family circumstances and the welfare of his children's education he decided to stay in the UK, but he still wishes to go back to his homeland and settle there.

8.38.4 Housing:

In the 1960's, the housing condition was not good enough compared to the present condition. There were no modern WC and central heating facilities. In the accommodation he was living in, there were no central heating systems, but the accommodation was in very good condition. The weather was just very cold. The houses in the 1960s sold at very good prices also, and the goods were sold at reasonable prices.

In 1989 he bought a four-bedroom house for £32,000 and an eight-bedroom house for £82,000.00. In 1990, he bought a three-bedroom semi-detached house for £39,000.00. In 2004, he moved to Crew and bought a three-bedroom house for £100,000.00.

In 2007, he moved to Manchester due to his child's job and the needs of the community. He bought a luxury 3-bedroom house in Long Sight, Manchester where he wants to stay for the rest of his life. He paid £245,000.00 and spent £50,000.00 to renovate the work.

8.38.5 Social & Family:

In 1971 he went to Bangladesh and got married. In 1978 his wife came to the UK. He has two daughters and three sons. Two of his daughters and one of his sons had gotten married in Bangladesh. All his children are graduates from the UK. His eldest son manages the property business, 2 of his daughters are qualified teachers and are working in schools, and 2 sons are lawyers working in solicitor firms. He has many relatives in Bangladesh, and he likes to help them. He maintains regular communication with his relatives and friends.

He said that the new generation is doing very well, and they will do even better. His children are very concise and independent-minded he added. He does not interfere with their personal affairs. He said that if his children are happy then he feels the same. They have adjusted to the British culture. His brother-in-law is a successful businessman who now has a business in Lincoln.

There was no mosque. People had to do their payers (Namaz/Salah) at home. He is a very good Muslim and always does his prayer (Namaz & Fasting). He likes to help poor people including his relatives. He is maintaining relationships with those relatives who are residing in Bangladesh.

He said, "I had a business partner known as Suruzzaman Chowdhury, he was a very simple person, and he used to forget things very quickly". He said, "There are many incidents where he was surprised and shocked to learn these stories". His partner used to send the laundry to the wrong address, and he used to play Littlewoods. On one occasion his partner sent a bill instead of a postal order. He received a reply from them saying "Mr. Chowdhury, what have you sent to us". His partner used to stay with him in the same room and his partner used to sing songs at night.

8.38.6 Independence of Bangladesh:

In Feb 1971, he went to Bangladesh. The war had begun on 25th March, and he returned to the UK on 26th September 1971. Whilst he was living in Bangladesh, he had seen many untold stories. At the time of the war, he was living at his village home in Bangladesh.

The village was very good, especially the people. There were no opponents of Bangladesh's independence; most of the people were involved in the war as freedom fighters. When he came back to the UK, he took part in a demonstration in London to support the independence of Bangladesh.

8.38.7 Conclusion:

In his conclusion, he said, "British Bangladeshis are doing better than before". The condition of living has been changed. His children like Bangladesh and frequently go there to see the country and people. The new generation of Bangladeshi people should take more responsibility to contribute towards the development of the Bangladeshi community.

He is spending his spare time with his family and children and is enjoying his retirement life in the UK. He would like to help the poor people in Bangladesh and like to spend some time there.

8.39 Alhaj Abdul Rouf Chowdhury
(Interviewed on 27 March 2008)

8.39.1 Life in Bangladesh:

Alhaj Abdul Rouf Chowdhury was born in the village of Gabdev, Nobigonj, district Hobigonj. His father's name was Mohammed Chand Miah. Their family was well maintained from the agricultural property's income. At that time their family tradition was that none of the Chowdhury family members would carry out any agricultural work. Workers would be used to do agricultural work. The pond found near their house would be ideal for fishing. At that time the cost of products wasn't very expensive. 37.5kg of rice would cost around six to seven taka.

Mr Chowdhury was only able to pass his primary school education and was not able to pursue any further. At that time students used to learn most of the things at School. There was no need for any Teachers at home to teach the students. At that time the Transport system was not that good, they had to walk on foot. Most of the School Teachers were Hindu. The Teachers were very good and polite. At that time there were not many Teachers at School. He was the only child of his mother and father. He doesn't have any brothers or sisters.

8.39.2 Immigration:

He had an interest in coming to the UK from the local Post Office. He found out that if you fill out a Postman or Postmaster voucher form and send it to the UK. He didn't believe that but still, he bought a form for 10 paisa from the Post Office. The Postmaster filled out his form and he sent it to the UK. Within 3 Months he got the Voucher which meant he could come to the UK.

Before that, they sent him another letter saying that they had accepted his application and within a few days they were going to send him a Voucher. After he received his letter, he made his Passport from the Sylhet Passport office. In 1963 he came to the UK. Including his ticket, it cost him 9 hundred Taka.

He had to sell his father's and father-in-law's paddy fields to pay for his ticket. His father, father-in-law and Uncle came to the Airport with him to say goodbye. His family was very upset to say goodbye to him. When he was on the Plane, he was very scared.

His cousin's brother received him from Heathrow Airport and took him to the restaurant. His cousin's brother worked in London in a restaurant and its name was (Golden Curry). Then he came to the Manchester Victoria station by train and his uncle (Firoz Chowdhury) came to receive him.

8.39.3 Employment:

He was taken to the restaurant where his uncle (Majid Chowdhury) was working. He stayed there with his uncle. He found another job in a restaurant called (Kohinoor), he used to work there as a Kitchen Staff. Then he had to get training quickly to become a chef because the Main Chef had to go to

Bangladesh. Then he used to work there as a chef and weekly he used to get paid 12 pounds.

As a Kitchen staff, he used to get 7 pounds per week. Free food but he had to stay in another house where 20-25 Bangladeshi people stayed together but no one had to cook in the house because they ate rice in a restaurant, they only slept in that house. On the day he was off he used to have only bread. He worked there for 6 months.

Then he found another job in Blackburn as a chef. He burnt his left arm in that restaurant. He stayed in the hospital for 6 months; they told him to go back to Bangladesh. The government gave him 900 pounds then he went to Bangladesh. He stayed in Bangladesh for 6 months and then he came back to the UK.

At that time, he didn't get permission to work in the UK, but he used to get sick note pay. After 3 years he started to work again. He went back to Bangladesh and then came back; he got permission from the doctor and started to work again. In Nottingham, he started to work in the (Kohinoor) restaurant as a chef.

After that, he went to Sheffield and worked in a restaurant as a chef. He burnt his arm again in this restaurant. He went back to Bangladesh again. He came back to the UK and started to work in the (Kohinoor) restaurant in Manchester as a chef. In the UK he worked for quite a few restaurants as a chef. His starting wages were 7 pounds per week and then he used to get 80 pounds per week and after that, he retired from work.

8.39.4   Housing:

From the council, he got a 4-bedroom house, and then after a few months, he bought his own house. Now he is living in this house. The council gave him a discount when he bought this house. At that time people didn't have radiators at home but there was hot water. They used to have coal to warm the house. They used to have a few blankets to warm themselves because of the cold. That time the weather was too cold, cloudy, and foggy.

8.39.5   Social & Family:

In 1951 he got married. He came to the UK after he had gotten married. He got married in his local area. In 1988 his wife came to the UK. At that time, he had 4 sons and 3 daughters. He couldn't get his daughters to come to the UK because their age was over, but he managed to bring his sons to the UK. His daughters got married in Bangladesh.

His younger 2 sons used to go to school, but his eldest son's age was 17 and 18 so they started to work. Due to the English Language, he didn't know how to get to his house. He used to write his address and keep it in his possessions. If he couldn't find the address, then he showed his address to someone then they told him.

He used to travel by bus or train, so he used to show the address at the counter. If he wants to buy something from the shop, then the people used to help him. He went to Bangladesh, and he got married again because of his first wife's medical issues. His first wife permitted him that he can marry again.

His first wife died in 1998 because of her illness. In 1994 he got married again and has another 2 sons from his second wife. His 2 sons got a visa to come to the UK. His second wife was in Bangladesh because he wasn't working at that time. So, he didn't have permission to bring his wife to Britain.

Every year he tries to go to Bangladesh once or twice. In Bangladesh, he has an old house, and his son bought houses in Sylhet. At that time there was a Pakistani shop to buy Halal food. There were not many shops compared to this time but there was cash and carry. When he first came to the UK more like English women would usually help, English men rarely did.

On his days off used to stay at home and he used to play cards with his friends. Sometimes he used to go to his uncle's house in Oldham. At that time in Oldham, they used to have a toilet and bathroom outside of their house.

8.39.6 Conclusion:

He thinks his life is well established because he came to the U.K. If he had been in Bangladesh, he would have had to face many problems. His sons are religious and they're living happily with their families. His eldest two sons got married and they're living happily. They have their own houses and are living with their wives and children, and he is proud of them.

Now he is retired and in his free time, he goes to his son's house and has fun with his grandchildren. Also, he prays five times a day. He goes to Bangladesh every year because of his wife in Bangladesh. He encourages his sons to help poor people in Bangladesh and, he would like to help poor people in Bangladesh.

He shares lots of experiences about his life in the UK. He also said the young generation should study and follow their religion. From his life story, we can get a good experience and, we can know about Bangladesh and Britain's past life.

8.40 Alhaj Amir Ali
(Interviewed on 20 July 2009)

8.40.1 Life in Bangladesh:

Alhaj Amir Ali was born in 1925 in the village of Ghabdesh, Nabigonj, Habigonj. His father's name is the late Iman Ali. His father was the only son in his family, and due to this, he inherited his parent's property. His father was maintaining his family, he had huge cultivation lands. His father used to do cultivation and generated a good income. On one occasion, he got involved with a legal battle and he had to sell 7-8 acres of his land to bear the cost of legal expenses. He has five brothers, amongst them, he is the third born.

He studied at "Muraura Primary School". He finished his primary education and took the responsibility to maintain his family because his elder brother used to work in the Police and his second brother used to work in the board ship and later settled in America.

8.40.2 Immigration:

In 1962, at the age of 37, he came to Britain with a labour voucher, during this time his two brothers were in the UK. His main intention was to look for employment in the UK. He was maintaining a good family life in Bangladesh; he had to leave his wife, one son, four daughters, and many other close relatives. After he arrived in Great Britain, his eldest son died. He could not attend his funeral; he is still deeply distressed by this.

He described his village life; he said the environment was good as his village was surrounded by small hills, and the price for goods was very cheap also. There wasn't enough money in people's hands, but they were happy. During the 1960s 40 kilos, paddy was 7 – 15 Rupees. The behaviour of people was good too, now fewer people are living in the village, due to the fact that many of them have gone abroad.

A minority of people are living in the village. If he ever goes to Bangladesh for visits, he used to go out but did not see many people in the village. He said that most of the villagers have gone to the Middle East, America, and come to Britain. He said there are about 70-80 families from his village that came to Britain.

There was some delay in obtaining the Employment Voucher, and due to this, he had to face some problems at Heathrow Airport. His brother was supposed to pick him up from Heathrow airport and because there was a flight delay in departing from Dhaka, Bangladesh, He could not communicate with his brother and inform him about the time and date.

When he came out from Manchester Airport, he was not able to speak English and was not able to ask, "How can I go to Manchester". He met a woman and shown his Manchester address, the lady then asked him whether he had any money in his pocket. He showed her that he had a £5.00 note, and the lady then told him to take a seat in the waiting area.

She arranged a flight to Manchester and duly he arrived at Manchester Airport. In the Manchester airport, he met with a Pakistani lady, that woman was in the airport to pick up her husband. The Pakistani lady took him to her house and from there she phoned his relatives living in Manchester.

8.40.3   Life in the UK:

The weather conditions were cold, more specifically he said that from 1962 to 1965 the weather was bad. It was hard when he found out that the water line became blocked due to the cold weather. The road surface was covered with snow and ice, it was very difficult to walk in this condition, he said.

One day when he was going to work, there was an incident in which he slipped and fell down a hill and he could not control himself for a quarter of a mile. He was slightly injured from this incident. He said the injury could have been a lot more serious and he could have died.

He used to take his prepared meals from home and used to go to the canteen to warm it up, he also said that a responsible person can earn a name and fame and success in his/her life. He worked with responsibilities; therefore, he earned the respect of the factories he worked with.

He travelled many times to Bangladesh, and every time in his return to the UK; he made inquiries about whether they had any vacancies. He was able to find employment with a sort of waiting. Some lady officials used to make jokes and say, "You came back so soon, you could have stayed there longer". The management was very friendly he added.

There was also a provision that with permission from the management they used to allow people to do their prayers. During that time, the machines were run by some other colleagues and that was arranged by the management. On one occasion, he was fasting, and the manager saw that he was not drinking any water or wasn't taking a lunch break.

His manager was pleased and granted two weeks of paid leave during Eid. The other colleagues heard this news and went to the manager and asked for the same thing. The manager replied to them that they did not do fasting, so they were not entitled to any leave. You can't make any comparison with Amir Ali, his manager added. You will see that in the religion the respect is there, he said.

8.40.4   Employment:

He started his first employment at the "Sun Paper Mill" in Blackburn. He worked there for about four years, then he moved to Oldham, and he worked at "Manjil Restaurant" for six months. He and his brother got involved with a restaurant business and ran it for about a year, and then he found a job in the paper mill.

The manager of this paper mill told him that there had been no black workers for the last 200 years and Amir is the first Bangladeshi who has been employed there. He also told him that Pakistani people work hard and long hours. The wages were good, £60.00 per week including overtime. The wages in the restaurant were only £7.50 per week. In this paper mill, he worked there for about four years.

In 1966, he went to Bangladesh and stayed there for seven months. He returned to the UK and saw the job demand and volume of work have reduced. He joined with his employment, and he used to receive £260.00 per week.

He worked in a cotton mill in Ashton-under-Lyne for two years and then went back to Bangladesh. He worked as a learner at the spinning section for two weeks then he was allowed to work with them. His wages were £80.00 per week without overtime. He utilised the opportunity given to work as a spinner, and he became an experienced spinner. The management was pleased to see his achievement and performance.

He went to Bangladesh again, then soon returned and joined another cotton factory in Ashton-under-Lyne. His wages were £80.00 per week without any overtime. He worked there for about two years and then went back to Bangladesh. In his return to the UK, he enquired about the same mill, and he rejoined with them. In the last job, he had the position of foreman due to his long-standing experiences.

In 1980, when was 60 years of age, he decided to take retirement from his long employment life in the UK. Whilst he was working in the restaurant, there were two shifts, the morning and the evening shifts. He used to have his breakfast, go to work and have his lunch at the restaurant. He had some rest in the afternoon before going to work in the evening. In the evening, he used to take his evening meals at the restaurant.

The employer was responsible for providing staff with free meals. Therefore, during this time, he did not have to prepare any meals in his house, but when he was working at the factories, he used to prepare his meals, until his wife came to Britain in 1979.

There was a language barrier while he was working in the factories, but the foremen were very helpful and very supportive too. He was able to understand the body language when someone was giving him work. Often there were many people, who used to come forward with help. They used to hold our hands to show us how to do the work.

He shared his first job experience at a paper mill in Blackburn. He said after completing his first two weeks, his supervisor (foreman) recommended he get full-time employment. So, he was able to get a permanent position. During his long employment with the factories, he said "Only older people used to come forward to help us". He also mentioned that British people usually didn't help in the factories (especially if they were younger), so it was quite difficult to do the job and live in the UK.

This manager later allocated an area with yellow ribbons; to do prayers and he had given the key to that room. His manager also told him that he could not do the prayer anywhere in the factory, as you used to do. Now you must use a clean place for prayer, his manager added.

He said his manager understood that for the prayer we needed a clean place. He said he earns this respect by showing responsibility and working hard, otherwise, it was not possible to get any respect from them. He said, if there were opportunities available, he could have continuously worked in the factory for the rest of his life.

8.40.5 Housing:

When he first arrived in the UK in 1962, the housing conditions were very poor; the toilet was outside, and there was no central heating system or any bathroom inside the house. So he used to go to the public bath once or twice a week. The charge was two and a half shillings. Usually, on Saturdays and Sundays, there was no work, so he used to do the bath every Saturday and do other necessary work on Sundays.

They used coal fires to make the rooms warmer and to make hot water people used to use kettles. There was accommodation with the restaurant, but he never lived there, he usually used to live in shared accommodation in rented houses. One of the foremen used to pick up and drop him off from his home and he used to pay him £1.00 per week for fuel expenses.

So it was very helpful and he did not have to travel by bus. The foreman was an African national and was very friendly too. In 1980 he bought a two-bedroom house from an auction and paid £60,000.00 for this. In 1984 the house was demolished by the local authorities.

During 1984 – 1986 he was living in Bangladesh. In 1986, he moved to Manchester. He had this house from the co-operative Housing Association. The local authority is paying the rent, and his children have their own home, but he is prepared to stay on his own. When he retired from employment, he became a British citizen along with his other four sons. He paid the Home Office a fee of £50.00 for registering as a British Citizen. His wife did not become British but she intends to do so.

8.40.6 Social & Family:

He married in 1948, then he came to Britain in 1962, but he did not bring his wife and children until 1979. He is a father of 5 sons and 4 daughters. Two of the daughters got married in Bangladesh. The rest of his children came to Britain with his wife.

When he arrived in the UK, he stayed with his brother. In the same house, two more people from the same village used to live with them. One of them was Firuj Miah and the other one was Noor Miah. He can't forget this; this is always in his memory and reflects on its own.

All his children are living in the UK. Five sons are involved with the catering business, and they have created about 100 vacancies. His children did not get any other opportunities, and they have chosen to do these businesses. All his children are now established, businessmen. Two sons got married in the UK, three sons got married in Bangladesh. He has 14 grandchildren, and he said: "I am very happy".

He had no intention of staying in the UK; his main primary objective was to work and save some money and return to his home country, but due to time and the changing of conditions he considered bringing his family. Since he brought his family to the UK, his family members (including children) don't want to go back, as they think; they have been brought up here and wish to settle in the UK. His wife at first didn't like the idea of moving to the UK but now seeing how her children have grown up she is very happy with the decision.

His sons made the wealth in the UK, and they are also investing money in Bangladesh. They have built up a shopping complex known as "Amir & Sons Shopping Complex". It has created an opportunity for local businesses i.e. general stores, banks, and community centres also with a children's play area. He went to Makkah with his wife to do the Hajj (pilgrimage).

8.40.7 Independence of Bangladesh:

He went to Bangladesh on 25th March 1971 and the war had begun on the next day. After the liberation war, he obtained a Bangladeshi Passport and returned to the UK. During the liberation war, he often had to hide near the hills to save their life. His brother was a local chairman, so their house was on target by the Pakistani Military. Their house was raided a few times by the Army, so he feels that they are lucky to be alive. His wife was pregnant during the war, so it was very difficult for her to move from one place to another.

8.40.8 Conclusion:

He has been living in Manchester for the last 30 years. Where he lives now is very close to his son's businesses, which was the main reason for him considering living in Manchester. He is the main person to establish the "Shahporan Mosque" in Manchester. Abdul Mannan also helped him set up this Mosque. At the Friday prayer in the mosque, there are about 600 - 700 people who turn up every week.

There is demand from the local community to extend the Mosque, due to the large population which had increased in that area. There is an extension plan under consideration by the committee and it is hoping to start the work very soon. Many of his colleagues and friends are not alive. At this stage, he is happy to live near the Mosque and he can go five times a day.

Finally, he said, I am serving the local community as a volunteer at the Mosque. He also said he goes to Bangladesh with his close relatives and friends. Due to his old age, he has many medical issues; therefore, he is unable to travel to Bangladesh at least for two years.

8.41 Alhaj Mokbul Ali
(Interviewed on)

8.41.1 Life in Bangladesh:

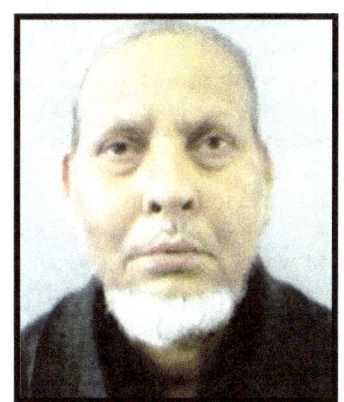

Mr. Haji Mokbul Ali was born in 1937 in the Singerwali village of Bishwanath. His late father's name is Mr. Haji Nasib Ali and his Late Mother Haji Apjan Bibi. Mr. Haji Mokbul Ali had 5 brothers and sisters, and he was the third of them.

His father was a businessman, and he owned a Cloth Store and a Grocery shop in his local Village Market. The business used to run smoothly as well. At that time people used to follow their belief in culture and were quite wealthy in that village. Any issues with the village were dealt with by meeting in the village's cultural meeting place. At present people do not follow these cultures as the tradition fades away with time and hence stays curved in history.

Mr Haji Mokbul Ali completed his primary school in a local village and continued secondary education till the 8th grade. After that, he spent the rest of his time helping his father with his farming in the village until he came to the UK.

8.41.2 Immigration:

His cousin Mr Montaj Ali was living in the UK and invited Mr Haji Mokbul Ali to come to the UK. Mr. Haji Mokbul Ali's younger brother Mr. Mortoj Ali and his Uncle Sowab Ali came to the UK before he did in 1969.

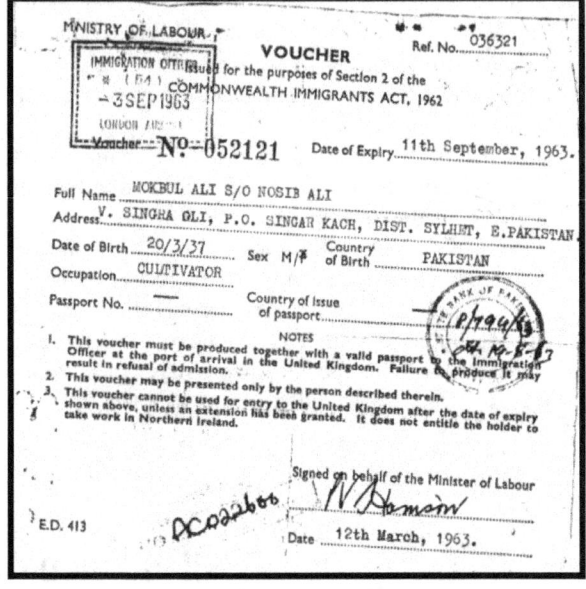

One of Mr Haji Mokbul Ali's friends was the first to know that British High Commission in Dhaka was offering Boucher's. After knowing this, Mr Haji Mokbul Ali contacted Mr Moboshir Khan from another village close to his, and Mr Moboshir Khan helped him in filling the form in the Boucher. After receiving the Boucher from the BHC, Dhaka, he prepared his passport through a travel agency in Sylhet.

He then submitted his Boucher and passport to BHC, Dhaka and after a few days he was invited for an interview, and he went to the interview with Mr. Mubarak Ali in Dhaka. He was very amused when he got the Visa. He made his ticket from the same travel agency with 160000 rupees and travelled from Sylhet to Dhaka to Karachi and Finally to Heathrow Airport.

When all the preparation for coming to Britain was done, his parents were a bit worried about him. Even though he was happy about coming to the UK, he was also feeling very sad leaving his relatives and friends behind. He also mentioned that he would sometimes shed tears when the thought of leaving his Family came across his mind.

He started worrying about his parents as soon as he got on the plane, and he became frustrated again. He was feeling very sad about the fact that he was leaving his Birthplace and all his family and friends and was setting off to an unknown country with a different environment than his own country.

His younger brother Mortuj Ali was waiting for him at Heathrow Airport. He hugged his brother as soon as he met him at the airport. He went straight to his brother's place from Heathrow airport. There were already about 7/8 people living at that home when he went to stay at his brother's place. The price for staying was 15 shillings per double bed and 10 shillings per single bed and everybody used to have lunch at dinner together. At that time there was no Bengali or Pakistani Grocery Shop in Oldham. The foods such as rice, pulses, cooking oil, vegetables, meat, etc were used to arrive through delivery. They used to shop once a week. Occasionally they used to buy chicken from the farm, and they also used to buy deer meat and salmon from English Grocery Shops.

There didn't use to be central heating in their home and the toilet was located outside the house and they used to feel very uncomfortable going to the toilet during the night. The house was heated up using charcoals. There wasn't any system for hot water, so they had to use the kettle to heat the water for their use. They used to go to a public bath and the price was 2 shillings per person. There was usually a long queue and at times they would have to wait hours in the queue. There wasn't any mosque at that time in the area. The first mosque in Oldham was built at 10 Churchill Street, Glodwick, in Oldham.

8.41.3 Employment:

After coming to the UK, he started looking for a job. Failing to find a job after searching for 4-5 months, he started claiming job seeker allowance. He used to get £2.50 every week. His first job in the UK was in LiliMil Factory He used to work 42 hours a week and was paid 11 pounds per week for his job. His job started from 6 am till 2 pm and in some weeks his job was from 2 pm till 10 pm. He worked there for about 7-8 years.

He then started working at Dee Mill Ltd. His weekly wage was 60 pounds. He worked there for about five years. He then started working at an Ash spinning mill. His wages were 100 pounds per week. He worked there for about 3 years. He then worked at Kent Mill in Oldham and his weekly wages there were 120/130 pounds, and he worked there for another 5 years. He then started working in Manor Mill in Oldham. He worked there for 5/6 years as well, and his wages were 160/170 pounds per week.

The factory was closed in 1991 and all the workers in that factory received 600 pounds for losing their jobs. While working in the factory he was often attacked by thugs of white origin. So, they had to stay in groups to avoid being a victim of them.

While working in a factory, he used to have lunch in the canteen and during the night shift he used to bring packed lunch from home. He used to use the microwave oven in the canteen to heat the food. He had good relationships with all his colleagues and his colleagues always helped him if he was in any trouble in the factory.

He didn't have any work experience before he started working in a factory. So, he took training for 2 weeks before getting the job. British women in the factory used to help him a lot.

8.41.4 Housing:

In 1966 he started living at 70 Middleton Road in Oldham and he bought the 2-bedroom house for just 70 pounds that time. After 2 years he sold the house for the same price and in 1968 he bought a two-bedroom house with Mr. Abbas Ali at 39 Benson Street in Oldham.

After one and half years he sold his partnership of the house to Abbas Ali in 1970 and bought a 2-bedroom house in 13 Tin Street in Oldham for 325 pounds. In 1971 he bought a 2-bedroom house for about 500 pounds at 225 Middleton Road, Oldham. In 1978 the house was demolished so he bought a two-bedroom house at 39 Marmaduke Street and stayed there for about 18 years and then that house was also demolished by the council. He bought a four-bedroom house at 16 Martha Street and he's living there at present.

8.41.5 Family and Social Life:

In 1968 the first Social Centre was opened in Oldham called the 'Pakistan Welfare Association' and its director was Mr. Mofojjul Husain and Manchester's Mr. Abdul Motin. He started working in the foundation ever since it was founded. When the battle with India-Pakistan Started in 1966, he provided some financial help for Pakistan and He always used to attend social meetings in time. After Bangladesh won the war in 1971, an organisation called Aomiligue was founded in Oldham, and he was the main founder of the organisation.

Oldham Bangladesh Association was founded in 1971 June. He participated in several activities in this organisation. Besides that, he provided a lot of financial support for the development of the Central Mosque in Oldham, and he was a respected Social Worker in Oldham.

He got married in 1968 and he brought his wife to the UK in 1968. He has 2 sons and 1 daughter. Among his 6 brothers and 2 sisters, 3 brothers and 2 sisters have passed away. His other brother is dwelling in America. He has lots of close relatives in Bangladesh. He visits Bangladesh to meet his relatives every 1 or 2 years and he also helps them by providing financial support.

His wife performed a hajj in 1994 and he performed another Hajj on behalf of his brother in 1996. He went to see his brother Nur Alahi and his family in 2001 in America. His brother Nur Alahi was a freedom fighter who fought during the war in Bangladesh.

In 2002 he started to receive a pension. His elder son Joynal Abedin gained a higher education in Accountancy and then founded the Indigo Restaurant. His second son Jahangir Alam started working at his brother's restaurant after finishing college. His daughter completed college and is currently looking after her father and mother.

8.41.6 Independence of Bangladesh:

While reminiscing about Bangladesh's independence, he remembered in 1971 when Sheikh Mujibur Rahman made his huge Conference in the Field of Red course he was listening to the radio at a coffee bar in Marker Street, Oldham. After hearing the news, his close friend Kacha Miah said that a scary time was drawing near, and Bangladesh had little chance of winning.

In 1971 on 25 March when the Pakistani Army attacked Bangladesh, War was declared on 26th March and His friend made a speech about the war in the Awomiligue organisation in Oldham, and through the organisation, he helped to gather funds for the Bangladesh war and provided financial support even though he couldn't participate in the war as a freedom fighter and due to his commitment in the support for the war, he self-claimed himself a Foreign Freedom fighter.

8.41.7 Conclusion:

Finally, Mr Haji Mokbul Ali says that coming to the UK has given his children the opportunity to gain an education. He was a successful man and spent 30-32 years working. When visiting Bangladesh, he was also involved in his father's business. Bangladeshi people are following the cultural system maintaining education and making a commitment to society. He stayed busy making a commitment to society Helping the Community and Hoping that our future generation will be successful in education and life.

8.42 Mohammed Kacha Miah

8.42.1 Life in Bangladesh:

Muhammad Kacha Miah, son of late Siddek Ali was born on the 1st of January in 1938 in the village of Chonawagaon, Bishwanath, Sylhet. He has 5 sisters and 1 brother. His mother's name is Musammeth Afthra Bibi, and she is still alive and can read the Quran without using glasses.

His father was a farmer and used to work on his land. His father studied up to 4th grade in the British era. He was able to read and write letters very well and he was also able to understand and interpret official documents of landowners. He often used to help interpret and understand non-literate people with their official landowning documents.

His father was always interested in education, and he always respected education and used to teach his son Muhammad Kacha Miah to read and write and how to do maths. He also used to bring storybooks for his son to read. His father was his best teacher. There wasn't any school in his village at that time. Therefore, his father admitted him to a primary school in their neighbouring village Battapara.

Another child from his village was also admitted to the school at the same time. The teacher in that school was Mr. Shrigobindo Proshonno. He was a greatly respected gentleman. While admitting he smiled at Mr. Muhammed Kacha Miah and said that he was also the teacher of his father, and he was happy to have Muhammad Kacha Miah as his teacher.

It was quite troublesome for Muhammad Kacha Miah to travel to school. He used to go to school with his friend from the village who was admitted with him at the same time. They had to cross a river over a very small and weak bridge made of bamboo and were often scared as neither he nor his friend knew how to swim. The regular pedestrians were good and often used to look after them so they could cross the bridge carefully. They studied in that school for one year.

In 1965, a voluntary primary school was built in their village in the northland of Makunda River. There were about 20-30 students in that school. All the student's parents had to pay 50 Paisa fees for each child going to the school. The money was paid to the teacher. Later the school became a government school. In 1958 he passed his primary education from that school. That time he started to learn how to write landowning official documents from Mr. Singerwali's relative Mr. Moulana Sikandhar Ali. After learning he used to work part-time on filing official documents and he was able to earn his own money needed for fees at school.

In 1969, he was admitted to class 6 in "Eklimia Junior High School". At that time the only high school in the Bishwanath district was "Ramshundhor High School". Luckily a current Politician Anam Shafiqul was a classmate in his High School, and they used to study together in High School. With his motivation, he became involved with the Awami League. He passed class 8 in 1961, and he was then admitted to class 9 in "Moinpur High School".

8.42.2   Journey to the UK & Immigration:

In 1963 during the school holidays, he went back to his village and the next day afternoon he went to visit the Singerkach Market and the post office. While visiting the post office he met a respected elder of the Village and said hello to him. The elder recognised him and was happy to see him and asked him when he came back to the village. They started talking and the elder asked him- "Nephew, a lot of people are going to England through the voucher, have you applied for a voucher? If you didn't, then you should apply as soon as possible. This could turn your fortune."

He then started thinking about it and he became very frustrated. His Metric exam was drawing near, and he also didn't want to miss the opportunity to come to England. He became confused and was having a hard time making the right decision. He then finally concluded and decided that he would go to England. In the evening, he went to see his cousin Rojob Ali. He was surprised to see Kacha Miah.

They started talking and Kacha Miah asked his cousin if he had heard that his cousin had formed for the voucher to England. Mr. Rojob Ali said that he did have some forms but there were none left now. There he gave the full address of the British High Commission in Dhaka and instructed him to write a letter to them for a request of application form for the Voucher and the British High Commission in Dhaka would then send a form to his home address within a few days. He had dinner at his cousin's place and returned home at about 9.30 pm. His parents were worried about him being usually late and he then had to explain the situation to them.

The application form for the Voucher was in the English language and he didn't have any trouble filling in the form. He posted the form the next day when he received the form. He kept his receipt from the post office and returned it to his student apartment. Even though he was living in the student apartment, his mind was always at the post office of his village, and he was very impatient for the reply.

Every weekend he went back to the village to enquire at the post office about his reply. After 10-12 days when I visited the Post office, I heard that I had a letter from the British High Commission in Dhaka. The Postmaster knew that Kacha Miah was still at his student apartment which is why he didn't deliver the letter to his home he knew Kacha Miah would come to enquire at the post office and thought it would be best and safe to hand Kacha Miah's own hands. He returned home with the letter completed the form and posted it to the British High Commission, 14/2 Tupkhana Road, Dhaka. That was the address in 1963.

After 5/6 weeks he one day went to the post office. That day about 20-25 other people were also waiting there as well. By the time the postmaster came in it was already evening and he said it was time to close the post office. After looking at the gloomy and depressed faces, the postmaster said that he would make an exception and said he would only say the names of the people whose Boucher had arrived, but he would do the delivery at 10 o'clock the next morning. About 15/16 vouchers arrived that day and he started calling out the names. After calling 5/6 name, Muhammad Kacha Miah's name was called, and Muhammad Kacha Miah became so happy after hearing his name that he couldn't express it in words.

As soon as he arrived home that evening, he informed his father about the news. His father became depressed after hearing this and said to him: "I understand, you won't be able to finish your Metric Exam then." The next day at 10.30 am he received his voucher, and he went straight back home. After a few days, he took the Voucher to Dola Miah, the owner of Masum Travels in Kajirbazar. He went there with all the necessary documents needed for the preparation of the passport and asked Mr Dhola Miah to prepare the passport. Within 4/5 weeks the passport was prepared.

A visa application was made at Dhaka High Commission and a date was given for interview. He had given his interview on the date, but his passport had a different date of birth than his date of birth in his application, so he had to fix the error in his passport and had to give an interview again and he also had to bring relevant documents such as school certificates to prove his date of birth.

He came back with his visa being issued and he gave this news to his father first. At that time the price of the Dhaka-London ticket was 1600 rupees. People had a hard time trying to earn their tickets.

So, in the end, a gentleman offered that he would lend him 1600 rupees, but his father would have to pay that within 3 months, and they would have to pay some interest too. His father agreed to this. He then handed the money to the travel agency and made his ticket from there.

His father always used to farm on his land, though he never asked his son to help him with his farming. His father didn't want his son to get distracted from his studies and therefore always thought of the best possible way to provide him an environment where he can study well.

He sometimes used to bunk school and go fishing with other boys. His father didn't like that. He was the youngest in the family therefore everyone in the family wanted him to concentrate on his studies.

On 23 December 1963, he came to the UK. He travelled from Dhaka to Karachi to Rome then to London. He left Bangladesh on 22nd December at 8 am after taking farewell from all his relatives. His father and his uncles as well as his teacher accompanied him to the train station. It was sorrowful for him to leave his family and friends behind in Bangladesh. We had to walk 5 miles from home to the rail station. After waiting for about 20-30 minutes, the village train that goes to Sylhet arrived and we departed on that train.

After arriving at Sylhet, he took his ticket and other relevant documents from Masum's Travels and bought the train ticket from Sylhet to Dhaka. His father, elder brother, and three teachers wanted to go with him to bid farewell, therefore he bought 6 tickets. The price of each ticket was 7 rupees at that time. The train departed at 7 p.m. and arrived at Dhaka at 6-30am. They rested at a hotel, and he met one of the people we know from Masum travels. He suggested the others should go home and that he will take him to the airport.

He met another person who was also going new there and they chatted all the way. While they arrived at Heathrow airport they had to wait in a queue for a medical check-up. After the check-ups, they both went outside together and the passenger who was travelling with him was delighted to see his brother. He hugged him and was happy to see his brother.

His brother asked him who was he, therefore he replied that we met together and travelled together. He showed him the address that he was going to go to. He replied that he would take him to that address. Therefore, they got in a taxi and about 40 minutes later they arrived there. The place was Bricklane in London.

They got something to eat and then they travelled to Fulham by subway train. He met his uncle there and was happy to see him. His uncle said to him that his other uncle was coming to London to take him to Oldham. Therefore, the next day his uncle arrived and from Euston Mainline; they took a train to Manchester Piccadilly. From Manchester, they took a bus to Oldham.

He arrived at 70 Middleton Road in Oldham. He started living at his Uncle's Place. About 7-8 people used to live in the 2-bedroom house. In 1964 he first claimed Unemployment benefits from the Local Labour. At that time the benefit per week for a single person was £2.10.

8.42.3 Employment:

He saw in one of the adverts in the newspaper that Dunlop Mill was recruiting people for employment. Therefore, he applied there and got a job. There were people from different backgrounds working in that factory.

In 1965 he started working at Delta Mill in Royton, near Oldham. He worked there till 1980. A first he was an assistant supervisor for the machine operator. Then he started working at Courtaulds Ltd Cedar Mill. He used to work there on the night shift. He started working there in 1986 and in 1991 the mill was shut down. In 2003 he was successful in receiving a state pension.

8.42.4 Housing:

He bought a house in 1986 at Eleanor Street. He is still living there with his family.

8.42.5 Social & Family:

He also volunteered in many community associations such as the "Pakistan Welfare Association". It was established by a union of East Pakistan and West Pakistan people. It was a combination of Bengali and Pakistani people, and it was established by Mr. Mofojul Hussain in Oldham. The first Mosque in Oldham was built with the help of this Pakistan Welfare Society.

In 1971, Oldham Bangladesh Association was established. Since it was established, he worked vigorously with the local community and took active participation. On 22 September 1998, the historical election was held in Oldham. Mr. Khacha Miah was voted as the press publicity secretary. No other historical event in Bangladesh politics happened in Oldham other than this.

In 1969 he got married in Chattok District. He has 5 sons and 2 daughters. His elder daughter got married in 2005. His youngest daughter has completed BA Honours in Management and Business. His eldest son is an electric engineer and a skilled builder. His second son is working in Manchester Santander Bank. The other two sons are still at college continuing with their education. He is living a happy family life.

8.42.6 Independence of Bangladesh:

He has been a supporter of the Awami League since high school. He was also involved in the establishment of 'Oldham Bangladesh Youth League'. Mr. Mokbul Ali and Mr. Assoddor Ali also joined after he invited them. In 1971 during September, he handed the cheque to Mr. Abu Syeed Chowdury at London Bangladesh House. That day Mr. Khacha Miah went there with three other people to hand in the cheque.

8.42.7 Conclusion:

Kacha Miah said, "we have to work together in the future to develop a better environment for our next generation so that they can all the facilities for better education".

8.43 Abu Taher Md Mohiuddin Chowdhury MBE, JP, B.Com
(Interviewed on 17 November 2007)

8.43.1 Life in Bangladesh:

Abu Taher Mohammed Mohiuddin Chowdhury was born in 1942 in the village of Ghopal in Feni, Bangladesh. He comes from a landlord (Jomindar) family. They have had sufficient wealth/income to maintain their family comfortably.

Abu is number 2 of 5 brothers and studied up to class 3 from a village Primary school. He then moved to Karaiya High School under the supervision of his uncle and passed Matriculation (SSC), thereafter completed "Higher Secondary Certificate" (HSC) from "Feni College" and Bachelor of Commerce Degree from "Chittagong Commerce College".

He used to like playing outdoor games and was elected Sports Secretary twice in his student days. He went to India several times to play football against Indian teams and found Indians very hospitable/friendly.

8.43.2   Journey to the UK:

He had early ambitions to go to England for higher studies like his cousin and nephew. Luckily for him, just at the time, his cousin returned from Britain after the completion of his Engineering Degree. He guided Abu, to an easy route to enter Britain through the "Chittagong Agrabad Employment Office" and completed the necessary forms to come to England. Within a few days Abu, received a priority Employment Voucher in Feb' 1964 to go to Britain.

Unfortunately, he lost the Employment Voucher and had to obtain a duplicate from the Dhaka British High Commission with the help of their HO in Karachi. At the start of his journey to Britain, he met an older person from Comilla, who was returning to Britain, who helped him a lot on his arrival in Birmingham.

8.43.3   Early Life in the UK

In 1964, most of the Bengali settlers were ex-seamen, either working in a factory or self-employed. Although there were a small number of educated professionals and semi-professionals, they were not visible within the community. At the time, he found Bengalis very supportive of one another. Abu used to help them in many ways including reading/writing letters/filling official forms. These voluntary supports were immediately known in the community, and he became very popular and had regular visitors on their days off from work. They used to address him as "Master Sahib" to show their mark of respect.

8.43.4 Employment & Achievements:

With the help of another Bengali named Yusuf, he secured a job in the hospital. They called him for an interview. In the interview, Hospital Chief Administrator asked him to read a paragraph from his Daily Times and after hearing him read, he was offered a job to manage a hospital store for a weekly wage were 12 pounds and 10 shillings. After a few months, Abu left the Hospital job to join an insurance company and began to study insurance at "Birmingham College of Commerce".

After the start of the war with India in 1965, Abu left an insurance job and join United Bank Ltd. After 6 months Abu was promoted to the rank of a manager of the Manchester branch and opened other offices in the Gtr. Manchester. He worked for the Bank up to Dec'71 and resigned on 11.12.1971, just a week before the Liberation of Bangladesh from Pakistan army occupation. After doing a few short-term jobs, he joined as Manager to set up Janata Bank Birmingham/Bradford, thereafter he resigned to go to Bangladesh for a long break.

On his return in 1973, he was looking for a new career and has received an offer to join DHSS/DWP towards the end of 1974 and joined Jan'75. In 1984 Abu was selected to become an Active Magistrate on the Manchester bench. While working as an Executive in DWP in 2001, Abu was honored by the Queen with an MBE. Abu was the first Bangladeshi elected Councillor to serve Manchester City Council in 2004-11.

In 2005 he was selected as an Adviser to the Gtr. Manchester Police Authority (Race) and served them for 5 years including about 2 years as chair. In 2006, he decided to retire early from his full-time job with the DWP to devote more time to his elected position as Councillor. Thereafter, in 2008 he was the first Bangladeshi to be elected as Governor of all Central Manchester Hospitals (CMFT) and currently serving his second term till 2013.

8.43.5 Family:

He got married in 1963. His wife joined him in 1967 and is a father of four children and Grandfather to Five. His Children are well educated in Britain are in professional jobs. Abu is happy and proud about its achievements in education and careers.

During his life in Britain, he tried to be involved with many local leaders of the community both in Birmingham and in Manchester. Notably Mr. Motin, Mr. N Uddin, Mr. M Rahman, Mr. Kabir Ahmed, and many others Bengali Community leaders in Gtr Manchester including many mature university students from Bangladesh.

In 1983, Abu became the Chairman of Gtr. Manchester Bangladesh Association and immediately started looking for a separate building or a permanent home for the association and managed to secure the present building in a few weeks only with a direct grant from the local authority and set up "Bangladesh House" at 19a Birch Lane, Manchester.

This achievement was possible as they had unanimous tacit and open support from all in the community and Councillors from all political parties. It was primarily set up to coordinate all social, welfare, educational, and training needs of all members of the community, centralised from one place so that it can be used as a resource centre to the wider community and Local Council. He managed to set up foundation work for all men/women/children. After 9years he handed over his position to the newly elected committee to carry on and advance from here in 1991.

8.43.6　Independence of Bangladesh:

When the war had started in Bangladesh in 1971, they did a lot to advance the Bangladesh movement here. He used to attend all meetings and help the movement while remaining in the United Bank. All war activities were centralised in Manzil Restaurant. They used to have meetings initially before the war in the Shalimar restaurant in Manchester. He was in the meeting when they first decided and resolved to be called the "East Pakistan (Bangladesh) Association" (1970). After the Awami League won the Election, Bhutto (West Pakistani leader) refused to hand power to a Bengali in the east and put pressure on the army to start the military operation on the then East Pakistani and the War started in March 1971. We then got rid of the word 'Pakistan' from the name of our organisation and the whole liberation movement remained in Manzil restaurant and coordinated work to include all Bengalis from Greater Manchester.

8.43.7　Conclusion:

Abu said that our new generation Bangladeshis are in a good shape eg, in education, job, profession, sports, business, and training, etc., and hope that with their help and support, it could go forward from strength to strength in the future.

He came to Britain with no practical life skills but managed to maintain his discipline in personal, family, and social life. He always believed in honesty and maintained integrity more than the accumulation of money. Politics was his hobby and has been so since his student days. He is proud and happy about his life here and has always tried to help others and give his knowledge and experience back to the benefit of the people and society at large. Abu is hoping that the future Bangladeshi new generation will give back something to society from their life skills.

Now he is living in Manchester with his family for part of the year and the rest in Bangladesh. He has always maintained a generous helpful manner towards the whole community who come to seek his advice or help in all matters of their concern and still maintains an open-door policy.

8.44 Alhaj Masrurul Hasan Choudhury
(Interviewed on 20 January 2009)

8.44.1   Life in Bangladesh

Alhaj Masrurul Hasan Choudhury was born in 1942 in the village of Parkul, Osmani Nagar, Balagonj, Sylhet. His father was a religious teacher; he was the head 'Maulana' in the 'Hailakandi School' in India. After India and Pakistan had been separated, his father came back to the 'Moulvibazar High School' in East Pakistan (now Bangladesh).

When Hasan was studying in class six, his father moved to 'Sylhet Government High School'. In 1965, he gave his matric exam (S.S.C) from this school, but due to illness, he couldn't achieve good results. He also used to enjoy sports very much when he was young.

Due to him being well educated, he had opportunities of working as an official in the tea garden industries, but his mother didn't want him to work for any relatives. Therefore, he didn't take the job, and he started to look for opportunities for coming to the UK. Right after the independence of Bangladesh, he migrated to the UK. Hasan mentions that the furious and frightening memories of the war still bring him pain and distress.

8.44.2 Journey to the UK & Immigration:

He first came to the UK with a student visa in 1962. Even though all his arrangements for coming to the UK were complete, he still had to wait till he had been given the graduation exam because his father's wish was to see his son as a graduate.

He first landed at Heathrow, and then he travelled to Manchester and from there he took a taxi to one of his relative's places in Salford. The taxi driver demanded six pounds but after his relative bargained with the taxi driver, he was happy with only four pounds. When he left his home, his grandfather gave him 5 pounds as a present.

8.44.3 Early Life in the UK:

Hasan said that the social culture of Britain was good at that time. Everyone was friendly and would always help each other. He said, "Really this country was one of the best in the world". He found the old Britain was much better than present Britain. He also said that when he first came to the UK, he felt lonely and sometimes tears would fall when he would think back on his memories in Bangladesh.

Everyone's lifestyle was good in the past, there were opportunities for employment and people didn't have to struggle for finding a job. He said that he came to know from some senior people who came before him; that there was a job crisis in Britain for a certain time and it was hard to earn money and maintain the household.

8.44.4 Employment:

Since he came to the UK for study, he was admitted to Salford Textile College. He used to go to that college in the morning and the evening; after class, he used to work at a restaurant. At that time after taking the career advice to consider the catering sector, he was able to work in a famous catering in the UK. As time went on, he gained more experience in his profession and later on in 1969, he became a general manager in a 5-star Hotel. He started a partnership business in 1969.

After coming to the UK, he was successfully able to find a job because he knew some Indian restaurants and the owners of the restaurants also knew him. Therefore, he didn't have to struggle to find a job. He kept working in the Indian restaurants for about four or five years, after that he started another business in partnership. The name of the business was 'Bombay Restaurant'.

The business was running well, and they were also making good profits from it but later on, he became a bit physically ill and decided to retire from the business for a few days. Due to this, the business wasn't making any profit. He had no other choice but to withdraw the partnership of the business.

Even though they were making good progress in the business in the beginning, it ended unexpectedly as their partnership in the business broke down. He said, **"When a business was making a good profit, one partner was happy with the other partners but when there was a loss in the business, one partner tries to blame the other partners".**

Some people don't understand the common practice that if you are willing to share happiness in a business, you must also be willing to share the sorrow. He said that lack of patience, experience, and the lack of trust; are facts that might be responsible for the breakdown of partnership in most businesses.

Besides working on Indian food, he also spends a significant amount of time at other various types of catering. This includes- 'Fried Chicken'; 'American Style Restaurant'; 'Spanish Restaurant'. But later, he sells them all.

After his bypass heart surgery and staying in rest for five years, he started the business of an Indian restaurant with permission from his wife in 1989. The business still exists, and it is also famous in the present time. Hasan said that he bought the building for about £70,000 and spent another £75,000 on setting it up.

8.44.5 Housing:

Hasan said that when someone works in an Indian restaurant, their living cost and the expenses of their food were free. Whereas someone has an English job, they had to bear their expenses for the food and accommodation. He also said, "during that time the only thing to do for entertainment was to watch a movie, usually at a cinema hall".

At that time people didn't have the facility to have a bath at home. They had to go to the public bath every week for having a bath or shower. Hasan also said that it used to get cold during the winter. It also snowed heavily during the winter and the council had to clean the snow off the road so that the roads wouldn't be blocked. He also said that in the summer in and around 80's the weather was hot, it can be compared with the summer of India. According to him, today's weather in Britain is different from the past.

8.44.6 Social & Family:

In 1969, he went to Bangladesh to get married. His father and his father-in-law discussed that after marriage Hasan wouldn't come back to the UK. He didn't know about this at first. During the war in 1971, he refused to go back to the village for his safety and stayed back at Sylhet town.

He has four children- two sons, who are both successful businessmen in the UK; and two daughters, who are currently living in Bangladesh. All his children have graduated. His wife was also a teacher in Bangladesh and after coming to the UK she was employed by the Salford City Council. Currently, she's doing an interpreting job.

In 1976 he brought his wife and his daughter to the UK. He was successful in performing Hajj with his mother in 1983. Hasan has reached the pension age; he was very active with his business and other things. He plans to go to Bangladesh and spend some time there. He also has a travel plan to visit some places. His greatest wish is to perform Hajj with his wife. Besides that, he also said that he'll go to Bangladesh for holiday every year as it is his birthplace and as he also has many sweet memories in Bangladesh.

8.44.7 Independence of Bangladesh:

Due to the business commitment, he couldn't find the opportunity to get involved with any community, but he still tried to help in every possible way. After Bangladesh became an independent country, he became involved with the mosques and the 'Greater Manchester Bangladesh Association'. He was selected as the Vice Chairman of the 'Shahjalal Mosque' and became the Chairperson of the 'Greater Manchester Bangladesh Association".

He is trying to do everything that he could do; so that the future generation will be able to practice Islam and leave them an enlightening future.

He said that the respected elders from the past have always thought and worked for the benefit of the community instead of thinking about how they would gain power and argue amongst each other.

8.44.8 Conclusion:

Hasan said, "I might go back to Bangladesh and settle there, this may be the correct thing to do". Because most of our new generation is losing touch with the relatives and their relationship between the relatives are also breaking down. Many properties are left empty in Bangladesh as the owners of those properties have migrated and settled in the UK. He is worried that a time might come when people will lose the Islamic and Bangladeshi Culture. He said that if we don't do something to protect the Bangladeshi and Islamic Culture, they will disappear forever.

Even though he is happy about the fact that he was able to settle in the UK, he is still concerned about the future generation. He is frightened of the fact that they might lose the Bangladeshi and Islamic cultures.

Even though many families follow the Islamic and Bangladeshi cultures, he is still concerned about if our future generation will be able to protect and hold the Islam and Bangladeshi Culture. At last, he wishes that the Islam and Bangladeshi cultures will live within the heart of the Bangladeshi and that they shall be passed on from generation to generation.

8.45 Lion Gulam Mustafa Chowdhury MBE
(Interviewed on 26 September 2010)

8.45.1 Life in Bangladesh:

Lion Gulam Mustafa Choudhury is a prominent community leader living in Manchester. He was born in 1946 in the village of Bodordi, Nabigonj, Habigonj. His father's name is late Alhaj Samsul Alam Choudhury and his mother's name is late Azizun Nessa Choudhury. He has three brothers and one sister; he is the third amongst all his siblings.

He completed his primary education at 'Bodordi Primary School'. He then moved to "Nabigonj JK High School", he studied there up to class eight and then he moved to "Habigonj High School", and there he studied class nine and ten. He then moved to "Moulvibazar Government High School" and he applied for his Secondary School Certificate (SSC) in 1963.

In the past, there was better education. In 1963 it was the first time an SSC exam had been taken after eighteen months; this was due to the adjustment of the examination times in December. The curriculum was more realistic, and Bangla, English, and Maths were the compulsory subjects in the curriculum but later, the English subject became an optional subject.

He said, the standard of education was very good and people who were educated in the 1960s had completed their SSC's, which is equivalent to a degree. Without receiving the results for the SSC exam, he migrated to the UK on 27th November 1963.

His father was involved with agriculture farms and some other businesses. With the income from the businesses, his father was able to maintain his family without any difficulties.

8.45.2 Immigration:

We asked him how he migrated to the UK. In his reply, he said, "my eldest brother "Alhaj Gulam Rabbani Choudhury" arranged the labour voucher, and his grandfather paid all the expenses for their journey to the UK. He did not have any objections before coming to Britain, as his eldest brother came with him, so he relied upon him". He had held his brother's hand and came to Britain. At that time, he was only 18 years old.

He and his eldest brother arrived at the London Heathrow Airport and took a taxi and went to a Good Place in London West. There was a relative from his brother-in-law in-law's family who was living in west London. There were 14 bedrooms, some people used to live there, in the morning some people would sleep, and some used to sleep at night. He and his brother stayed there only a few nights.

8.45.3 Life in the UK:

When first arrived in the UK he has seen the snow and white ladies wearing skirts. The weather was very cold; people used coal to warm up the room. The snow and ice were common weather everywhere.

After that, his brother's uncle-in-law known as "Gulam Mustafa Raja Miah", came from Southend-on-Sea and took them with him. His brother's uncle-in-law took him to Southend-on-Sea and arranged admission for him to learn English. He studied at the college for a year on a part-time basis. He

learned Basic English for communicating with others on a day-to-day basis.

During the period of his employment, he met the renounced community leaders, Tosodduk Ahmed OBE, Gous Khan, Abdul Mannan Sanu Miah, and Minhaj Uddin. He became closer to these people.

In 1965, there was a war between India and Pakistan. The community leaders had taken initiative to raise funds for Pakistan. At that time, Tosodduk Ahmed formed a Pakistan Society (Committee). Tosodduk Ahmed became the chairman, and he became the Treasurer of this Society. He said, "Since then he became actively involved with community work and the politics". He also said he is using his experience and working with many charity organisations to raise funds for them.

8.45.4 Employment:

While he was studying in London, he started his working life from there. He worked as a kitchen porter in a local restaurant, then he worked as a trainee waiter and then was promoted to manager. He was employed until 1973, and then he started a restaurant business in Manchester. When he worked as a kitchen porter, his weekly wages were £4.50. He worked in the Allahabad Restaurant, Tandoor Mahal Restaurant, and Bombay Restaurant.

He started his first partnership business in November 1973, still, now he is involved with this business. During this time the name of the business had been changed many times. The first name was the Momotaz Restaurant, then Curry Queen Restaurant, and finally Showdagor Restaurant. He did not encourage his

sons to get involved with the curry business.

In 1973, he started a Restaurant business with Abdul Matin and Anis Ullah. The business is situated in Gatley, Manchester. They paid £18,000.00 and bought the building. In 1994, he retired from the business due to health problems. Both of his partners have passed away and their children had taken over the management of this restaurant.

He is one of 10, who were able to build a hotel in Dhaka, called "Osmani Hotel International". There was a good background story behind this development. He organised his friends to form a co-operative group and decided to save £10.00 every week and they built the eight stories Hotel building.

In 1982, the retired army General MAG Osmani also known as Bongobir Osmani came to visit the UK. On one occasion, they met with him and discussed

their plan. The retired army general was impressed to hear that story and agreed to assist them in purchasing land in Dhaka. They provided the necessary fund to him.

In 1984, the retired general came to the UK again with the land registry deed and handed it over to them. On that visit, he came for medical treatment, and apparently, he died in the London Hospital in 1985.

In 1985, his partner Abdul Matin passed away and he became the managing director of this group. He took the initiative to make further progress to complete the project; therefore, he had to go to Bangladesh to get possession of this land, as the land was occupied illegally by other people. After a long battle with the group of people, he was able to take possession of this land.

In 1987, the building construction had begun, and it was completed in 1990. On 25th March 1990, the opening ceremony of Osmani Hotel took place. The vice president of Bangladesh Barrister Moudud Ahmed was the chief guest to conduct the ceremony. He also said the president was supposed to attend this ceremony but due to his very busy schedule, he had to send the vice president instead. He also said the foundation was laid down by Prime Minister Mizanur Rahman Choudhury in 1987.

He said "Initially we had plans to name the Hotel as Probashi Hotel but due to the involvement of Retired Army General MAG Osmani and his death before the opening of the Hotel, they had changed the name from Probashi to Osmani Hotel International.

He was able to unite 50 people to establish cash and carry in Rusholme, Manchester. The business was known as Bangladesh Cash and Carry. After running the business for about 5 years he had a second heart attack and then he decided to sell the cash and carry.

In 2004, he had a heart bypass surgery and since then he has retired from business activities.

In 1973-2011, 38 years which is a long time, he is successfully running this business. This is the success story in his life. He strongly believes that he had a long-lasting partnership with the Bangladeshi Community.

8.45.5 Social & Family:

In 1971, on 23rd March he got married to Syeda Raushanara Choudhury, but the marriage function did not take place due to the political tension at that time. He had to go to Dhaka on the same day of engagement after receiving a telegram. On 1971, 25th March the war had begun, and he was advised to leave

Dhaka and go to his hometown in Habigonj.

After that, he left Dhaka, and it took a month to go to his hometown. After arriving at his home, he decided to bring his wife. He brought his wife, without having a marriage ceremony.

In 1974, he went to Bangladesh, and he stayed there for about six years. In 1980, he returned to the UK re-engaged himself with the business and became involved with the community work.

In 1967 and 1969, Dr. Amin Uddin came from Sylhet TB Hospital to collect donations and he assisted him personally to raise funds for this hospital.

In 1980, he was engaged with the Shahjalal Mosque in Manchester. In 1982, he became a joint secretary of this mosque's committee. Thereafter, he became the General Secretary, vice chairman, and chairman. In 1998 and 2000, twice he was elected chairman of the mosque committee.

During his chairmanship period, he carried out the major development work (reconstruction) for the Mosque building. About 800,000.00 had been spent on the reconstruction work. There was plenty of work that needed to be done; the current committee is continuously carrying out this development work such as an improvement of the hall room.

In 1985, the Greater Manchester Bangladesh Association was formed; he became a founding member and Treasurer of this Association. There were few other people also involved, such as Abdul Matin, MM Bakth, Kabir Ahmed, Gulam Nurany (Humayun) Choudhury, and other community leaders he added.

In 1985, he had to go through an ulcer operation. At that time, he realised, for a few hours he was lying in a bed like a dead man, if the operation was not successful then his children would become orphans, then what would happen to them? Since then, he decided to do something for the orphans.

As soon as he returned from the hospital, he discussed this matter with his wife, brothers GR Choudhury & GK Choudhury, and other close family members and convinced them to support his will. He then went to Bangladesh to discuss this issue with his six uncles, who were the joint owners of the lands which were inherited from his grandgrandfather (fourth generation) Daim Uddin. His uncles supported his good intentions and registered the land for the orphan's project known as "0Daim Uddin Ethimkhana & Hafizia Madrasha" in Badordi, Nabigonj.

He said altogether, he got 300 decimals of land for the Orphan Project. He decided to do a Shelter house and Madrasa (Islamic Institution) for the orphans. He carried out the building construction and finally, it was opened in March 1989, by Alhaj Samsul Alam Choudhury. He also managed to get 600 decimals of paddy fields for this project. There were so many trees that had been planted so that in the future, these trees could be sold and generate further funds for this project, he added.

He also created a fund from his savings and opened a fixed deposit account, so that for the future the running costs can be met from this fund. At present, his family is contributing every month to meet the running cost of this project. He is also involved with setting up an Islamic Institution known as "Darul Hadis Latifia" in Oldham.

He is the father of two sons and three daughters. All his children have obtained higher degrees from university.

He had his first heart attack in 1996 his doctor advised him to take full rest. Since then, he is not working but continuing to do his voluntary work as a community worker.

His eldest son designed an aircraft; this was approved by the Air Force authority and the Second son went to the highest mountain (Himalayas). These are the achievements of his sons. Many other people have achieved different things, so these are the positive steps forward for the second generation and future generations to follow.

He spends his retirement time with his family and friends. Also, he continuously does his community work throughout the UK and Bangladesh.

He said if he would have never had come to Britain, then he could have completed his degree in Bangladesh, but it was very difficult to get a good job. He came to Britain; he sees this as a positive step towards developing many businesses and getting involved with community work. He had the opportunity to do these kinds of businesses and carried out charity work.

He is also involved with establishing a diabetic hospital in Habigonj. Up to now, they have spent 4, 00, 00,000.00 Taka for the construction of a building and they have been able to build a three-story building. He said "We have a plan to develop this project as a medical college along with a diabetic hospital.

He also said, "There was no electricity in his village, where he established the Shelter House for the orphans; he had taken the initiative to get the electricity supply set up in that area and now all the villagers are getting the benefits". Due to the success of setting up the charity project, many people like local politicians, doctors, lawyers, bankers, engineers, and successful businessman gave their

wholehearted support towards the development and advancement of the charity project.

8.45.6 Independence of Bangladesh:

He admitted that he is involved in Bangladeshi politics. He said, that in 1966 Awamileague declared a six-point demand to the Pakistani ruling party, he supported this demand and since then he has been actively involved with Bangladeshi politics.

He said in 1967 when Sheikh Mujibur Rahman was alleged by a false case by the Pakistani authority, known as (Agortola Conspiracy Case) and Sheikh Mujibur Rahman was arrested.

He said, "I was involved in arranging solicitors and barristers from the UK to deal with this case and Sheikh Mujibur Rahman was released from their custody". When Sheikh Mujibur Rahman was released from custody, he wished to meet with those people, who arranged the legal assistance. As a result, Sheikh Mujibur Rahman came to London to meet with them.

In 1968, when Sheikh Mujibur Rahman came to London, he took a Limousine on behalf of the London Awamileague to bring him from the hotel to a party conference in Exeter. He met with Sheik Mujibur Rahman at the hotel. At that time, he was having his morning tea. He sat there for a few minutes when

Sheikh Mujibur Rahman was waiting for a phone call from Bangladesh.

He asked Sheikh Mujibur Rahman a question to break the ice; the question was "Uncle when you went to jail, do you get the same treatment as the other people did?" Sheikh Mujibur Rahman replied to his question and said to him "I've been to jail so many times, almost all my life, most of the time I was in a different jail, so which one should I tell you".

We asked him, why he called Sheikh Mujibur Rahman's uncle if he related to you. He said no "I used to call Gous Khan and Abdul Mannan (Sanu Miah) my uncle and they were a very close friend of Sheikh Mujibur Rahman, which was the main reason to call them uncle on that day".

In 1969, the London Awamileague donated a 12-seat minibus to Sheikh Mujibur Rahman for the 1970 general election. He had taken the minibus with him when he went to Bangladesh. He endorsed in his passport that he was taking a minibus and went to Bangladesh.

He went to the party office on 52 Nobabpur Road, Dhaka, and met with the party chief Sheikh Mujibur Rahman. Sheikh Mujibur Rahman then requested another senior leader Gulam Sarwar; the organising Secretary to go with him to

Chittagong to release the minibus from the seaport.

On the next day, he went to Chittagong to get the minibus to Dhaka and handed the keys to Sheikh Mujibur Rahman. On behalf of the London Awamileague, he also gave 10,000.00 rupees to Dewan Farid Gazi, a local MP candidate from Habigonj.

On 23rd March 1971, he received a telegraph from the party office in Dhaka and he went to Dhaka on the same night. He went to Dhaka at the party office and found only 4/5 people in there. Then they went to Sunargah Hotel to meet with the other political leaders. He met Ismoth Chowdhury and Farid Gazi.

In 1971, on 25th March the war began, and everyone left their houses and looked for shelter, where they could save their own life. He was advised to leave Dhaka and go to his hometown in Habigonj. After that, he left Dhaka, and it took a month to go to his hometown.

After arriving at his home, he decided to bring his wife. He brought his wife, without having a marriage ceremony function. At that time, during the liberation period, one of his relatives was the chairman of the Peace Committee in the Habigonj area. He received a letter from him.

In this letter, it was mentioned that after receiving this letter, he should leave his home immediately and find a safe place for shelter. At that time, a few leaders were living at his house, Ali Amjad (Moulvibazar), Abdus Salam, Dr Hasim, and Suroth Miah from Habigonj. He had taken these people to a safe place for shelter.

He realised that living in that situation was not safe, so he returned to the UK in June 1971. In August 1971, they organised a demonstration in France. He was amongst others, who were showing their support for the country. They demonstrated in front of the World Bank in France, they raised their voice with slogans such as "Do not provide any financial support to West Pakistan, who invaded East Pakistan".

8.45.7 Conclusion:

He said the Bangladeshi community has been doing community development in many ways. Many young people are getting degrees from university and doing good jobs like Doctors, Engineers and so on. This is a great achievement for the Bangladeshi community in general.

He also commented on the curry business in the UK. He said considering the economic downturn, although many businesses have been affected this industry has grown and has a good position in the British economy. The young people are also taking responsibility for running this industry as curry has become a very popular dish in the UK. He said, "The young businesspeople will be able to hold this industry, as they are working hard to maintain the good quality food".

He invited the Bangladeshi community to come forward to work towards community development work. More specifically he said, "Everyone should get involved in setting up schools, colleges, mosques and Madras's in their village and town.

He also encourages young people to get involved in community work and politics to do better in the future.

8.46 Alhaj Sazzad Khan
(Interviewed on 29 March 2008)

8.46.1 Life in Bangladesh:

Alhaj Sazzad Khan is living in Manchester. He was born in 1940 in the village of Thilok, Jagannathpur, Sunamgonj. His father's name is the late Mosoddor Khan, and his mother's name is the late Ayubun Nessa. He has three brothers and one sister; he is the third among all his siblings. He completed his education at 'East Tilokh Primary School' and "Digolbag High School.

He then moved to Mirpur High School, and then Tilokh Sarpara Shahjalal High School. He studied till class nine in high school and after that, he migrated to the UK. He was more involved with sports; therefore, he could not complete his education. On one occasion, his eldest brother guided him to do further education but was not successful.

After leaving the school in class nine, he was unemployed for 2/3 years. Then he had taken the initiative to come to Britain. His father was not happy about this, so his father used to give him a lecture about this. When his father was giving the warning, his eldest brother saw this situation and started crying.

8.46.2   Immigration:

In 1939, his father went to Singapore, at that time he was not even born. When his father returned to East Pakistan (Now Bangladesh) in 1948, he was eight years old and had seen his father for the first time.

His eldest brother did not tolerate that his brother was having a hard time due to being interested in sports. His mother used to say to his eldest brother why don't you go abroad, you could have taken him with you, and then this situation could have been avoided. His eldest brother did not give any reply to his mother; he finished his vacation and then went back to his workplace.

After two weeks his brother returned home with a Passport. At that time, the year was 1961. His eldest brother obtained a visa and came to Britain. His eldest brother's main intention was to bring his younger brother to the UK.

His eldest brother came to know that all the people came from Karachi to the UK. He came to the UK on 22nd February 1962. The visa was processed by the British High Commission in Karachi, Pakistan. He received a letter from the Karachi British High Commission and in this letter, it was mentioned that he should contact Glove Travels based at (Jinnah Avenue now called Bongobondu Avenue), Dhaka, Bangladesh.

He went to this place and was just given his passport-size photograph. Three days later, he received another letter, and he made the arrangements to leave Bangladesh for the first time. He went to Dhaka by train and met the official at the Glove Travels. They arranged the flight, and he flew from Dhaka to Karachi, Pakistan.

In Karachi, he stayed for one night, and the next day he flew from there to London Heathrow by KLM Airlines. 5/6 Bangladeshi people were travelling with him. When he arrived in Karachi, he had seen his Passport for the first time. Before that, no one received any passports in his group.

The authority called the name and handed the Passport just one day before the flight. The flight and tickets cost £350.00 paid for by his eldest brother. Asghar Khan and Afruj Miah helped his eldest brother to do the visa processing.

After arriving at the London Heathrow Airport, he had seen a gentleman with a list in his hand and waiting for their arrival. He was an agent of Afruj Miah. Afruj Miah sent this agent to receive these passengers, who arrived at the London Heathrow Airport. There were about seven people in their group. They arranged two cars and went to Birmingham.

They did not have any destination address and were not able to show the taxi driver the address. They were just able to understand that the Taxi driver was saying, "We arrived in Birmingham and whereabouts in Birmingham do you want to go". One of them had his relatives' address and showed this address to the Taxi driver and he dropped all of them off at that address.

Except for one person, all of them felt uncomfortable because they were not being welcomed by the other Bangladeshi people residing there. Then they asked all the Bangladeshis "Do you know Afruj Miah and where does he live". The people replied, "We know Afruj Miah very well but do not know where he lives". Then he asked a question "whether any of them know Kazi Mozommil Ali". One person replied, and said, "I know him, and I will take you down there". On that he did, he took us to Kazi Mozommil Miah's house in Birmingham.

When they arrived there, Kazi Mozommil Ali wanted to know who they were and where they came from. He was the relative of Kazi Mozommil Ali, but they never met before. When Mozommil Ali came to know that he was a relative of Ali, he embraced him. Then Kazi Mozommil Ali phoned Afruj Miah, and he came to pick them up from his house.

All of them arrived at Afruj Miah's house and had their meals. He found so many relatives and he embraced them all. On the next day, he went out with Afruj Miah in his office. Afruj Miah received a phone call from Sazzad Khan's brother; he was sitting there and was able to recognise his brother's voice. He did ask permission from the staff and had spoken to his brother.

His brother was surprised to know that he had arrived in the UK, without informing him by letter or by any means. His brother also said he was worried about him to know whether he would be able to come to Britain. Then his brother said to him, "Anyway, at last, you have arrived and now I am free from tension".

Then Afruj Miah took him to the train station and purchased a ticket for Bradford, where his brother was residing. When he arrived at his brother's house, he stayed there for three months and did not do any employment.

8.46.3   Employment:

Then, one of his relatives from Burry came to see him and his brother in Bradford. They had a conversation about employment and his relative was saying if he goes with him, then he would be able to find employment for him. He convinced his brother and went with him. He had a meal with his relative, and then his relative told him that he could go to sleep as he was going to work, and it would be quite late when he returned.

He was quite surprised to hear this from his relative and he was thinking about how he could stay on his own in the house. He told his relative that he was not able to stay on his own and he said, "I will go back today". His relative replied to him and said, "If you want to go now you may not be able to find the bus for Bradford, because it was a quiet late evening".

Then his relative had no choice but to take him to the bus station. He took a bus from Burry and arrived in Rochdale and from there he took another bus to Halifax. When he arrived in Halifax, he did not find any bus for Bradford. He was in a very difficult situation and was thinking the only alternative transport was to catch a taxi, but it would cost him a fortune and his brother would have to pay for this, but it would not be a wise decision.

At that time a Police Officer arrived there and asked him "Why you are standing here and where do you want to go"? He replied to the Police that he missed the bus for Bradford and now thinking about what to do. The police then asked him whether he had enough money in his pocket, so they could call a taxi for him. He said, "No I do not have enough money to pay for the Taxi".

The police officer took him to one of the Asian houses and asked him to knock on the door. He knocked on the door quite a few times. No reply and no one came out or opened the door. Then the Police officer told him, "Do not knock on the door anymore, as everyone is working people and might be sleeping".

Then a white man arrived there, the Police officer had a conversation with this man and convinced him to stay with him tonight. So, in the morning he would be able to catch a bus. He accepted his advice and stayed with him for a night. In the morning when he woke up, he gave a heartfelt thanks to the gentlemen who provided the accommodation and left the house.

Finally, he arrived at his brother's house. His brother used to work in the cotton factory. About two weeks later, his relative arrived again to visit their house in Bradford. They discussed employment and accommodation. Then he came to Burry again for the second time and started a job in the cotton factory.

A few days later he found accommodation owned by Pakistani and moved there. He lived there for a few days found a Bangladeshi house and moved there. His wages were £6.00 to £7.00, and he worked there for about a year. He used to pay £1.00 for accommodation and £2.00/£3.00 for the food. He was very careful when spending money, as he was thinking of saving some money.

He thought that his brother spent £350.00 on his travelling and visa processing costs. He said he is quite sure that he must have borrowed some money from someone to pay this amount and he needs to pay this back. He was thinking of saving to pay back to his brother.

At that time life was hard. He had seen many people working hard in Great Britain, which he had not seen before. He said working in the cotton mill was not that hard, the management used to give training. Once or twice, they used to show how people could handle the machine, and the worker was able to learn very quickly.

He used to take packed lunches he made from home and used to eat them at lunchtime. After finishing his job, he used to wash his face and hands and take his evening meals at home. There was no boiler for the hot water; he used to use the kettle to boil the water. The toilet was outside in the backyard. When there was bad weather then it was very difficult to use the outside toilet. Two /three people used to cook together to make their evening meals.

He used to have his breakfast in the morning and used to take 2/3 pieces of toasted bread with butter for his lunch. There was a canteen, but halal food was not available therefore Bangladeshi and Pakistani people used to take a packed lunch from their Homes. Eight nine months later he went to the canteen and saw there some food such as Beans, Mash Potatoes, Chips, etc which are halal and can be eaten. Since then, he used to go to the canteen instead of taking his lunch.

A few days later he left his factory job and took a job in the restaurant. Then he left the restaurant job and went to Halifax, where he worked in a carpet factory.

In 1965, he moved to Rochdale and searched for employment. He found a job with the Turner Brothers. There were about 2,500 Pakistani and only 3 Bangladeshi people who used to work there. The weekly wages were £13.00 to £14.00. He worked there until 1967. In 1967, he went to Bangladesh, and he got married there. He stayed in Bangladesh for one and a half years in the area called Shibgonj, Sylhet.

In June 1968, he returned to the UK. At that time, his brother was employed at the Wilkinson Glass Factory Limited in St Helens. His brother's weekly wages were £35.00. His brother felt that working in the UK was very hard as he was employed by the government of Bangladesh, and he was planning to go back to Bangladesh.

In 1969, his brother returned to Bangladesh. His brother was planning to take 5 trucks with him. At that, the procedure was to obtain permission from the Pakistani Government. His brother made several inquiries and found that it was impossible to take the trucks with him.

In 1970, there was a problem caused by a group skin skin-headed people in the St. Helens area. This group was very aggressive and used to attack black people on the street. Therefore, for this reason, he left the job and moved to Birmingham and found employment in the engineering workshop.

In 1974, he started a business under the provision of the wage earner scheme facilitated by the Bangladesh Government. He was involved with three other people and imported 40,000 Tons of salt. Their unit was raided by the authorities and the salt was crooked. He made a loss in this business.

8.46.4 Social & Family:

In 1975, he brought his wife to the UK. At that time, he was living in Oldham, therefore he was involved with the Bangladesh Welfare Association.

In 1978, he moved to Manchester and worked at the Aligor Restaurant. The owner of the Aligor Restaurant was Mannan Miah; he was a treasurer of the Mosque Committee. Through Mannan Miah, Sazzad Khan became involved with community work.

In 1980, there was the first election held to elect committee members amongst 372 members. In 1994, he was elected as a treasurer of the Shahjalal Mosque in Manchester. Then in 2000, and 2004 he was elected as chairman of the Mosque Committee. He was actively involved with the Greater Manchester Bangladesh Association - GMBA.

His first daughter died one month after she was born. He is the father of three daughters and two sons. His eldest son is involved in the Property Business, his two daughters are working in the Job Centre, one daughter is

employed as an IT Instructor and one son is in University.

About 8-9 years ago, he retired from work. Most of his spare time was dedicated to community work. More specifically, he spent much of his time on the improvement of the Shahjalal Mosque in Manchester. His contribution will be remembered by the Bangladeshi community in Manchester.

He said all his children have obtained better qualifications, most of them have gotten married and are staying in Manchester. He has 5 grandchildren, and he gives them some time to play with them. He regularly travels to Bangladesh to see his brother's family.

8.46.5   Independence of Bangladesh:

When the six-point movement of independence started, he followed the events very closely. At that time a student named Asad was injured by the bullet, this news was covered by the Bengali newspaper called "Janamot". He was involved in raising funds for this student for his medical treatment.

He was hopeful as Ayub Khan stepped down from power, and Yahya Khan came and declared the election schedule. He said "The BBC and Janomot were the main sources of information and news.

He mentioned that in September 1970, there was news in the Guardian newspaper that the Awami League would get the majority of seats in the parliament, but Sheik Mujibur Rahman would not be able to become the Prime Minister of Pakistan and get the power from the Pakistani authority, the reporter doubted.

In 1971, Farid Gazi's brother Ashraf Gazi came to Birmingham for a visit and to see Mr. Khan. Mr. Gazi told him that the election of Pakistan was over, and the president of Pakistan called an assembly on 3rd March 1971 in Dhaka, East Pakistan. The visitor guest proposed he visit East Pakistan to see all the political leaders.

On 22nd February 1971, he went to Bangladesh. Whilst he was on the aeroplane, he met a navy official and asked a question "How many Bengali army personnel are employed by the Pakistani authority". He replied less than 10%.

His trip was wasted due to the cancellation order made by the Pakistani authority and the first seating of the parliament did not go ahead. Thereafter, the opposition party called for the non-cooperation movement. He decided to take part in the demonstrations in support of the independence of Bangladesh. On 25th March 1971, the West Pakistan military attacked East Pakistan.

In April 1971, the Pakistani military attacked the village market known as "Fesir Bazar". They distorted houses and killed many people in that area. He had seen this operation and realised that staying in the house was not safe and he might be killed. He decided to become a freedom fighter to resist the Pakistani army's atrocities in his village. He contacted his cousin's brother and decided to go to India.

He left home with his cousin and some other people and went to "Karimgonj" (a village close to India) and found a hotel where other leaders were staying including the local MP "Rois Uddin Advocate". Unfortunately, he did not get an opportunity to get involved with the Bangladesh Liberation Force (Mukti Bahini). He eventually had no choice but to return home.

He then went to Chelar Bazar with his cousin and some other people. There they met a local businessman called Deb Das. Deb Das organised a meeting with the residents, who wished to go to India for their safety. In that meeting, a Cornell from the Indian army was present to give support to the local people.

The Army Officer then informed the public that he did not get an order from the Indian Government, until then he was not able to permit the Bangladeshi people to enter the Indian Territory. He was disappointed in the meeting and had no choice again but to return home, as he thought, by force, no one could do anything.

Later, with help from "Farid Gazi", he was able to obtain a membership to join the Bangladesh Liberation Force (Mukti Bahini) and received a border security pass to go to India for training. Thereafter, along with others, he went to the "Megaloy Sector" to join the force. The Sector commander was "Mir Shawkat Ali". They were welcomed by the sector commander, and he asked them to bring more people with them and they would be able to join the Force.

They had to return home, to find some more people who were interested in getting involved in liberating the country from the Pakistani military. As a result of their hard work, they were able to recruit 31 people from their village area and arranged to go to India.

The 31 people were divided into 5 groups, there were six people in each group, and they began their journey from Chattak to Chelar Bazar. At that time, it was raining and 18 of the people with help from the villagers went to a house. They had given some money on behalf of the group to arrange food for these people and villagers had organised the rest. They had their meals and went to sleep.

In the morning, they saw seen their hands had been tightened with rope and their house had been captured by the Pakistani Army. He was caught up in the turmoil of the War of Independence. He said one of the local chairmen from the area of Betura was the informer of this group. Many people were planning to escape from there by hiding but he told all of them it would not be possible, therefore, they needed to stay in one group.

He also said, "I have had three cousins with me; I am not going to leave them alone and run away with you". Then they were arrested by the Pakistani military and were taken to Chattak Cement Factory for house arrest. Amongst them, there was one person, who was the son of Abdur Rouf (School Teacher).

The school - teacher had this confirmation that his son had been arrested by the Pakistani military. At that time the manager of Chattak Cement Factory was a Bihari man. He had influences with the Army and he was a good man. The manager recognised the son of a school - teacher.

There was a police officer from a local police station known as Siddikur Rahman. The Police Officer recognised him, and he regretted what had seen. The Police Officer told him, "I am very sorry, but please tell the truth, as the truth will eventually win". The Police Officer had been given the authority to record individuals' statements.

He told the half-truth and half-lied to the Police Officer. The first question was when the Pakistani Military was attacked in Sylhet town, whether he was involved with the Bangladeshi Liberation Force. He admitted his involvement with the BLF. With the help of the manager of Chattak Cement Factory, a request was put forward to the Pakistani Military Officer (Cornell) for their release. The manager also told the Army Officer that whoever had been arrested in the middle of the war, had been killed and it has been damaging the image of the Pakistani Army.

They had been taken to the local Police Station by the Police Officer. At that time the Police Officer spoke to a newly appointed Officer-in-Charge (OC) and arranged some food for them to eat. The Officer-in-charge told the people that they should pray to Allah (God) for their life and he also said to them that he had no authority to release them.

On the next day, they were relocated to the "Sylhet Cadet College" by truck. Brigadier "Iftekhar Ahmed Rana" made this order. At that time one army officer was saying to another that you did not have the bullets and why you brought these people here. Thereafter, they had been locked up in a room in the "Sylhet Cadet College".

On the next day, 2/3 people's names were called at a time and all of them had been interviewed by Army Officers. When he entered the room for the interview, he had been offered orange juice and a bed to sit by a Major. He was waiting for the last moment of his life, as he thought he was going to die. So, he decided to take some rest and drink some juice.

He was then called for an interview in another room. There was one Major, one Cornell, and a Captain in that room. He told them, he lives in the UK and shows some evidence. They were pleased to see these papers, he said.

Then, they asked him a question, "From the UK, how much money did you donate to the Political Party known as the Awami League". He replied, "I did not make any contribution and did not find the opportunity to donate any money to the Political Party Fund". He informed the officer that on one occasion, he raised some money for an injured student Asad for his treatment during the anti-Ayub movement.

Then, they asked a second question, "You are a resident of the UK, why do you want to go to India?". The third question was whether he supported the Political Party known as the Awami League. He admitted that he is a supporter of the "Awami League". The fourth question was "Why do you support the

Awami League". He replied that the "Awami League" was demanding the interests of the Bangladeshi people.

The fifth question was "Have you seen the manifesto of Awami League, they did not mention anywhere the name of Bangladesh – now they have declared". He replied to the Army Officers that he was bound to give support to the Party as he had seen many innocent people being killed in his village by the Pakistani Army; the houses had been destroyed. He also said "I could be killed like many other people; therefore, I want to go to India and have some training, so I can save my life.

Then they asked the sixth question, "Do you know who belongs to the party in your area". He told the army officer those he knew were MLA Haque and Rois Uddin MP. They told him, they knew about them, and they asked him again "Are there any other people who are involved with the Awami League?" He replied to the Army Officers and told them he just got back in February 1971 and everyone was supporting Awami League, how many names he would be able to tell.

Thereafter, he was locked up in a toilet. He found a part of the cigarette was left in the toilet. He was just going to pick up the cigarette at that time but then an Army Officer (Cornell) saw that he was picking up the cigarette. Cornell asked him "Do you smoke". He replied, "I do but I do not have any Matchbox". Cornell did not say anything to him but left the area. A few minutes later, Cornell came up with a packet of Star cigarettes and gave it to him.

He was not afraid of death and didn't know why all the 18 people were kept in the same room, they discussed the situation and decided that if they were going to kill, then they would chant "Joi Bangla" (victory to Bangladesh) as the last word of their life.

He had been taken again to Cornell's room and they told him "We have enough information from you, and I am trying to release all of you, but I need more cooperation from you". Cornell also told him that we were trying to prove that if we had to arrest anyone, we did not want to kill them. Cornell also told him that if they win the war "the members of the Peace Committee will be in danger".

He also helped many other colleagues and other people, who were in their custody by providing interpreting. He was shocked to see that many people were tortured by the Pakistani Army and instead of asking for water, he asked for cigarettes.

He also said some Bangladeshi people supported the Pakistani Army in carrying out much killing of innocent people. Those groups were known as Al-Sams, Al- Badar, and Razakar. He also said the people who were killed, did not affiliate with any political party or neither of them was a member of the liberation force (Mukti Bahini).

Therefore, still, now, he hates those people, who carried out the many killings and co-operated with the Pakistani Army. He had seen these people, who betrayed the nation by cooperating with the Pakistani Army.

He said, "When someone was being tortured by the Pakistanis, they had to come to me and many of them told me `You are the one son of Bengali and you can save us".

Thereafter, the Army Officers made up their minds and told them that many of them were students if they went back to school and college, then they would be released. All of them also needed to sign a blank deed for security purposes and they had to agree with them that no one would go to India.

Cornell told him that he would send an Army Officer to inform them that all of them were alive and that the Army Officer would bring all his parents and guardians. The guardians are also required to give assurance that their children will not go to India. Then your release will be quicker.

He replied to Cornell and said that when your Army Officer arrived at their house, their parents would leave the house, and they would hide anywhere to save their life. So, the Army Officer would be able to find anyone in the house. Instead of sending the Army Officer, he advised them to send a Bengali Police officer to their house, and then they would be able to meet with the officer.

Cornell then said to him "I am a Muslim, and you are Muslim too, but if I kill you, I do not have to give the reasons to anyone, do you understand". Cornell then said to him "As a Muslim, I promise you that I will not shoot you, but you need to tell me that you must have some relatives in your town".

He was puzzled by this statement made by Cornell, and he was thinking about what he could do or what he should not do, and which one was the better option. He was determined that he was going to die, anyway but considered the proposal made by Cornell. He was thinking about helping Cornell and willingly he disclosed the information that his brother-in-law was working in the office as a clerk.

By that time two people already had been killed among the eighteen people by the Pakistani Military. On the next day, they brought the entire guardian from the remaining sixteen to the Sylhet Circuit House. A Brigadier and Syed Ali Advocate were there. The brigadier told them, "You will be released on the condition that you will be admission in colleges again and Mr. Khan will remain in the town". Syed Ali Advocate objected; he said, "If you release all of them, they will become stronger". He also said in Jagannathpur the Bangladeshi flags are flying.

While they were in prison, in one night, the Pakistani army 6 or 7 in numbers wanted to charge bayonet on them. They had struggled for their life. They thought the Pakistani army might have been planning to kill them that night. But suddenly, Major Salim entered the room and ordered them to halt. He then ordered them to get out of the room and ordered the sentry not to allow anybody, without his permission.

When he was caught it was May 1971 and detained by the Pakistani army for six months. In September 1971, the President of Pakistan Ahilya Khan declared a general amnesty to prisoners' war, who was arrested during the war. After a few days later they were released from prison.

After the liberation war, he returned to the UK and started a cloth shop in Oldham. After that, he joined the Turner Brothers. He used to work and run the business at the same time.

8.46.6 Conclusion:

He was asked to give us a reflection about his life between 1962 to 2009. He said his first intention was to settle in Bangladesh but considering the social-economic condition of Bangladesh wasn't good, he thought it would be better after the liberation. He does not think that he has achieved his goals. He said, "I think Bangladesh is my mother, I was born in Bangladesh, and I am very much attached to my mother, soil, and the country".

He very sadly said, "when the first-generation people will pass away, the second generation is not going to learn Bangla". He is worried that the culture might get lost by the next generation or future generations to come.

He said with emotion that his children did not learn Bangla, because they are all in the UK. He did not think it would happen to his family. Similarly, there are thousands of children who will be disconnected from the Bangla language like his children.

He is appealing to these people, to take care of their children, otherwise, the nation and country will be affected by them. He also insists that the Bangladeshi community should do more cultural practice and encourage them to get involved in British Politics. The community also needs to take care of their children to

make sure they have a better education so that they would have a better life in the future.

He said, "I cannot leave my family, all the children, and live in Bangladesh on my own. Therefore, I have decided to stay with them for the rest of my life".

8.47 Shamsuddin Ahmed MBE
(Interviewed on 11 April 2010)

8.47.1 Life in Bangladesh:

Shamsuddin Ahmed, son of Late Komor Uddin Ahmed, was born in Sataihal village of Nabiganj, Habigong. His father's economic condition was better compared with other people. His father used his agricultural lands and a substantial amount of income from this. His father had a business as well. Shamsuddin Ahmed completed his primary education at Sataihal Primary School, went to Dinarpur Junior High School, then went to Habigonj High School, then again went to JK & HK High School and completed the Secondary School Certificate (S.S.C) planned to come to Britain.

8.47.2   Immigration:

Shamsuddin Ahmed came to the UK in 1958, at that time there was no immigration control for the Commonwealth Citizens, and it was easier to enter and remain in the UK without any difficulties. He was very keen to come to the UK; he arranged to obtain the passport without telling his family anything about this. At that time, it was very difficult to obtain an international passport. This is because if his family or any of his relatives knew about it, then they would try to stop him from going to the UK.

After a lot of effort, he was able to find an officially recognised person who helped him get a passport. Since he was only 15-16 years old, he had to admit to high school again. At the time of the Second World War, his uncle was working on the Merchant ship. That ship was bombarded, and his uncle escaped from the ship by using the lifebuoys. Therefore, there was always worry in his family.

Shamsuddin Ahmed says that, when he first got his passport, he was worried about how he will manage the travel expenses for the journey. But later, after trying hard, he was able to convince his family and his relatives, and they helped to arrange the money needed for him to travel to the UK. Shamsuddin mentions that it took him about £1700 to travel to Heathrow Airport.

During that time there was no requirement to get a visa to come to the UK. The requirement for a visa system started in 1982. Before that, a passport as a commonwealth citizen was enough to obtain entry to the UK but for the Europeans, there was a visa requirement for them to enter the UK.

Shamsuddin Ahmed flew from Dhaka to Karachi and finally arrived at Heathrow Airport. From there he got on a bus and went to one of his relatives' places in Earls Court. He spent a night with one of his friends and they provided him with good hospitality during his stay. On the next day, he left his friend's place and took a train from Euston, London to Manchester Piccadilly.

One of his uncles and cousins received him from the Piccadilly and went to his uncle's house by a black taxi. He was surprised to see the meter fitted at the Black Taxi, which he had seen for the first time. He was more surprised to see that when people came to see him, they gave him money as a gift, one pound to five pounds he received from everyone. At that time people were very loving and caring. Some people gave him good advice, which he remembered.

8.47.3   Life in the UK

He was very keen to continue his studies, therefore he was admitted to a language school in Mosley Street, Manchester, and attended Commerce College in Cheetham Hill. He used to attend meetings with Malik Bokth of "Jomiotul Muslimin" in Manchester. At that time Malik Bokth was the General Secretary of Manchester-based "Pakistan Association" and "Jomiotul Muslimin". Mr. Bokth was impressed with his work, he showed affection and treated him as a

younger brother. Sometimes Malik Bokhs used to take him far away from work. He used to help the Bangladeshi community throughout the Northwest by reading and writing letters.

The restaurant known as "Shalimar Restaurant" in Manchester city centre, was the centre place for all the community leaders to meet on a regular basis to discuss many issues and provide services to the Bangladeshi Community. This restaurant has been demolished. The people used to come to the restaurant if they lost their way or were in need to get a service.

The restaurant owners also gave support to those people who arrived new to the UK with no jobs or a place to live. It was a shelterhouse for food and accommodation. They also assisted to find a job for the newcomers. His business partner was very keen to help others. His partner used to visit the ill people, even though they were living far away. It was not easy to travel anywhere like it is now. There were only a few private car owners. Just for that reason, his partner was seen as a respected person in the community.

The restaurant business was not good at that time but there were free meals for the visitors. They provided community services rather than concentrating on business. During that time, he had the opportunity to work along with the senior

community leaders to deal with any community matters.

During that time Asian people did not get job in places like Tesco or any other big stores. Also, there were difficulties in purchasing houses; the estate agents did not provide any information to the Asian customers as they do now. There was also a condition attached from the vendor that no black buyers.

At that time, he had to struggle a bit to find a job. There was a crisis of finding employment. Since he was educated, some people advised him to take the job of a contractor on the bus and some advised him to carry on with his education.

The radio in the black taxi, double decor bus, and the non-co-operation from your colleagues were his first experiences outside of his home country, but he tried to adjust to the new experiences, and he soon got used to it. When the winter season began, he was feeling very cold as it was his first winter in the UK. He was struggling to cope with the first winter.

8.47.4 Employment:

He had an opportunity to meet with another well-known community leader, Abdul Matin. For the goodwill and the reputation, he was working with along with Malik Bakth, he was given the partnership for a restaurant in Blackpool for just five hundred pounds (1961).

In 1962 – 63, he became a partner of Shalimar Restaurant, situated in the heart of Manchester City Centre. His uncle's friend Rois Miah also liked him, he was a very well-known community leader and respected person. He advised him to go to Blackpool, his uncle also welcomed his suggestion, and it was agreed that he should go to Blackpool. He went to Blackpool and got admitted to the Catering School.

At the same time, he was working in the restaurant as a part-time waiter. The head waiter was not keen on teaching him how to become a good waiter. A few days later he was able to become a full-time waiter without receiving any training.

He used to get one pound per week working as a waiter, customers used to give tips for the services. He was enjoying working seven days a week. He was a responsible and hard-working person and earned a good name for himself in a few days. Therefore, he was able to find a job in the Everest Restaurant in Manchester. The weekly wages were seven pounds and fifty pence.

In 1962 – 72, he became a partner of Shalimar Restaurant, situated in the heart of Manchester City Centre. In 1972, he purchased a restaurant called Samiul Kosher in Dickenson Road, Manchester and he ran this business for a short period and sold the business. He became a managing partner of Babor Restaurant in Preston. While he was running this business, he had the opportunity to become a sleeping partner at Gate of India in Chester. In the same year, he left the Babor Restaurant and moved to Chester and got involved with the Gate of India Restaurant.

In 1977, he decided to end the partnership with Gate of India and purchased a restaurant called Roman Garden. He was successful in running this restaurant until 1984. In 1985, he opened a restaurant called "Monsoon" and ran this restaurant until 1993.

In 1994, he purchased a restaurant known as "Agra Port" in Ellesmere Port, Cheshire. In 1999, he sold this restaurant and purchased another restaurant known as Country Spice, Hope, Flintshire, North Wales. Till now he has been running this business successfully.

Currently, he is working with a local authority in the Social Service department as a home visitor. Shamsuddin Ahmed shared an experience of racial discrimination. He went with one of his English friends for a holiday. They had been enquiring about the bread and breakfast hotel when they came to know that an Asian is going to stay there, they replied no vacancies.

His English friend then wrote an article in the newspaper saying that the English people were receiving treatment from the Indian doctors, but Asian people refused to get a place in the bread and breakfast which wasn't right.

He also added that during the late 50's and early '60s people in Blackpool did not like Indian food. They used to say that the smell of Garlic stays in their mouth and many other things, but Indian Curry became a famous food in the UK.

8.47.5 Housing:

While he was working in Blackpool, he used to live in a terrace house, and he used to share the accommodation with other colleagues. The landlady used to provide bed sheets and cleaning services. When he moved to Manchester, he used to live in private rented accommodation in All Saint, Manchester. He purchased a two-bedroom house in Ardwick, Manchester, he paid £350.00 for this.

He then moved to Chester and purchased a semi-detached house with 3 bedrooms with other modern amenities, he paid £9,500.00 for the freehold price. In 1982, he sold this house purchased another 4 bedrooms detached house in

Chester. In 1992, he sold this house and purchased 4 bedrooms detached house in the same area, where he is residing now.

8.47.6 Social & Family:

In the beginning, the first-generation people had the intention to earn money and go back to their home country and to be settled there, but when people brought their families to the UK, the original intention to leave the UK had changed.

In 1968 he got married but he did not bring his wife to the UK until 1972. Many other people had done the same thing. When he brought his wife and son, he received advice and suggestions from many of his friends that Chester was the best place to live. He moved to Chester and found that there was no Mosque or any Association where people could hold any meetings and community activities.

In 1977, General MAG Osmani came to Chester, and as soon after that meeting, a Bangladeshi Association was formed. Don Miah became the first Chairman, and he was elected as a General Secretary.

In 1967, he was also involved in establishing a Mosque in Manchester. Malik Bakth, Dr Din, and Abdul Matin also took the leading role in establishing this Mosque known as the "East Pakistan Islamic Centre". It was also known as a religious institution. He always played a supportive role with the senior leaders.

He is also involved with many organisations in the Northwest. He was the founder chair of the Bangladesh & Asian Development Council. He was serving as a director at the "Citizen Advice Bureau". He was a member of the North Wales Police Diversity Forum, a member of the Cheshire Police Constabulary, and founder vice-chair of the Cheshire, Holton, and Warrington Racial Equality Council. Besides that, he was involved with the National Federation of Pakistan Association UK, Lions Club International, Chester Chamber of Trade, GSDWC, and many other organisations in the UK and Bangladesh.

In Chester, he was the first person to organise Arabic Lessons for the children. The lesson took place in the front room of his staff quarter. At a later stage, Johirul Haq managed to find an Imam (Religious Teacher) to do the Islamic teachings and run the five times prayer. In the beginning, the Imam did not get any wages or salary, but food and accommodation were provided.

He received many awards for his outstanding contribution to community work including MBE. He was nominated for an MBE award in 1990 by an English person and he was awarded one in January 2001. He came to know this person in 2001 and now this gentleman has passed away.

8.47.7 Independence of Bangladesh:

During the liberation moment of Bangladesh, he played an active role. Although he was not affiliated with any British political parties or wings, he maintained communication with British higher-up officials like MPs and Lords.

In 1971, Muhbubur Rahman returned from East Pakistan (now Bangladesh) and told him that the situation in Bangladesh is not very good, if the political situation gets worse then we must do something for the nation.

Later, when the independent movement developed in East Pakistan then they first proposed to organise a meeting to get support for the independence of Bangladesh. Duly to the public meeting was called and an Action Committee was formed from this meeting.

There were about thirteen action committees in different towns and cities in the whole of the Northwest and his restaurant became a central meeting place to co-operate with other action committees.

At a later stage, this location had been changed to "Manjil Restaurant" owned by Najir Ahmed. The Action committee played a vital role to lobby the British government to get their support for the independence of Bangladesh. At that time, it was very difficult to meet with the higher-up government officials such as British ministers, MPs, Mayors. There was a lack of race relation policies exit at that time.

Mr. Uddin also mentioned that in April 1971, Abu Syed Chowdhury (First President of Bangladesh) convened a meeting in Coventry, where Mr. Chowdhury took the responsibility to take the leading role to manage and co-ordinate 5 regional committees (this committee also known as the steering committee). Each regional committee nominated a person to work with Mr.

Chowdhury for the campaign of the independence movement in the UK, Dr. Kobir Chowdhury was elected as a member of the steering committee from the Northwest.

Mr. Uddin stated that during the liberation war, Mr. Abdul Matin was a president of the Northwest region played a vital role to lead the Action Committee throughout the UK. Mr Mohibur Rahman, Latif Ahmed, Bosarat Ali, Khondaker Nazir Uddin, Moksud Ali, Nazrul Islam, Abdul Wahid and many others played an important role as well.

8.47.8 Conclusion:

Mr. Ahmed is a successful businessman, also known as a community leader for his outstanding community and voluntary work and fundraising for various disaster charities. He has worked tirelessly on welfare, race relations, and integration issues for many years raising the profile of human rights and race issues locally and beyond.

Recently Mr. Ahmed was invited to Buckingham Palace by Her Majesty the Queen and the Duke of Edinburgh in recognition of his services to the British Hospitality Industry. The Mayor of Wrexham said, "It is no exaggeration to say that you are a true ambassador for Wrexham". Also, Mark Tami MP said, "Mr. Ahmed is the ambassador for this area".

In his concluded remarks, he added a bit of advice to the community. He said they should concentrate on education, take care of the young stars and not get addicted to drugs, respect the elderly and all the institutions including mosques and religious schools (Madrasa). He also acknowledges his wife's contribution to providing inspiration and support for the community work.

8.48   Alhaj MA Aziz Nunu Miah
(Interviewed on 11 April 2010)

8.48.1 Life in Bangladesh:

Alhaj MA Aziz Nunu Miah was born in 1948 in the village of Motukuna, Bishwanath, Sylhet. His father's name is late Mohammed Tormuz Ali and his mother's name is late Ahmeda Khatun. In 1958 his father came to Britain. His father had huge amounts of agricultural land and his father was engaged in cultivation. His father used to employ the workers to do the farming work.

8.48.2   Immigration:

His father came to Britain in 1958. He followed in the footsteps of his father and came to Britain in 1966 with a boy voucher. At that time, he was a student at the high school in class seven.

His father wanted him to come to the UK. He could not continue his studies; he feels very unfortunate for not completing his education. He was only 13 years old when he first came to Britain. He used to do some part-time work and attended school for some days.

8.48.3   Life in the UK:

During the first three months, he stayed in Walsall, west midlands, and went to Oxford and then to the Ridding area in Berkshire. Between 1966 and 1973, he was able to do some study besides his part-time employment. When his

father came to Britain there were many job vacancies in the engineering and factory field. There were many Bangladeshis employed in these two sectors, his father was among them.

Many of the Bangladeshi people were employed at factories. The landlord used to provide beds and some other furniture. Due to the low earnings, the people were not even in a position to think about bringing their families to the UK. He remembered that one of the Gujarati men used to supply them all with the grocery items including live chickens.

The Bangladeshi fishes were not available at that time. If anyone had wished to have fish, then English fish was the real alternative. At that time, the grocery shops were the only shops in the Walsall area, there were about 2-3 shops in the Birmingham area.

Nowadays you will see there are many Mosques in every town, where the Asian or Muslim peoples are residing, but during the 1960s there were only a few Mosques in the UK. At the time of Eid Prayer, the people used to hire the hall to do the Eid Prayer. There was one occasion when he was in Riddling; they had to hire an Imam from London. There were no Muslim funeral services, so it was very difficult to organise funerals when people died. Nowadays, everything has been improved and life has become easier.

The first Bangladeshi funeral service had begun in the Mosque in London. At that time Haji Taslim Ali oversaw the Mosque. Now, this part of the Mosque's services became full funeral services.

The people who worked in the board ship and came to Britain for settlement, he remembers those elderly people with his deepest heart. Since his arrival to Britain, he met some of the first-generation immigrants i.e. Ayub Ali Master, Abdul Matin, Gous Khan, Afruj Miah, and so on. He was not able to remember all the people's names.

He said that if those people had not come to Britain for settlement, then it would have been impossible to come to Britain. They were the genuine people who did the community work.

8.48.4 Employment:

While he was living in the Redding area he was employed at the "Karachi Restaurant", his weekly wages added up to £5.00 per week. The restaurant owner was one of his relatives. He was young; therefore, he did not get the opportunity to work as a waiter. He used to work in the kitchen as a kitchen assistant.

The accommodation and food were free, this was due to the relationship with the employer, and he was young, therefore he took the advantage of not doing any work during the daytime as he was studying at school. This opportunity was good, he added. For about a year he worked as a kitchen assistant, then he was promoted to a cook and he worked as a cook for two years. Then he had the opportunity to work as a chef. His wages were increased too.

He said "in 1968 his wages were £20.00 per week. He was employed until he set up his own business. His relative employer is one of his cousins known as Hafizur Rahman Tera Miah. His cousin's brother was able to set up an electronic industry in Bangladesh known as "Surma Electronics Industry" situated at Newmarket, Dhaka.

He said this was probably the first electronics industry in Bangladesh. His cousin used to import TV parts from Japan and assemble the TV in Bangladesh. He mentioned this to show that his cousin is not doing the catering business, but he is contributing to the Bangladesh economy by setting up this industry.

His cousin was the owner of three restaurants, the first one is known as "Karachi" and the second one "East Bengal" both were in the Riddling area, and the third one which was the "Kohinoor" was in the Canterbury area. He had the opportunity to work in all the restaurants. Therefore, he did not require finding employment elsewhere.

In 1973, he bought a restaurant known as "Asia" in Chester and he moved there since then. That was a partnership business, fifty equal shares amongst partners. He paid £7,000.00 for this partnership. The business was good; the weekly takings were £300.00 to £400.00. The income from the business was sufficient to maintain him adequately and the price of goods was very cheap too. The weekly rent was £20.00, and the rate was also very cheap.

During the period 1973 – 1986, he was running the "Asia Restaurant". In 1979 he opened another restaurant in Preston known as the "Asha Restaurant". Firstly, they bought the lease and paid £30,000.00. Later, they bought the freehold. The weekly takings were up to £4,000.00 to £5,000.00.

He was involved with this business for about five years, and he sold his share to his partner. In 1980 he entered another partnership and opened a restaurant in Darwin, it was known as the "Anan Restaurant". He bought the share from his partner and was able to run this business for five years.

In 1986, due to his problem, he sold the business and went to Bangladesh. He opened a shared shop at the Shukria Market was known as "Rubi Sharee Bitan" and opened another shop which was known as the "Runa Fashion" at London Mansion. Both shops much closed and were situated in Zindbazar, Sylhet. After spending a year in Bangladesh, he returned to the UK in 1988.

Since he came to the UK, he stayed for five years and in 1970 he went to Bangladesh for the first time. In 1970, he observed the general election. At that time, the majority of East Pakistani voted for Sheikh Mujib. There were several political parties such as Awamileague, Muslim league, PPP, and NAP headed by Moulana Bhasani.

In 1992, he opened a takeaway business known as "Ahmed Takeaway"; his eldest son is running this business now, now he is semi-retired. His eldest son does not wish him to work there. His children have obtained degrees and are working in different offices.

In 1960 – 62, the restaurant businesses had begun. In the Redding area, he has only seen three restaurants. Those were the Karachi, the Bombay, and the

Tajmahal. In every town, there were one, two, or three restaurants. The people who had restaurant businesses were able to bring their families to the UK.

During the 1960s people were very busy with their work. One day was the day off for many Bangladeshi workers. While he was living in the Redding area, on his off days, he used to go to London to see his friends and relatives. At that time the social culture was very effective.

8.48.5 Housing:

Many of the Bangladeshi people were employed at factories. At that time most of them were single, therefore, they used to live in shared accommodation. He said, "I have seen 10 – 15 people living in one house". He said in a bedroom house, about 8 – 10 people used to live there. The rent for a single bed was higher than a double bed, so people used to share the beds. The rent for the single bed was £1.00 and sharing a bed was £0.50.

The landlord used to provide beds and some other furniture. Due to the low earnings, the people were not even able to think about bringing their families to the UK. He remembered that one of the Gujarati men used to supply them all with the grocery items including live chickens. The Bangladeshi fishes were not available at that time. If anyone had wished to have fish, then English fish was the real alternative. At that time, the grocery shops were the only shops in the Walsall area, there were about 2-3 shops in the Birmingham area.

Since his arrival to the UK, he bought and sold many houses, the house where he is residing was purchased by him. In 1977 he bought this house for the price of £9,000.00, the current market value is about £200,000.00 he added. This house consists of five bedrooms, and it is semi-detached.

He said the road communication and the housing have been improved compared to the 1960s. There were no baths inside the houses; the people had to use the public bath. The new generation is not going to believe it as they have not seen the past.

8.48.6 Social & Family

During the liberation war in 1971, he got married. He is the father of two sons and two daughters. He brought his wife to the UK in 1977. One year later, since his wife's arrival in the UK, they travelled back to Bangladesh. In 1986, he and his wife returned to Bangladesh. His wife remained in Bangladesh until 1990, and he returned to the UK.

In between, he travelled several times to see his wife and children. His young son was suffering from illness and according to the doctor's advice, he had to bring his family back to the UK. He said he had two brothers and two sisters and amongst them, he was the third-born. They enjoyed a very happy family life with their parents.

Since he was living in Chester, he was involved with the Bangladeshi Association. He attended many meetings in Manchester to represent Bangladeshi living in Chester.

When retired Army General Mohammed Ataul Gani Osmani came to Britain on behalf of the Janata Party, he organised a reception party in Chester.

When President Ziaur Rahman came to Manchester, he was part of the organising committee. He was also engaged in community work. He served as a treasurer and now is serving as the chairman of the Shahjalal Mosque in Chester.

In 1990, he performed the Hajj (pilgrimage to Makkah) along with his wife. In 1998, he and his wife performed the Umrah. In 1999, he took his wife and young son to do the Hajj for a second time.

Sometimes, he goes to Bangladesh to see his close relatives. His spare time is dedicated to the Mosque and his family. His mother and other siblings are residing in Bangladesh, so he intends to retire from his life in Bangladesh.

In the past, the leaders from the community had done the real community work, without any self-interest. Those people, many of them are no longer alive, but he remembers their hard work.

8.48.7 Independence of Bangladesh

He was in Bangladesh during the liberation war. He left Bangladesh just a few weeks before the victory day. When he flew from Sylhet Airport, the military was there, he was afraid at that time that they could have been killed by the Pakistani Military. The messages were given by the Army officers to those people, who flew from Sylhet that they should tell the others on arrival that the condition of the country is safe, and war is not affecting the public.

On arrival to the UK, he saw that Bangladeshi people, who were living in the UK, tried to put up demands to the British authorities to gain their support for independence.

On 26th March 1971, when the war was declared, he had the intention to join the liberation force called Mukti Bahini (freedom fighters) but unfortunately, he did not get any channels to communicate. The people who joined the force must have been joined before he said.

Bangladeshi people who were living in the UK during the liberation war, did everything they could to put their wholehearted support for the independence of Bangladesh. From demonstrations to collecting funds for the purchase of firearms, many people had given their full week's wages, and some people had donated their savings too.

He remembers 5 senior leaders, who worked hard to unite the people and organised demonstrations. He said they were called Gous Khan from London, Afruz Miah from Birmingham, and Matin Miah from Manchester; those are some key people who led this independent movement in the UK.

He recognised the support received from Russia and India to the Bangladeshi Mukti Bahini (freedom fighters) to win the war. After a long battle with the Pakistani army, Bangladesh became an independent state on the 16th of December 1971.

8.48.4   Conclusion

He made the comparison remarks of the 1960s and current times, he said that the old days were a hard life, but many things have now been improved. In 1966, when he first came to Britain, there were not many Bangladeshi families who arrived in the UK. At that time only boys came to Britain with a boy voucher. The main employment sector was at factories for the Bangladeshis and Pakistanis.

There are about 500,000 Bangladeshis that are residing in the UK. Some people have obtained higher degrees and are working as Doctors, Engineers, Barristers and contributing to local politics. He encourages the Bangladeshi community to come forward and work as a team to advance the community even further. New-generation British Bangladeshis have some interest in the country of Bangladesh, but due to lack of support, they are reluctant to get involved in community work.

Besides that, he encourages parents and community leaders to play vital roles in motivating young people to make some connection to their roots. The Bangladeshi community is living in a multicultural society, and they need to maintain and improve their relationship with the British society to get the best outcomes, which will benefit their life in the UK.

8.49 Alhaj Makhon Miah
(Interviewed on 11 April 2010)

8.49.1 Life in Bangladesh:

Alhaj Makhon Miah was born in 1952 in the village of Att Para, Bishwanath, Sylhet. His father's name is late Alhaj Monuhor Ali and his mother's name is late Arobun Nessa.

He has four brothers and two sisters. One sister remains in Bangladesh and the rest of them are in the UK. He went to "Habra Bazar Primary School" and studied at "Ramsudar High School" in Biswanath.

8.49.2 Immigration:

In 1966, he came to Britain at the age of 14 years old. He came to Britain with a boy voucher. At that time, he was a student in high school in class seven.

He stayed at 9 Fourth Street in Walsall, West Midlands. He said, "After 18th months when he was born, most probably in 1954, his father went to Singapore". His father worked there for about 7-8 years, and after that, his father came to the UK. In 1964 his father went to Bangladesh, he was only 12 years old. He went to high school and studied there for two years.

8.49.3 Life in the UK:

The new generation of British–Bangladeshis is getting the right education and has gotten used to the advanced life in the UK. However, the old generation has worked hard to bring their families to the UK. The generation is far more advanced than the older generation.

8.49.4 Employment:

In the UK, he started his part-time employment at the "Royal Bengal Restaurant" in Walsall. The owner of the restaurant was called Shamsu Miah, and he was from Vadeshor in Sylhet. He worked there as a part-time employee just at the weekend, he used to get £2.00 just like pocket money.

When he was able to do some work in the restaurant then the days of work were increased to three days; Friday – Sunday and wages were £5.00. He was able to become a waiter in a few days and he worked there till 1970. In 1970, he worked in another restaurant in Lichfield. That employment was the last job of his life.

In 1971, he became a business partner with Abdul Aziz Nunu Miah and opened a restaurant in Chester known as the "Asia Restaurant". He invested £9,000.00 in the business. He said he had some savings, and the rest of the money was borrowed from his relatives. He was working as a manager/waiter and his partner MA Aziz Nunu Miah worked as a chef.

They worked hard right from the beginning and were able to improve the business. They did not think about the wages at the beginning as their main aim was to pay the loan money, which he borrowed initially to improve the business. They were able to meet the aim. They ran this business for a long time.

He was able to establish another restaurant in Preston. He took another two partners before opening the second venture. The name of the restaurant was "Asha Restaurant". This business was successful because his partner Majid Miah was a very good chef, and the other partner Moklisur Rahman was a good waiter.

Then he opened the third restaurant in Darwin, known as the "Anondo Restaurant". They had taken another partner to run this business. This business was profitable too but due to his problems, he had to come out of the partnership.

He was a brave young boy who came from Bangladesh, with no previous business experience but he was able to set up businesses in the UK. He said, "If anyone needs to succeed in setting up businesses then obviously you have to work hard and take extra care of the business."

He is still involved with the restaurant business at Brook Street, Chester and his children are running the business. Now it is time for retirement he said, and he is insisting his children take full responsibility to run the business.

His eldest son, after completing his "A levels" got involved with him to run the business. His second son completed his degree and is working in a Bank. Now he is showing interest in getting involved with the business. His two daughters are married and three of them are still in education.

There used to be good training for the chefs in the past. One-to-one training, one chef used to create another chef. The new generation of businessmen needs to look at these early chefs as role models and consider this training issue seriously. Otherwise, the catering trade is going to suffer. He also said, "The community leaders need to look into the issue and take necessary steps to develop the Bangladeshi community in the UK".

During his working life, he never faced discrimination, but he had some experience of dealing with bad customers, whilst he was involved with the business.

8.49.5 Housing:

He bought a three-bedroom semi-detached house in Chester. He paid £45,000.00 for this house. He was able to buy another house in the same area and paid £100,000.00 for this. Later, he sold these houses and purchased another 5-bedroom house in the same area where he is residing now. He paid £150,000.00 for this house.

8.49.6 Social & Family:

His first intention for coming to Britain was to earn some money and support the family in Bangladesh. Also, he said "I was thinking of earning and saving some money and then going back to Bangladesh" but considering the reality and for social reasons, he had to change his mind.

In 1974, he went back to Bangladesh for the first time. In 1977, he went again and got married. He brought his family to the UK in 1978, and he is the father of two sons and five daughters.

Whilst he was living in the Walsall area, he used to go to the public bath. He used to visit friends and relatives when he had a day off from work. At that time there were not many families who came to Britain. He used to share the accommodation and food with other people.

Nowadays, most of the people have got their families in the UK. It has improved the lifestyle, compared with the 1960s and mid-1970s. There is a lack of time due to family commitments, the people cannot move around like they used to do in the past.

One of his sisters is residing in Bangladesh; he goes to Bangladesh with her family and other relatives and friends. In 2008, he performed his Hajj (pilgrimage to Makkah). He had the ambition that he would spend his retirement life in Bangladesh, but he is unable to do so due to his family being in the UK.

Now all his family members are residing with him in the UK. He wishes his children to have a better education and to have a peaceful life in the UK. In considering religious education, they have been working towards developing the old Mosque and creating the facility to do five times prayer and Islamic studies.

He took the initiative to facilitate a mother tongue (Bangla) class but was unable to do so for some reason. He said the parents are not taking an interest in sending their children to the Bangla School. But he is hopeful, that maybe in the future the young generation will take some interest in learning their mother tongue.

When he moved to Chester, he was serving as a chairman for the Chester Welfare Society for many years. He said "Chester Welfare Society" is still active and he attends many events organised by the Society. While he was serving the

CWS, he tried to encourage the local councillors; Mps to take part in many of the activities and events.

He said, "I used to support the Awami league but one instant he supported the BNP MP candidate from Biswanath & Balagonj". As he thought that BNP MP M Elias Ali would be able to do the development work in this area.

There was a public reception party held in Manchester, where President "Ziaur Rahman" was going to attend but he could not attend this meeting due to his problem.

He liked to do socialising; in doing so he enjoyed and liked to attend any social gathering. He said while he was living in the "West Midlands" area, he was a member of the Birmingham "Jubo Shongo" (youth organisation) and "Birmingham Action Committee".

8.49.7   Independence of Bangladesh:

During the liberation war in 1971, he was in the UK. At that time, he was not old enough to get involved with any activities, but he can remember that many people were involved with the liberation movement in the UK. The people had given their emotional and moral support in the independence of Bangladesh.

In 1969, although he was young, he still attended a meeting in Birmingham where Sheikh Mujibur Rahman delivered his speech. He met with him for the first time. He was convinced with the speech, and he felt that the support should be given to the movement which he was the confident leader of at that time.

In that meeting, one of the Pakistani men shouted and said, "Sheikh Mujib is the agent of India". Then other Bangladeshis requested that man to leave the hall, he was trying to interrupt the meeting. After listening to Sheikh Mujib's speech, he realised that people and the country's interests are well connected. For example, he said, "Sheikh Mujibur Rahman told the audience that the paper is produced in East Pakistan and it goes to West Pakistan and returns to East Pakistan for selling with a higher price".

Thereafter, the general election was held in Pakistan. Sheikh Mujib and his party had most seats in the Parliament. Sheikh Mujib was arrested. He took part in a demonstration for the release of Sheikh Mujibur Rahman. At that time the Pakistani Cricket team came to Birmingham to play, he joined the demonstration and people shouted slogans like "go away, go away, release Sheikh Mujib and recognise Bangladesh". He had seen one person become very emotional and was throwing stones at the Pakistani Cricketers.

After the liberation war, when Bangladesh became an independent country, one of the ministers "Abdus Samad" came to Birmingham to attend a public reception party, along with the minister "Pir Habibur Rahman" he came as a companion of the minister. He gave a lift to "Pir Habibur Rahman" from Heathrow to Birmingham. He saw that "Pir Habibur Rahman" was wearing the lungi and he asked him why he was wearing this. "Pir Habibur Rahman" replied by saying that the lungi is the national dress of Bangladesh, and he prefers to wear the national dress as he loves Bangladesh.

He said that the minister of Bangladesh "Abdus Samad Azad" addressed the public meeting and informed the audience that they are receiving recognition from many countries in the world and he is also hoping that all of the countries will recognise Bangladesh as a new independent state.

At the time, when "Ziaur Rahman" was in Power, Retired Army General "MAG Osmani" came to Chester and stayed in Chester for a week. General "MAG Osmani" also addressed a public meeting in Chester, which he attended. Community leader "Don Miah" chaired and "Abdul Matin" conducted the meeting.

There was a question raised by the public about the father of the nation, why do some people say "Sheikh Mujibur Rahman" is the father of the nation? General "MAG Osmani" replied to the audience that as far as he is concerned, he knows that "Sheikh Mujibur Rahman" is called "Bongobondu" (friend of Bangladesh) not the father of the nation, the public will decide who the father of the nation is. General "MAG Osmani" also said that "Sheikh Mujibur Rahman" was a good leader, who played a vital role in liberating Bangladesh from Pakistan.

He left Bangladesh just a few weeks before the victory day. When he flew from Sylhet Airport, the military was there, he was afraid at that time that they could have been killed by the Pakistani Military. The messages were given by the Army officers to those people, who flew from Sylhet that they should tell the others on the arrivals that the condition of the country is safe, and war has not affected the public.

8.49.8 Conclusion:

He also blames the Bangladeshi Politicians for their insincere work. Politicians are often seen that they only think for themselves, not for the country. He also said one party put a name, the other party changed it. This is not called politics. If the leaders are working for the country and working for the people, then Bangladesh eventually will be developed like other countries in the world.

From his own experience being an ex-chairman of the Chester Bangladeshi Welfare Society, he said people need to work together as they did in the past.

The old and young generation needs to work together to achieve the goals of the community.

8.50 Abdul Kadir Jilani (Bodor Uddin)

8.50.1 Life in Bangladesh

Abdul Kadir Jilani was born in 1955, in the village of south Bhadeshwar, Gulapgonj, Sylhet. His father's name is the late Hazi Nehar Ali, and his father was a Sub Inspector of Police based in Dhaka. He attended his first primary school at "Bhadeshwar Primary Model School", then he moved to Dhaka due to his father's employment and it was for better education, he studied at "Gendaria Primary School" yet he didn't enjoy it at all.

He was thinking about home whilst at this school, he completed his primary school education, then he moved back to Bhadeshwar to "Nasir Uddin High School" and completed his secondary school qualifications there. The education back then was better for studying; the "Nasir Uddin High School" was very good and had a very good reputation for giving people a good education.

There was no need to employ private tutors because the school delivered such a high standard of education, very different from nowadays. His parent's family was moderate; they had some land and properties. The road communication system wasn't bad at the time, the main roads were all tarmac, and only the main roads were tarmac.

The village people were very lovely, kind and down to earth, they also had an excellent sense of humour. Most of the people were dependent on cultivation, growing rice, and vegetables and there was a small village Bazar (market), the village is surrounded by a river and has a very nice environment.

It was a very lovely place, and he states that birds were singing, the trees were beautiful, flowers blossomed everywhere, and the farmers were doing their jobs in this beautiful climate. Every Friday they would play football on a large field, other activities would be done on this field also. Whilst he was a student, he was involved in a variety of school activities such as cricket, football, and scouting, he used to enjoy it.

When he was a young boy he had a pet monkey, dog, goat, and a sparrow. When he used to come back from school all his pets would come to him, and he used to play with them. His monkey used to go on his shoulder and steal bananas and share them with him, where he lived there were plenty of bananas, his monkey's name was Shampoo and his dog's name was Sham. He loved the time he spent in his village; there would be festivals in the village celebrating different cultural activities.

8.50.2 Journey to the UK & Immigration:

He came to the UK on the $17^{th\ of}$ June in 1970; this was because his father was in the UK at the time (he migrated there in the early '60s). It was his parents who had pushed him to migrate to the UK because they wanted him to have a better life and a better education, he was influenced by his uncle also, they all told him that going to Britain would be best for him.

His father applied for a settlement and had to go to the interview twice at the British High Commission Dhaka, finally, he got a settlement visa then flew from Dhaka on British Airways and arrived at Heathrow airport very early in the morning, he travelled with his parents, his siblings and some other parts of his family.

Before he flew to Britain, he wasn't very happy about it, he didn't want to come to Britain because he had no experience of what Britain was like, but he had no choice. When he arrived at Heathrow airport, he was very surprised to see tall, nice and attractive people, especially the ladies with short skirts, he nearly got caught out having a look now and again also.

He went to the clearance officer, and he was asked "What is your name? What is your date of Birth?" he answered in English without any difficulty, he was also asked, "Where are you coming from?" His Father's cousin was at the airport to receive them, and he had taken them to Birmingham, he was amazed by what he had seen on the way, the cars and the buildings amazed him.

There was a house that belonged to his father, and this was where he stayed; it was 197 Mansel Road, small heath, Birmingham. When he arrived in Birmingham it was a very tight fit at the house, there wasn't nearly enough space for him, he was very tired once you arrived, he had something to eat and then went to sleep.

8.50.3 Life in the UK

Whilst he was in small heath, the following day he went to the park and said that the weather was very nice, it was just like home. There was a small lake there and on the other side of the lake, there were gardens. One time when he looked over, he witnessed a couple getting very close and kissing, so he used to climb a tree and watch, he had never seen anything like this, his mother would ask him if he enjoyed his day, and he said it was very nice.

He wasn't settled in Britain, and after a few months he was upset and wanted to return to Bangladesh, but his father wouldn't let him. Most houses didn't have central heating; all houses had toilets, usually outside though. The people were very nice and helpful; the elderly people were also nice.

There was a limited amount of Asian people, and they would be stared at, the British would see the Asian community as a newcomer. The Asian children would be pushed around and bullied by the British and Jamaican children; they would always have a problem if they went to a new place.

The road service was very good, the public transport was excellent also, he used to travel by bus all the time, not many people owned cars, so the roads were very quiet, there weren't many motorways either, public transport was the main form of transport at the time.

The trains were also very good as well. He also witnessed that many Asian people would usually be working 7 days a week with a very paid job, the British people would never do this job so it was left for the Asian people, and there would be a very limited social life for these workers, going to the cinema and visiting each other's houses were the only social activities.

8.50.4 Education in the UK:

In September 1970 he attended a language institute in Spark Hill, he stayed there for a year, and it was full time. After that in 1971, he went to a Technical College in Birmingham, he had to study GCSEs in English and Maths; he completed these within a year.

Then he started BTEC in Business, which was a full course in 1972, and then in 1973, he did an HND in Business. Then his education was stopped. Then in 1990, he wanted to complete a level one and two in accountancy, but he stopped it because of a family and business commitment, he said that one day he would certainly finish his education.

8.50.5 Employment:

His first job was at a vegetable shop in a small heath in 1973, he started as a shopkeeper and manager. He worked there for 3 months, and his weekly wages were £5. It wasn't enough for him though, his shifts were 9 am to 5 pm and worked Monday to Friday. He decided to leave that job and started looking for a new job, he applied for jobs in Birmingham City Council, and he tried and tried yet he couldn't a job there.

He worked for an agency that was cooperating with the City Council in 1973, his job was to let out the properties and collect the rent, his salary was £290 monthly which was good wages. After 6 months he decided he wanted his own business, he had an idea to start a restaurant, and he started to work at a restaurant called "Royal Bengal Restaurant" in Walsall as a waiter. He started working there in 1974.

On his days off he used to work without pay in the kitchens to learn how to cook and to help the chef, with this he would be learning the skills for it. Then in 1975, he opened his first restaurant in Bromsgrove in Worcestershire called "Bay of Bengal", he invested £9000 to start the restaurant, he was a sole trader, it was a very good profitable business.

In 1976, he bought the freehold, he sold the first restaurant, and then in 1985 he bought another property in Hollywood, Birmingham, and started another restaurant business called the "Red Fort". There was another established restaurant called "Red Fort" in London and they didn't want the restaurant in Birmingham to have the same name, after court action, he changed the name to "Rajasthan".

In 1986, he opened another restaurant called "International Balti House". The business didn't do well so he ended up shutting it down. In 1988, he sold the Rajasthan restaurant and went to London, Croydon because the business prospects in London were better. He bought another restaurant in London and called "Kaddirs Indian Cuisine".

He stayed there until 1990, and he sold the restaurant and went to Ellesmere Port. He opened another restaurant called "Agra Fort" and stayed there until 1996. Hold the restaurant and open another one called "Village Indian" in Tattenhall, Cheshire, near Chester.

He ran that restaurant until 2007; he then opened another restaurant called "Red Fox", then in 2009 he sold the "Village Indian". The "Red Fox" is still running and from 1970 until the present time he was also involved in the property business. He had chosen the restaurant because it was a popular business within Britain, although he didn't have the business experience, education, and working confidence to set up his own business.

8.50.6 Housing:

All the restaurants he had year by year he would always move, his first house was in Croydon, he bought it in 1998, and it cost him £95,000 and it was a 3-bedroom house. He sold his old house and then moved to Ellesmere Port, he bought a house in 1990, and it was a 3-bedroom semi-detached house, that cost him £49,000.

He sold his second house and bought another house in Ellesmere Port in 1996, it was a 4-bedroom detached house, and it cost him £145,000. In 2006 he moved from Ellesmere Port to Neston, Cheshire, and bought another newly built house which was detached, it was a 5-bedroom house and cost him £350,000 which is where he is residing now.

8.50.7 Family & Social:

In 1981 he married Hazera Begum Jilani in the same area he was raised. In the same year, his wife came to Britain, he has 4 daughters. The ages of them are 28, 27, 24, and 18. The oldest has done her master's degree from Birmingham University and is now working at the Queen Elizabeth Hospital.

His second daughter completed her master's in international banking and finance at Salford University; she is now married and is now working in London Docklands at an American Bank. His third daughter is a teacher working at a secondary school; she's done a BSc at Manchester University. Also, she has a PGCE. His fourth daughter is doing her A levels and is aiming to do a law degree.

When he was in Birmingham he was involved in the Bangladesh Welfare Association, he was the cultural secretary, and he was the organising secretary of the Midland Catering Association in Birmingham. He did a lot of voluntary work, he helped at the Racial Equality Council, and he helped with the administration.

When he moved to Ellesmere Port in 1990, he was heavily involved with lots of charity work, he helped at the Citizen Advice Bureau. He has been actively involved with the Labour Party since 1990. In 1994 he participated in the local election, he lost that one but in 1995 he was elected as a Councillor for Ellesmere Port and Ashton Council.

He stayed there until 2004 due to him losing the election by 3 votes; this was because of the Iraq war. In 2007 he stood in Neston and was elected again as a Councillor of Neston and has been the councillor since. He was one of the founding members of the Racial Equality Council in Cheshire also; from 1994 and still going he is the school governing body in high schools and primary schools in Ellesmere Port.

8.50.8 Independence of Bangladesh:

In 1971 he was a student in Birmingham and his involvement was attending various meetings and was collecting donations from various people to support people in Bangladesh in winning the war. Also, he was in a youth movement in Birmingham; he was the cultural secretary in Birmingham also. He organised

many demonstrations himself also, such as organising coaches going to Hyde Park in London and Downing Street.

8.50.9 Conclusion:

The Community now has improved in every section of the UK, especially in education; our children have a higher education. They're working in all sectors of the country. He says he anticipated that his community would be the best, yet the other Indians and others have improved quite a lot more than Bangladeshis. He said, "In the future, our community will do more and will be in a better position".

He would like to see his culture and language be appreciated by more people and continue to educate our generation about these matters. Also, he would like to see more young people come forward (especially women) to involve themselves in politics, he wants to see more Bangladeshis become Members of Parliament and councillors.

8.51 Syed Ansaf Miah

8.51.1 Life in Bangladesh

Ansaf Miah was born in 1953 in the village of Syedpur, Jagannathpur, Shnamgonj. His father's name is late Syed Abdal Miah, and he was the landowner (Farmer). He completed his primary education at "Syedpur Primary School", and then he went to "Syedpur Pilot High School", where he studied up to class 8.

The condition of the village was very good with plenty of rice from the paddy fields and cows (Milk), fish, and horses being available in his house. He used to ride the horses, and his family was involved in the boating competition every year. Although the economy wasn't very good the people were very happy and what they needed was there.

There wasn't very good road communication within that area, and he used to use the boat for transport (even going to school). His family also had a fighting bull, and they used to organise events to celebrate for cultural reasons. He used to do the fishing and there was plenty of fruit and vegetables available in his home area.

At that time the education system was very good compared to this time. The people were good and there was less corruption, if there was any problem in the village then the villagers would help to resolve any issues. If the Villagers found that someone was guilty of doing wrong, then the punishment was to shave their head or to put a shoe necklace on and they had to run around the pond 7 times and they also had to swear that they would never do it again.

8.51.2   Journey to the UK & Immigration:

In September 1966 he came to Britain, he had used a boy voucher to come to the UK, and the reason for coming to Britain was because his father was living there. In 1965 there was a conflict between India and Pakistan and his father thought it would be better for him to come to the UK to settle.

When he received the declaration from his father, he had taken one of his cousins and went to the British High Commission in Dhaka to process the application for settlement. On the same day, he obtained the visa and then after two months, he came to Britain. He flew from Dhaka airport by PIA and arrived at Heathrow airport. When he first arrived in the UK he went to see one of his uncles in London and then was taken to Birmingham where his father was living. The address was 35 Dickens Road, Hay Mills, Birmingham.

8.51.3 Life in the UK

His father used to work in a car factory making Jaguars based in Birmingham, the weather was very cold, and during the wintertime, there was always snowfall. The people were very nice and friendly. The housing conditions weren't very good, there was no central heating system, and no hot water, and people would use coal to heat the house.

The toilet was outside, the people used to go to the public bath once a week. There weren't many Asian grocery shops at the time, so people used to do their shopping from the English markets, there was a very limited supply to get Asian vegetables. The price of goods was good, the life was good.

There were fewer private cars, and the main transport was public buses, trains, and taxis. There was a very limited number of mosques at the time also. The people used to go to the cinema once a week and would also visit each other's houses. The TVs were black and white, and they only had one channel so people would prefer to go to the cinema. There was no carpet in the house so they would use liners and people had a really hard time with the weather.

8.51.4 Education in the UK:

He went to Golden Hillock High School in 1966 in Small Heath, Birmingham; he finished in 1969 with an SEC (Secondary Education Certificate). In 1969 he went to college to study photography and to learn English. After finishing his studies, he studied for a GCSE in law, and after about a year he finished his studies.

8.51.5 Employment & Business:

His first job was an apprenticeship with a garage in Birmingham; he did it for a week and stopped because he didn't enjoy it. His uncle then offered him a job in a restaurant and offered to teach him how to do it. He started working in the restaurant in 1969, he worked as a training waiter and earned £7 a week, 12 pm to 3 pm and 5:30 pm to 11:30 pm were his working hours, he worked there for a year.

In 1970 his father opened a grocery shop, and he helped within the shop. He used to get £20 a week as pocket money. He worked there until 1974 and then his father bought a restaurant, and he sold the grocery shop, he then started work within the restaurant. He worked there as a waiter and earned £35 a week; his working hours were 5 pm to 12 pm.

His father sold the restaurant in 1975 and then he found a job in an English restaurant and started work there in 1976, the restaurant was called Steak House. He earned £25 a week and the working hours were 7 pm till 12 pm. In 1976 he bought a building and renovated that place into a restaurant and opened it in 1977, It was in New Brighton.

The building cost £4500 and he spent £4500 on the restaurant. The profit was reasonable. He owned the restaurant until 1991 because the MDC council said that the building came under CPO and took it. In 1992 he opened a takeaway in Wallasey Village in Merseyside.

To set up the business it cost him £20,000, the profit was reasonable. In 1999 he had given up the lease and bought a new restaurant/takeaway just opposite the old business. It's still there now and he is still the owner, it is called MAK Syed Restaurant & Takeaway.

8.51.6 Housing

His first house was a 3-bedroom townhouse in New Brighton, Merseyside. He paid £13,500 and he bought it in 1979. In 1986 he bought a new house and let out the old one, it was a 4-bedroom detached house, he paid £33,000 and it was in Wallasey Village, Merseyside. In 1989 he bought a new house; it was a 3-bedroom semi-detached house, and he paid £33,000. It was in Prenton, Birkenhead, and Merseyside. In 2010 he sold the first house to his son; he is still living in the semi-detached house.

8.51.7 Social & Family:

In 1975, he went to Bangladesh for the first time, and he got married to Syeda Rabeya Khatun, they were from the same area where he was raised; in 1978 he brought his family to the UK.

He has 6 sons and 2 daughters, His first 3 sons have done higher education and their profession is teaching, his 3 other sons are attending schools, one of his daughters is going to university and his other daughter is attending secondary school. He has got some close relatives living in Bangladesh, so he regularly travels there to see them.

Since 1966, when he came to Britain, he used to help people write letters, In 1970 he provided help and support to the people who didn't have transport and struggled with their language, he offered support to those people by taking them to hospitals, job centres, etc. In 1970 he was serving as the sports secretary.

In 1975 he joined the Bangladesh Welfare Association in Merseyside, where he was the Assistant Secretary. He served there for 5 years. He became the General Secretary in 1980, in 1985 he became the vice-chairman and was a founding member of a Bangla School, and in 1995 he became the chairman of the Wirral Bangladesh Association.

In 1995, he joined a Bangladeshi political party called Jonoforum headed by Dr. Kamal Hussain. In 2006, he retired from the chairmanship. During his involvement with all these organisations, he carried out several projects helping local communities. From 2006 to 2009 he was the director of the "Shajahal Mosque" in Birkenhead. In 2010 he was serving as a treasurer of the "Development Council for Bangladeshis in the UK". In 2012 he was appointed as the "Voice for Justice in the UK".

8.51.8 Independence of Bangladesh:

During the liberation period, he was involved in supporting the action committee collected donations, and attended meetings and demonstrations organised by the group. Recently he received an award from Channel I in recognition of his participation in the liberation time.

8.51.9 Conclusion

The first generation of Bangladeshi immigrants did not have higher education but at present, the new generation of the Bangladeshi community is doing very well and making progress. The community needs to have the facility for Bangla classes to be added to Arabic classes. That is the improvement he wants to see; this affects the outcome of the Bangladeshi community.

8.52 Conclusion

The project initially started in 2007 and finally concluded in 2012, the information gathered had been a long process of talking to separate people who had different views, different experiences, and so on. The first generation of Bangladeshis had an intention to go back to Bangladesh to settle but due to the political situations and the aftermath of the liberation war, they could not return and therefore changed their plans.

There was also a change of immigration rules which had given people the opportunity to bring their families into the UK; this all had taken place during the early '70s and it had continued until the late '80s. Today's Bangladeshis are integrated into mainstream society, playing their part in shaping Britain.

There is a lot of information within this chapter, and we aimed to collect valuable historical information for those people who have a rich history and experience they had since their arrival in the United Kingdom. Many of the people had been through a very hard time in their early life experience in Britain.

The new generation must be aware of what the first generation had been through because if it weren't for them, there would be no Bangladeshi people living in Britain. So, these people must be acknowledged and respected for what they have done for the Bangladeshi community. If there is any nation, it should never forget its roots and history; it is what establishes everyone's national identity in the present.

8.53 Muhammad Abdul Matin Chowdhury
[M.A. Matin]

8.53.1 Life in Bangladesh:

Muhammad Abdul Matin Chowdhury was born in 1929 in the village of Sreeramshi, Biswanath, Sylhet. His father's name was late Moulana Abdul Azim Chowdhury and his mother's name was late Shamsun Nehar Chowdhury. He was the only child.

He went to the local Primary School and Secondary School and studied up to SSC. Due to the early death of his father,

he left his studies and became a teacher at the local Primary school.

MA Matin's grandfather came to Sreeramshi from Fitwah, Nobigonj in the early 1900s and acquired the present "Bari" and agricultural land to support the

family.

8.53.2   Journey to the UK & Immigration:

In 1949, he entered the UK. He was living in Birmingham and moved to Manchester and settled here. He went to Assam for obtaining his passport and went to Karachi for a flight to the United Kingdom.

8.53.3 Family and homes:

MA Matin married Syeda Nurun Nehar Begum in 1964, they have 6 children, a son & 5 daughters. He bought his first house in Victoria Park Manchester and then Cheetham Hill, before moving to Didsbury in 1974.

8.53.4 Employment & Business:

On arriving in the UK he started working in a restaurant and then opened a small cafe with a dear friend, Mr. Lal Miah. Moving to Manchester, he opened the Oriental Restaurant on Oxford Road, Manchester. When the Oriental Restaurant was demolished, he opened the Motijheel in Deansgate, Manchester. In 1964 he moved to Leeds opening Taj Mahal Restaurant. Moving back to Manchester in 1967 they opened the first Bengali Grocery" Asian Food Store" on Stockport Rd which relocated to Landcross Road, Fallowfield. In 1971 he opened a travel agency "Sylhet Travel Services" on Oxford Road – the oldest surviving Bangladeshi Travel Agency in the UK and the first Biman-appointed agent in the UK.

8.53.5 Life in the UK:

The weather was very cold; people used coal to warm up the room. The snow and ice were common weather everywhere. There was good understanding and cooperation amongst Bangladeshis, if there was a death in the community, the people came forward to raise funds to arrange funerals in the UK or by sending the deceased back to Bangladesh.

8.53.6 Social & Family:

MA Martin spent most of his life organising the unity of the Bengali communities to realize their objectives here in Britain as well as at home.

In 1951, he organized and founded The Pakistan Welfare Association in Birmingham, Leeds, Oldham, and the Caterer's Association in Manchester. He was also a founder member of the Pakistan Welfare Association for Britain in London. He also organised the first Muslim burial facilities in Birmingham.

In 1955, he organised a historical public meeting attended by the late H S Shuhurawardy, Bangabandhu Sheikh Mujibur Rahman, and Maulana Bhasani at St Pancras Hall, London which for the first time initiated the movements of the Bengalis in the UK.

In 1965, as President of the Pakistan Welfare Association for Britain at a meeting with Ayub Khan, he ensured that East Pakistanis [Bengalis] received a just and fair share of Catering Vouchers [visas] and that Bengalis completed Immigration & Customs in Dhaka and not Karachi.

In 1966, he organized and launched the first historical public demonstration as the president of the Pakistani Federation in Britain against the totalitarianism of the Ayub regime.

In 1968, he organized the demonstration in London, for the release of the Bangabandhu from the Agartala Conspiracy Case.

In 1969, he also organised and led the Hyde Park Speakers Corner demonstration against Yayha Khan's regime within 3 days of the takeover from the Ayub regime. As President of the Pakistan

Welfare Association, he met with President Yahya Khan for the immediate release of Bangabandhu.

In 1969, to help people send money back to their families in Bangladesh, he persuaded Habib Bank to open a branch in Manchester, working there himself, he ensured that people used the Bank and thus ensured the profitability of the branch; after the independence of Bangladesh, the state owed Pubali Bank opened a branch - Manchester being the second worldwide branch after London.

Recognising the need for the rights of Bengali-speaking East Pakistani Muslims he founded the East Pakistan Muslim Society in Manchester which led to the purchase of the building now known as Shah Jalal Mosque & Islamic Centre. He was also involved in the foundation and development of the Shahjalal Mosque in Manchester. Bosroth Ali, Malik Bakth, Syed Abdul Hannan, and MA Matin were the first Trustees of the Shahjalal Mosque. He also took the initiative to unite the Bengalis and to focus on their problems by publishing a Jagaron Bengali newspaper from Manchester.

In 1971, when independence was declared he fully devoted his time to organising the movement of liberation in the UK. Along with other respected elders, he organised The Action Committee for Bangladesh in the UK (24th April 1971 at Coventry) and persuaded Justice Choudhury to become the advisor of the movement. Those who were closely connected with the movement were aware of how much he contributed to keeping the unity of this movement.

During the Liberation War, he founded The Lancashire Awami League Action Committee which held many rallies throughout the North including at the Shalimar & Manila restaurants. The organisation convinced many Bengalis to contribute a month's salary towards the arming of the freedom fighters.

In 1971, it was reported that The Lancashire Awami League Action Committee has the historical honour of being the first depositor in the account of Bangladesh. The cheque was handed over to Bangabandhu at Claridge's Hotel during the famous press conference in London after his release from imprisonment in West Pakistan on 8th January 1972.

MA Matin recognised the fact that Bangladeshis needed to quickly create an identity in the UK and formed the Lancashire Bangladesh Association [which later became the Greater Manchester Bangladesh Association - GMBA].

After independence many Bangladeshis holding Pakistani passports could not provide the necessary documents to obtain Bangladeshi passports; MA Matin convinced the Bangladeshi Government to accept Declarations of Nationality witnessed by community elders [including himself]. Leading to the first official visit to Bangladesh by the UK Awami League, he was honoured by Bangabandhu for his role during the war of liberation.

Manchester was the first city outside London to give The Bangladesh High Commissioner S.A

Sultan to UK a civic reception and MA Matin as President of the Lancashire Awami League organised a conference at the Free Trade Hall Manchester.

In 1975, he ensured that proper representative for Bangladeshis in UK North, he ensured that offices of Pubali Bank, Bangladesh High Commission, and Bangladesh airlines were opened in Manchester.

In 1976, he observed the political instability after the tragic death of Sheikh Mujibur Rahman, along with Late Tayebur Rahman joined the Jatiya Janata party being the joint UK co-ordinators.

In 1981, MA Matin recognised the need to improve the image of Bangladesh following the many coups in the fledgling history of Bangladesh, uniting many of the political factions of the community he held the first state visit to Manchester by a Bangladeshi Head of State.

1981 – Sheikh Hasina discussing the future of Bangladesh with UNCLE MA Matin 1981 - Skeikh Hasina visited Manchester after becoming President of the Awami League while in Self-Exile

In 1983, he was instrumental in the purchase of Bangladesh House, the Community centre in Longsight Manchester. He also helped the development of many Bangladeshi communities to establish Bangladesh Welfare Association in Hyde, Oldham, Rochdale, Leeds, Bradford, Birmingham, and London.

1983 - MAG Osmani 1983 Presidential Election

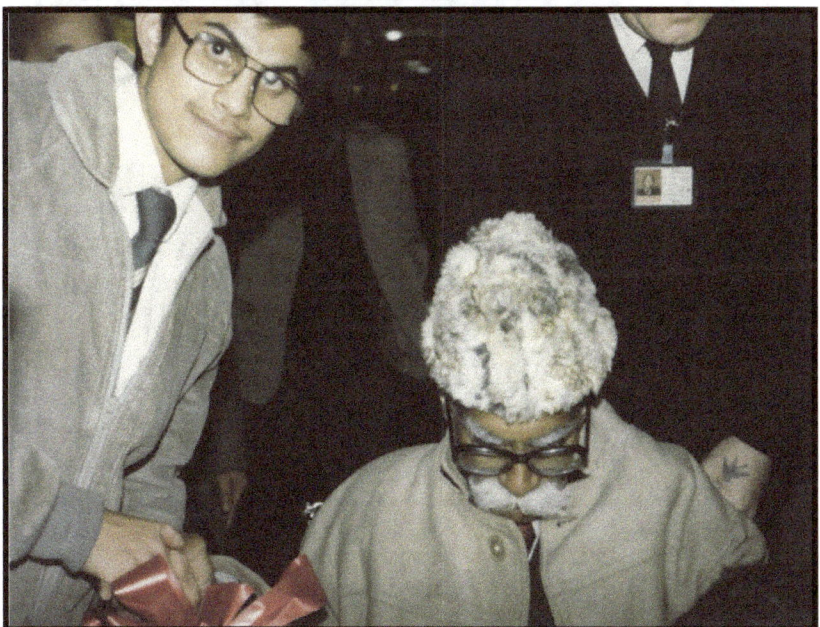

1983 - MAG Osmani is brought to the UK by M A Matin for treatment

On 16 February 1984, after the death of Bangabir MAG Osmani in London, M.A. Matin was given the honour of escorting the coffin back to Bangladesh. President Ershad received the coffin in Sylhet.

MA Matin died on 19 September 1985, at the age of 56, over 2000 mourners attended his funeral held in Platt fields near Shah Jalal Mosque, Manchester, he was buried in his birthplace village of Sreeramshi, Sylhet,

8.53.7 Independence of Bangladesh

MA Matin was one of the pro-active leaders amongst others who earned respect for his hard work with the Bangladeshi Community. It is not long ago, that Bangladesh as a nation emerged with other nations. Bangladesh had gone through a political and physical battle with West Pakistan. Ordinary people like MA Matin played a vital role in seeing the new nation should be established, as Bangladeshi can exercise their own culture and communicate with the same language.

In 1947, when Pakistan became independent from India, the Bangladesh independence movement began. In 1952, students were killed when they were demanding that Bangla should be a language in East Pakistan, not Urdu. In 1966-69, the movement became very strong and Yayha Khan was bound to declare the election.

In 1970, there was a national election where East Pakistan's leaders won the majority seats, but the authority did not call the parliament, but they had chosen to kill the whole nation. The Pakistani Army attacked East Pakistan (now Bangladesh) and killed 300,000 Bangladeshis.

The people were very scared and did not know what to do. But the Bangladeshi people did not just sit down and observe the killing of ordinary people, they decided to save the nation by getting support from other nations. We are going to share the life experience of a man with a vision and mission for Bangladesh Nation, who has done so much for the community and nation but sadly no one has given any recognition for his hard work.

At that time of liberation, there were Mr Matin, Dr Kabir Chowdhury, Mr Shomuj Miah, and Mr Moksud Ali worked together to achieve the goals of independence. Col. MAG Osmani and Abdus Samad Azad came to the UK to unite the Bangladeshi people. Justice Abu Sayeed came to the UK and appealed to all the Bangladeshi people to help the freedom fighters.

In 1971, at the time of the Bangladesh liberation war, he played a vital role in uniting the Bangladeshi Community in the UK. Mr. Matin was a very active and intellectual person to organise community meetings, seminars, and talks. He approached British MPs and Ministers for their support for the independence of Bangladesh. At that time there was a massive public meeting in Hyde Park, London. He was one of the key organisers to take a leading role in this meeting. Through his active involvement and participation, he became a very popular leader in the northwest and the UK.

During the period of the independence movement in the UK, there were some problems with the leadership. He initiated a meeting in Coventry where Chief Justice Abu Syed Choudhury (first president of Bangladesh) was present to form a coordination committee. We have not seen any evidence of how much money was raised from the UK but the Northwest Bangladeshi community was able to raise £75,000.00 to help the Bangladesh interim authority to buy arms, food, and medicine.

During the liberation movement, there were about eleven demonstrations throughout the UK, including Manchester. Manzil and Shalimar Restaurants were the meeting point for all of the community members to meet regularly to review the war and draw further action according to necessity.

At that time of the liberation, all the Bangladeshi people who were living in the UK supported the war against West Pakistani aggression. The Bangladeshi people organised a rally and demonstrations at Trafalgar Square, Hyde Park, and Downing Street in support of the independence. He said, "The Pakistani people often tried to get involved in an argument and tried to stop us from doing our Campaign in favour of our native country".

There were very limited telephones and televisions at that time. People used to gather in their houses to hear the news about the war. Some people got together and bought second-hand television sets to watch the news.

8.53.8   Conclusion

In conclusion, we would like to see the history of Bangladesh should be written in the correct format. During the '60s and '70s, there were only a limited number of people living in the United Kingdom. With the help of the Bangladeshis living in the UK, it was impossible to think about our existence today. But sadly, the Bangladesh government has not recognised the people who devoted their lives to the nation.

It is a shame when we see people get a reward for harming others. We strongly recommend that many people like him contribute to the country and nation as a whole; we must give national recognition and insert their story at the academic level so that future generations can learn from this.

Acknowledgements:
1. Melonie Tebbott – Manchester Metropolitan University.
2. Dr. Robert Light – Huddersfield University
3. Jalal Uddin – ITC – Xtreme PC
4. Shofique Miah, Nazia Kadiri, Nor Tasneem Abdul Wahab – Blue3print
5. Ahad Ullah Shah – City Brokers UK
6. Iqbal Ahmed – Sonali Bank UK Ltd
7. Yousuf Miah – Event Management
8. Khukon Maskub – Supreme & Co
9. Andrew Schofield - Northwest Sound Archive
10. Jamal Uddin – Westwood Restaurant
11. Murad Chowdhury – Photography.
12. Jamal Uddin – Degnasoft
13. Shahel Chowdhury – Infinite Marketing
14. Abdul Hamid – PBL Exchange UK Limited
15. Hasan Ahmed Chowdhury – Sylhet Travel Services
16. Juned Ahmed – Probash Bangla & Spice City
17. Phil Carey – Rathbone
18. Shahid Zaman – Regulus Training & Employment.
19. Abdul Mannan - Oly Oli Ltd
20. Muzahid Khan – Sylhet Times
21. Shahid Miah – Jonosheba Group
22. Nep Islam Shaek – British Asian Media Group
23. Koyes Shikder – Bangla Transcription Services
24. Fahima Sultana – Admin & Event Management
25. Abul Hasnath Shamin – Awards & Presentation
26. Hamidul Kibria Chowdhury - Publication

Bibliography

- *Bangladeshi Restaurant Curries*, Piatkus, London — ISBN 0749916184 (1996)
- *Curries* - Master chef Series, Orion, London — ISBN 0297836420 (1996)
- *Curry*, Human & Rousseau, South Africa — ISBN 0798131934 (1993)
- *Kerrie*, in Afrikaans, Human & Rousseau, South Africa — ISBN 0798128143 (1993)
- *Petit Plats Curry*, French edition, Hachette Marabout, Paris — ISBN 2501033086 (2000)
- *2009 Cobra Good Curry Guide*, John Blake Publishing, London — ISBN 1-84454-311-0

References

Alam - 1988
Ali – 1996
Ahmed Kaufman & Naim – 1996
Bangladesh Bureau of Statistics – Government of the People's Republic of Bangladesh
Badawi, Zaki (1995): 'Muslim justice in a secular state' In Michael King (ed): *God's law versus state law: The construction of Islamic identity in Western Europe.* London: Grey Seal, pp. 73-80.
Ballard, Roger (ed.) (1994): Desh pardesh: *the South Asian presence in Britain.* London: Hurst & Co.
Ballard, Roger (1996): '*Panth kismet dharm te quam*: continuity and change in four dimensions of Punjabi religion'. In: Pritam Singh and Shinder S. Thandi (eds.): *Globalisation and the region. Explorations in Panjabi identity.* Coventry: Association for Punjabi Studies, pp. 7-38.
Ballard, Roger (2001a): 'Popular Islam in northern Pakistan and its reconstruction in Britain'. Paper presented at the International Workshop on Islamic Mysticism in the West, Buxton, Derbyshire, 22-24 July 2001, also at www.casas.org.uk.
Ballard, Roger (2001b): 'The impact of kinship on the economic dynamics of transnational networks: reflections on some South Asian developments'. Paper presented at Workshop on Transnational Migration, Princeton University, 29 June – 1 July 2001, also at www.casas.org.uk and www.transform.ox.ac. the UK.
Ballard, Roger (n.d.): 'Common law and uncommon sense: the assessment of reasonable behavior in a plural society, at www.casas.org.uk.
Chiba, Masaji (1986): *Asian indigenous law in interaction with received law.* London and New York: Kegan Paul International.
Carey & Shukur – 1985
Carroll – 1997
Chiefly, Menski - 1993
Drabu, Khurshid and Stephen **Bowen** (1989): *Mandatory Visas. Visiting the UK from Bangladesh, India, Pakistan, Ghana, and Nigeria.* London: Commission for Racial Equality.
Eade, John, Tim **Vamplew** and Ceri **Peach** (1996): 'The Bangladeshis: the encapsulated community'. In: Ceri Peach (ed.): *Ethnicity in the 1991 Census. Volume two. The Ethnic minority populations of Great Britain.* London: HMSO, pp. 150-160.
Fransman, Laurie (1986): 'Family settlement cases: a denial of statutory rights. In: Vol. 1, No. 1 *Immigration and Nationality Law and Practice*, pp. 5-15.
Fransman, Laurie (1989): *British nationality law.* London: Format.
Gardner, Katy (1993): '*Desh-bidesh*: Sylheti images of home and away'. In: Vol. 28, No. 1 *Man*, pp. 1-15.
Gardner, Katy (1995): *Global migrants, local lives.* Oxford: Clarendon.

Gardner, Katy and Abdus **Shukur** (1994): "'I'm Bengali, I'm Asian, and I'm living here": the changing identity of British Bengalis'. In: Roger Ballard (ed.) (1994): Desh pardesh: *the South Asian presence in Britain*. London: Hurst & Co., pp. 142-164.
Gillespie, Jim (1992): 'Maintenance and accommodation and the immigration rules: recent developments. In: Vol. 6, No. 3 *Immigration and Nationality Law and Practice*, pp. 97-100.
Glenn, H. Patrick (2000): *Legal systems of the world*. Oxford: Oxford University Press.
Griffiths, John (1986): 'What is legal pluralism?' In: No. 24 *Journal of Legal Pluralism and Unofficial Law*, pp. 1-55.
Haddad - 1986
Hooker, M. B. (1975): *Legal pluralism*. Oxford: Clarendon Press.
Hussein, Raza and Duran **Seddon** (1996): 'Recourse to public funds and indirect reliance'. In: Vol. 10, No. 2 *Immigration and Nationality Law and Practice*, pp. 50-53.
Joint Council for the Welfare of Immigrants (1987): *Out of sight. The new visit visa system overseas*. London: JCWI.
Jones, Richard and Gnanapala **Welhengama** (2000): *Ethnic minorities in English law*. London: Group for Ethnic Minority Studies, SOAS, and Stoke on Trent: Trentham.
Juss, Satvinder S. (1997): *Discretion and deviation in the administration of immigration control*. London: Sweet and Maxwell.
Kenny - 2002
Mayss, Abla (2000): 'Recognition of foreign divorces: unwarrantable ethnocentrism'. In: John Murphy (ed.): *Ethnic minorities, their families and the law*. Oxford, UK, and Portland, Oregon: Hart, pp. 51-70.
McKee, Richard (1995): 'A burden on the taxpayer? Some developments in the role of 'public funds' in immigration law'. In: Vol. 9, No. 1 *Immigration and Nationality Law and Practice*, pp. 29-31.
Menski, Werner (1988): 'Uniformity of laws in India and England'. In: Vol. VII, No. 11 *Journal of Law and Society* (Peshawar), pp. 11-26.
Menski, Werner (1993): 'Asians in Britain and the question of adaptation to a new legal order: Asian laws in Britain?' In: M Israel and N K Wagle (eds.): *Ethnicity, identity, migration: the South Asian context*. Toronto: Centre for South Asian Studies, University of Toronto, pp. 238-268.
Menski, Werner (1994): 'Family migration and the new immigration rules. In: Vol. 8, No. 4 *Immigration and Nationality Law and Practice*, pp. 112-124.
Menski, Werner F. (1997): 'South Asian Muslim law today: an overview'. In: Vol. 9, No. 1 *Sharqiyyat*, pp. 16-36.
Menski, Werner F. (2000): *Comparative law in a global context: the legal systems of Asia and Africa*. London: Platinium.
Menski, Werner F. (2001): 'Muslim law in Britain'. In: No. 62 *Journal of Asian and African Studies*, pp. 127-163.

Menski, Werner and Tahmina **Rahman** (1988): 'Hindus and the law in Bangladesh'. In: Vol. 8, No. 2 *South Asia Research*, pp. 111-131.
Mistry, Hiren Bhana (1999): *Diaspora and* sadacara: *the legal reconstruction of Hinduism in ancient and classical India*. MA dissertation, School of Oriental and African, London.
Modood, Tariq and Richard **Berthoud** (eds.): *Ethnic minorities in Britain*. London: PSI.
Monsoor, Taslima (1999): *From patriarchy to gender equity. Family law and its impact on women in Bangladesh*. Dhaka: The University Press Ltd. **Nielsen**, Jorgen (1988): 'Muslims in Britain and local authority responses'. In: T. Gerholm and Y. Lithman (eds.): *The new Islamic presence in Western Europe*. London: Mansell, pp. 53-77.
Naim- 2003
Nielsen, Jorgen (1992): 'Islam, Muslims, and British local and central government'. Paper presented at a conference on Muslims in Europe, Turin, 4-5 May 1992.
Peach - 1990
Pearl, David (1986): *Family law and the immigrant communities*. Bristol: Jordan & Sons.
Pearl, David, and Werner **Menski** (1998): *Muslim family law*. London: Sweet and Maxwell.
Poulter, Sebastian (1986): *English law and ethnic minority customs*. London: Butterworths.
Poulter, Sebastian (1990): 'The claim to a separate Islamic system of personal law for British Muslims'. In: Chibli Mallat and Jane Connors (eds.): *Islamic family law*. London: Graham and Trotman, pp. 147-166.
Poulter, Sebastian (1998): *Ethnicity, law and human rights*. Oxford: Clarendon Press.
Sachdeva, Sanjiv (1993): *The primary purpose rule in British immigration law*. Stoke on Trent: Trentham.
Shah, Prakash (1994): 'Legal pluralism – British law and possibilities with Muslim ethnic minorities. In: Nos. 66/67 *Retfærd*, pp. 18-33.
Shah, Prakash (2002): 'Attitudes to polygamy in English law'. Unpublished paper.
Shah-Kazemi, Sonia-Nurin (2001): *Untying the knot: Muslim women, divorce and the* shariah. London: Nuffield Foundation.
Samad & Eade – 2002
Salazar – 2001
Sek Pye Lim - 2001
Wray, Helena and Mahmud **Quayum** [1999]: 'Entry clearance application for spouses where the sponsor is on benefits. In: 13(4) I&NL&P 133-135.
Willet - 1998
Wrench & Qureshi - 1996

Yilmaz, Ihsan (1999): *Dynamic legal pluralism and the reconstruction of unofficial Muslim laws in England, Turkey, and Pakistan.* Ph.D. Thesis, London: School of Oriental and African Studies.

Yilmaz, Ihsan (2000): 'Muslim law in Britain: reflections in the socio-legal sphere and differential legal treatment'. In: Vol. 21, No. 2 *Journal of Muslim Minority Affairs*, pp. 353-360.

Yilmaz, Ihsan (2001): 'Law as a chameleon: the question of incorporation of Muslim personal law into the English law'. In: Vol. 21, No. 2 *Journal of Muslim Minority Affairs*, pp. 297-308.

Source of Information from Internet:

[i] Wikipedia
http://en.wikipedia.org/wiki/list of countries and outlying territories by total area

[ii] Bangladesh Bureau of Statistics – Population & Housing Census 2011 Preliminary Results July 2011

[iii] The Economist Intelligence Unit
http://country.eiu.com/article.aspx?articleid=218456206&Country=Bangladesh&topic=Summary&subtopic=Fact+sheet&subsubtopic=Factsheet

[iv] Greater London Authority Intelligence Update – 20th June 2010 (issued 30th June 2011)
http://www.london.gov.uk/sites/default/files/Update%2011-2011%20mid 2010%20population%20estimates.pdf

[v] CIA World Fact Book
http://www.cia.gov/library/publications/the-world-factbook/geos/bg.html

[vi] BBC
http://www.bbc.co.uk/news/world-south-asia-14967857

[vii] The Economist
http://www.economist.com/blogs/dailychart/2011/01/comparing us states countries

[viii] The World Bank Data Bank
http://search.worldbank.org/all?gterm=bangladesh

[ix] Population Division of the Department of Economic and Social Affairs of the United Nations Secretariat, World Population Prospects: The 2010 Revision

[x] Human Development Reports – United Nations Development Program
http://hdr.undp.org/en/statistics/

[xi] Transparency International – Corruption Perceptions Index 2010
http://www.transparency.org/policyresearch/surveysindices/cpi/2010/results

Photo Album

Oral history of Bangladeshis in Greater Manchester celebrtation parties.

Party 1: Programme held on 17th July 2011

Some of the participants on the stage

Councillors from Rochdale, Oldham, and Manchester City Council.

Chairperson Mustak Ahmed Mustafa & General Secretary Faruk Ali with European MP Sajjad Karim.

Yousuf Miah introducing the honourable community leaders – Alhaj Khandoker Abdul Musabbir MBE, Samsuddin Ahmed MBE, Gulam Mustafa Chowdhury MBE.

Yousuf Miah Miah taking to Philip Carey & Rahat Ahmed Mustafa

Yousuf Miah & Mustak Ahmed Mustafa

Yousuf Miah (Host) & Faruk Ali (General Secretary)

Community Award presented by First Secretary of BAHC, Ohidur Rahman & Cllr Farooq Ahmed

Abdul Aziz (Nunu Miah)

Alhaj Makhon Miah

Samsuddin Ahmed MBE

Abdul Aziz

Alhaj Tozomul Ali

Alhaj Nosir Ali

Mustak Ahmed Mustafa

Alhaj Ali Anjob

Boshir Ali

Alhaj Azmal Khan

Faruk Ali – General Secretary

Alhaj Eklasur Rahman Chowdhury

Alhaj Khodoker Abdul Musabbir

Alhaj Gulam Mustafa Chowdhury

Alhaj Masrurul Hasan Chowdhury

Bangladeshis in Manchester

Alhaj Shah Husiar Ullah

Alhaj Ismail Hussain Shiraji (Jomir Ali)

Alhaj Munsif Ali

Alhaj Noorfor Ali

Alhaj Rois Ullah

Alhaj Muslim Ali

On behalf of Atar Miah Chowdhury – Nurul Chowdhury

On behalf of Kari Abdul Baki - Abdul Kashim

Mustak Ahmed Mustafa

Speakers

Sajjad Karim MEP

Cllr Neil Emmott – Rochdale MBC

Cllr Abdul Jabbar – Oldham MBC

Cllr Shoab Akhtar

Cllr Olwen Chadderton

Cllr Lutfur Rahman

Phil Carey - Rathbones

Mrs Carole England – Dr Kershaw's Hospice

298

Guests at Millennium Centre

Some of the guests including Cllr. Abdul Kadir Jilani - Chester

Musicians

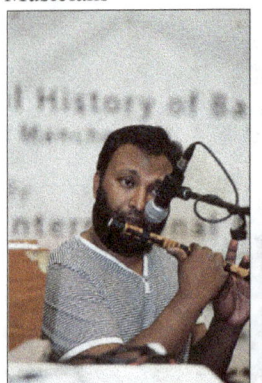  

Party 2

Hamza Arshad – [Volunteer] – reciting the Holy Quran

Bangladeshis in Manchester

Idris Ali – [Volunteer] - delivering the speech

Mustak Ahmed Mustafa – [Project Manager & Chairperson]– delivering the speech

Phil Carey – [Sponsor – Rathbones] - delivering the speech

Shahid Zaman – [Sponsor - Regulus Training & Volunteer] delivering the speech

Amin Babor Chowdhury – sponsor – Probash Bangla Newspaper

Mayor of Oldham Cllr. Professor Richard Knowles Delivering the speech

301

Mustak Ahmed Mustafa

Alhaj Muktar Ali receiving the documentary, Award & Certificate

Alhaj Nosir Ali - receiving the documentary, Award & Certificate

Alhaj Ali Anjob - receiving the documentary, Award & Certificate

Alhaj Ismail Hussain Shiraji [Jomir Ali] - receiving the documentary, Award & Certificate.

Alhaj Boshir Ali receiving the documentary, Award & Certificate.

Fozlu Miah receiving the documentary, Award & Certificate.

Shaeid Hamid – [Volunteer] - receiving the Award & Certificate.

Koyes Sikdar – [Volunteer] – receiving the Award & Certificate.

Bangladeshis in Manchester

Sahied Miah – [Volunteer] receiving the Award & Certificate.

Mizanul Alom – [Volunteer] receiving the Award & Certificate.

Zakaria Islam – [Volunteer] receiving the Award & Certificate.

Hamza Arshad – [Volunteer] receiving the Award & Certificate.

Shabana Yasmin – [Volunteer] receiving the Award & Certificate

Rosie Hamid – [Volunteer] receiving the Award & Certificate.

Dipu – [Volunteer] receiving the Award & Certificate.

Rezaul Karim Chowdhury– [Volunteer] receiving the Award & Certificate.

Juned Ahmed – [Sponsor – Spice City] receiving the Certificate.

Amin Babor Chowdhury – [Sponsor - Probash Bangla] receiving the Certificate.

Sahied Zaman – [Sponsor – Regulus Training & Volunteer] receiving the Certificate.

Faruk Ali – [General Secretary] – delivering his speech including the vote of thanks.

Some of the Oldham Participants and Volunteers of the TIA Oral History Project with Mayor of Oldham Cllr. Richard Knowles & Mayoress Valerie Knowles.

From Left (standing) Ali Akbor Liton, Nasir Khan Shueb, Idris Ali, Salah Uddin, MA Mustak, Abdur Rakib, (seating) Abdul Aziz, Cllr. Raja Miah, Mayor Cllr. Joe Kitchen, Mayoress Shirley Kitchen, Md Delwar Khan, Mobosshor Ullah. Programme held on 21st October 2013

From left Md Rofiq Uddin, Hafiz Ekhlasur Rahman, Rochdale Mayor Cllr Peter Rush, Azamal Khan, Atar Miah Chowdhury, On the back MA Mustak, Phil Carey, Idris Ali. Programme held on 14 October 2013.

History of Bangladeshis in Greater Manchester meeting in Rochdale. Programme took place at BACP on 14th October 2013

From Left - Yousuf Miah, Zokey Ahad - Asst. High Commissioner of Bangladesh, Cllr John Hatson Mayor of Oldham Council and MA Mustak. Celebration party took place at Oldham TIA office on 5 November 2013

Assistant High Commissioner of Bangladesh Zokey Ahad attended a presentation ceremony at TIA office in Oldham. Programme held on 5th November 2013

History of Bangladeshis in Greater Manchester book launched at Sylhet Auditorium on 5 June 2013

Mustak presented the history book to Ateeque Ur Rehman (Mayor of Oldham)

MA Mustak presented the History book to Mc Mahon MP in Oldham

MA Mustak presented the history book to Mayor Ariful Haque Chowdhury, in Sylhet Bangladesh.

From the left local studies officer Roger Ivens, Shammy Akter, Archive officer Joanne Robson, Moklesur Rahman and TIA chairperson Mustak Ahmed Mustafa handed over 50 videos to Oldham Library.

Here are the author's other publications

This is the author's collection of poetry and was his first publication of his creative writing.

This was the first part of the Oral history book. This was published before the 2nd part in 2021

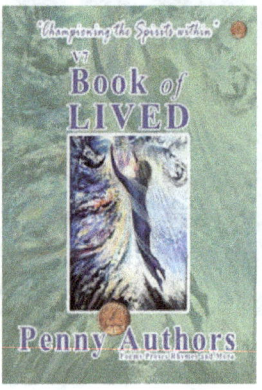

The author also participated and got few of his poetry in the Penny Authors Anthology, titled the "Book of Lived.

For more information about Penny Authors visit: www. pennyauthors.org.uk

For information about the books and service, visit: www.mapublisher.org.uk